16-11

OEDIPUS REX

A MIRROR FOR GREEK DRAMA

Wadsworth Guides to Literary Study
Maurice Beebe, General Editor

OEDIPUS REX

A MIRROR FOR GREEK DRAMA

Albert Cook

Western Reserve University

Wadsworth Publishing Company, Inc.

Belmont, California

TO

ED DOLIN

AND

FRED LOCKE

L.C. Cat. Card No.: 63-15505
Printed in the United States of America

or the student, *Oedipus Rex* is a play of signal richness. In itself
occasion endless discussion about character and situation, man
e gods, leader and people, consciousness and motivation. And
its e mplary artistry makes it an excellent introduction to the Greek
theater and to the technique of the drama in general.

Oedipus Rex was taken by Aristotle as a formal model for tragic
drama. Freud considered it the key representation of the parent-child
relationship, which, as he says in discussing the play, has the chief
role (*die Hauptrolle*) in determining a man's unconscious life. Hence
both the artistic technique of the play and its original thematic material are regarded as particularly exemplary. The play exhibits a
highly civilized use of diction and idea and dramatic structure while
drawing on deeply primitive sources of feeling in a more obviously
direct way than many works do.

And so, if we ask of the play, "Was Oedipus responsible for his
action; was it free will or fate?" the play itself returns us to its art, to
its primitive sources. Aristotle and Freud alike follow the Socratic idea
that to know is to do, and so free will may be said to imply consciousness. Hence the thought of Aristotle's treatise would, in effect, bring
the conscious features of the play to light: he conceives of the dramatic
art as a conscious one, if only because the philosophical categories that
he adduces themselves attest to the function of a consciousness—both
in the critic and, as the critic spells out the poet's implications, in the
playwright too. On the other hand, if fate implies unconsciousness,
Freud's reading of the play makes it the very model of our unconscious
life. As he says:

> The presentation of the play consists in nothing more than the revela-
> tion—heightened step by step and artistically protracted, comparably to the
> work of a psychoanalysis—that Oedipus is himself the murderer of Laios,
> and is also the son of the murdered man and of Jocasta. Shaken by the
> abomination he has unconsciously committed, Oedipus blinds himself and
> abandons his homeland. The statement of the oracle is fulfilled.
>
> *Oedipus Rex* is a so-called tragedy of fate; its tragic effect is supposed
> to reside in the opposition between the overpowering will of the gods and
> the vain striving of men who are threatened by disaster. Acquiescence in the
> will of the godhead, insight into one's own powerlessness, is what the deeply
> gripped spectator is supposed to learn from the sad spectacle.[1]

---

[1] Sigmund Freud, *Die Traumdeutung* (Vienna: Franz Deuticke, 1950, original
edition, 1900), p. 180. Translated by Albert Cook.

Without even invoking the relevant context about Greek notions of free will and fate, without scrutinizing more closely the text of the play, we can bring this complex question to a mighty impasse just by invoking Aristotle and Freud.

This question—fate or free will—may not be the ultimate one to ask of the play, but it is one readers have often asked. It is a question the play raises, by including oracles, by speaking of blindness and sight, by suggesting the appropriateness of punishment. This particular question is inexhaustible, and the play itself offers an interest that is inexhaustible beyond this question.

The aim of the present handbook is to provide for the student a context through which he can study the play and its many aspects. In addition, the inclusion between these covers of material on all phases of a Greek dramatic production, together with the text of Aristotle's *Poetics,* enables the student to get what is otherwise hard to come by, a full introduction in brief compass to the classic Greek theater.

Greek drama was presented in a theater quite different in appearance and in convention from ours. The very fact that *Oedipus Rex* stands as a model in that theater makes an understanding of the theater relevant to the play itself. And so this collection begins with a summary of Greek theatrical practices.

The second section, "Oedipus—The Myth and the Play," prefaces the text of the play with the most ancient statement of the myth, Homer's, and with a modern rendering of it, the poem by Edwin Muir. Robert Graves' exhaustive summary of what we know of the myth incorporates syncretically much of the material that anthropologists have thought or discovered about it. What Graves says about the myth, then, constitutes an introduction in itself to one of the most compelling modern approaches to the play, the anthropological approach.

The third section, "Criticism," consists of comments about the play or discussions of it from antiquity to the present. This material is so varied that chronological sequence seemed the most manageable order to impose upon it. The section begins with Aristotle's *Poetics,* substantially complete, a work which takes *Oedipus Rex,* more than any other play, as its model for what a tragedy should be. Following two samples of the ancient marginal notes or *scholia* on the play, there are a series of diverse reactions and views about it from Voltaire's hostile comments down to Arrowsmith's plea for a more adequate criticism of Greek drama. The interesting tradition of German theoretical criticism is represented by Schiller's classic statement, and by a selection from Karl Reinhardt's *Sophokles.*

Of the modern essays in English, Lattimore's essay is informed by exact Greek scholarship and by a critical awareness of poetic overtones. James Schroeter takes a Freudian context as his starting point for a literary discussion, and his essay can be used more serviceably than this or that psychologist's discussion as exemplifying what may be done with a Freudian approach to the play. Crossett, provided with the tools of literary criticism and of analytic philosophy, approaches some of the classic questions about the play by reasoning his way clearly and deliberately through the whole text, moment by dramatic moment. His essay, of those included here, most resembles the bulk of modern literary discussion of the play, though he is far more cogent and persuasive than many of the standard critics. Arrowsmith's essay proves itself an example of the kind of criticism it asks for, and meets the standards it sets up. The student may take it, as well, for a review of the present state of criticism on Greek drama. And since most of the material Arrowsmith discusses is readily available, he might wish to look up this or that critic mentioned by Arrowsmith.

There should be enough material here for the study of *Oedipus Rex* from any point of view.

To help him with the technical details of the research paper, the student will find the original page numbers of reprinted articles entered in brackets following the last word of the original page. Unspaced ellipses (...) are those that appeared in the original texts; spaced ellipses (. . .) indicate my omissions. I have not indicated omissions of words or passages of Greek in certain essays, however, because to have done so would have cluttered the text unnecessarily.

I should like to thank Kingsley Widmer for his advice, and also Flora Levin and John Crossett, who generously offered me access to material in advance of publication elsewhere.

A. C.

Contents

OEDIPUS REX

A MIRROR FOR GREEK DRAMA

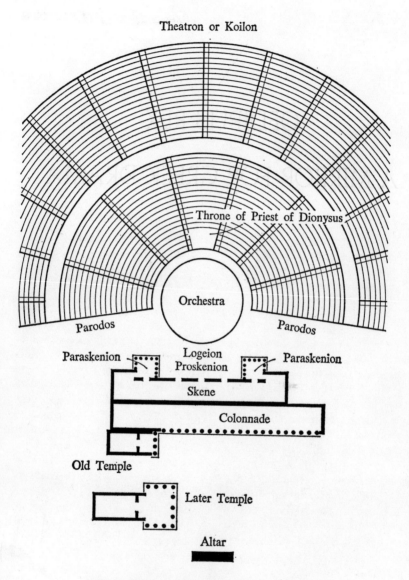

THEATER OF DIONYSUS AT ATHENS
AS IT MAY HAVE BEEN

Albert Cook

PERFORMANCE OF PLAYS IN THE THEATER OF DIONYSUS AT ATHENS

Greek dramatic performances took place on the special occasion of an annual spring festival for Dionysus, a god of wine and fertility who was symbolically present at the annual performances in the form of a statue which stood beside the stage. His altar was a permanent part of the theater precinct.

The plays were performed during the daytime under the open sky. The audience, seated on the semicircular tiers of stone benches, consisted of many of the citizens of the city; and at Athens they could be visually aware of the city, actually and symbolically, by looking over their shoulders and seeing the Acropolis, with the Parthenon and the other sacred buildings, against which the theater arena was built.

The performance possessed some of the tension of an athletic contest, as well as some of the aura of ritual, because the plays were entries in a dramatic contest, and judged on performance. Usually plays were given not as individual units but as parts of a trilogy. *Oedipus Rex,* like other plays of Sophocles, was a notable exception to this rule, being a single, self-contained play from the time of its first production.

The city government from first to last supervised the production of plays during the festival. A poet who wished to compete had first to submit the manuscript of his plays to the *archon* (leader), an important city official, who selected from those submitted the number to be performed—three for the largest festival, the City Dionysia.

The *archon* also maintained ten *choregi,* or leaders of the chorus, one from each of the ten tribes of Athens. The *choregus,* usually a rich man, selected a chorus and flute players and organized them, bearing the expenses for this himself.

The actors, at first chosen by the poet, were later chosen by the state, though individual actors came to be associated with individual poets.

1

After all preparations had been made, some days before the performance, the poet and his actors presented themselves to the public at the Odeon, a smaller theater next to the main one. There, in this fore-action (*proagon*), they gave the public a selected preview of the play they would soon be presenting.

On the day of the performance, which began very early, various civic ceremonies were performed before the plays, including the pouring of libations in front of the statue of Dionysus. The order of plays was determined by lot, and each poet was called up in turn by the public herald and commanded to put on his play.

After a round of plays, ten judges, chosen by vote of the council and the *choregi,* voted for the winner of the dramatic competition. Five ballots were chosen at random to determine the victor, who was then proclaimed by the herald. He and the *choregus* were crowned with ivy on the spot, and the winning poet was awarded a substantial money prize. Afterward he celebrated with a sacrifice and then a banquet attended by the *choregus,* chorus, and actors.

Although the three greatest playwrights (Aeschylus, Sophocles, and Euripides) often won first prize, failing most notably when in competition with one another, *Oedipus Rex* at its first performance lost to the work of a very minor playwright.

The theater itself, at the base of the arena, centered on the *orchestra* or dancing place, where the chorus stood or moved during the performance. Alongside the circular orchestra, slanting along in front of the stage building, were two passages (*eisodoi* or *paradoi*), which served as entrances for the chorus. The fact that they were also used as entrances to the auditorium by spectators before the play indicates the profound psychological difference between Greek and modern attitudes toward the stage area.

Behind and a little above the *orchestra* stood the stage building (*skene*), which probably consisted of (1) a stage platform (*proskenion*) on which the actors stood, (2) a stylized back wall with a central door that could be used for entrances and exits of actors, and (3) side-wing structures (*paraskenia*) high enough for the manipulation of machines like the *mechane* and the *ekkuklema*—by which, for example, Medea rode off in a chariot at the end of Euripides' play.

Aristotle says that Sophocles introduced scene painting (*skenographia*). But however elaborate this may have been, its presence on the back wall—somewhat detached from the actors, who often carried on dialogue with the chorus in the *orchestra*—gave it a different, more purely formal character from the street or palace scene of the Baroque theater, the fourth wall of the nineteenth-century proscenium theater, or even the scene of the Shakespearean stage, which, though largely imaginary, still environed the actors as a Greek *skene* did not.

The action was always conceived of as taking place in the open air, before a house or a temple; and so the spectators, with the symbolic citizens of the chorus dancing between themselves and the actors, could envision themselves almost in the role of civic participants in the action. They looked down—at an angle often steeper than that of a modern sports arena—on the actors, who stood at the foot of the auditorium declaiming at the singing or dancing chorus.

The actors, in a counterthrust, as it were, faced back at them aided by three devices: the platform; the stylized masks, which were larger than life; and the high boots they traditionally wore—boots that were built higher with each generation of performers. The other standard feature of the actor's costume was a stylized tunic.

There were no more than three actors on stage at a time, and Sophocles is said to have introduced the third actor. As in the Elizabethan and Kabuki theaters, men probably took the roles of women.

Throughout the classical period, the performance retained some of the character of its origin as a ritual recitation of poems to music. As in opera, music was essential to the performance, along the lines that Mrs. Levin fills out in the next essay. The actors stood and declaimed in long set speeches or in stylized line-by-line repartee (*stichomythy*). Violent action characteristically took place offstage and was reported by a messenger.

The chorus entered in some sort of regular formation, after the *prologos* or initial section of the play. After their *parados* (danced and sung entrance song), they would dance, divide into parts, sing, and go through formalized motions in their "standing" choral sections or *stasima*. The *stasima* alternated with the recitative dialogues of the actors, the *epeisodia*. The points in the dance at which the chorus turned are marked as *strophe* (turn) and *antistrophe* (counterturn) in the text of the play. These designations also constitute structural stanzaic divisions in the verses. The chorus concluded the play in an exit song and formation, an *exodos*.

Flora R. Levin

MUSIC IN ANCIENT GREEK DRAMA

Ancient Greek drama, provided as it was with a musical component, has often been held to be similar to the modern opera. A superficial examination of the evidence concerning the music of the Greek drama, evidence deriving mainly from secondary sources, may incline one to this view, especially as regards the role which the vocal element played in such dramas. But any serious attempt to compare the two would soon show that whatever musical correspondences one might find would be extremely tenuous; far from finding significant similarities, one would be struck by fundamental differences.

Generally, in the modern opera, everything is subservient to the music. The music supersedes the text, interrupts the action, and requires the sonority of a large orchestra. In the Greek drama the role of music, both vocal and instrumental, was quite different. There the music was subservient to the text. It was invoked to heighten, not interrupt, the action. Moreover, the instrumental accompaniment consisted of only a single flute.[1] For the Greeks, poetic language was the prime material of the drama.

The Greeks' preoccupation with the dramatic texts did lead, however, to a remarkable fusion of music with poetry—as well as with dancing and recitative. The fusion of music with poetry was founded in the very nature of Greek poetic practice. Greek poetry was quantitative, the rhythmic unit being the syllable. The rhythmic contours of Greek music were in their turn also determined by the syllabic structure of the poetry.[2]

Greek drama is composed essentially of three elements, which may be observed in the verse forms of the plays. There is first the lyric element which underlines the moods and feelings aroused by the re-

[1] The lyre was used rarely and probably only for special effects. Cf. scholiast on Aristophanes' *Frogs* 1264. Aristotle, *Problems* 19.43, states that the flute blends better than the lyre with the human voice on the grounds that both are dependent on the same factor, the breath, for their production.

[2] It is possible, furthermore, that the pitch accent of the Greek language determined the melodic line of the music, but evidence on this question is conflicting. See D. D. Feaver, "The Musical Setting of Euripides' *Orestes*," *American Journal of Philology*, 81 (1960), 1–15.

percussions of the dramatic events. This lyric element is confined to the chorus, and is expressed in various and complex meters. These lyrics were sung throughout to an instrumental accompaniment. Second, there is the scenic or mimetic element—the drama itself—comprising the discourses and colloquies distributed among the various personages of the play. The chorus also frequently participates in these discourses through the voice of its leader, the *coryphaeus*. For this running dialogue, the equivalent of the *recitativo secco* of the old Italian opera and the prose of the *opéra-comique*, tragedy employs the iambic trimeter. Generally, this spoken dialogue was unaccompanied by music. Lying between these two modes of execution there existed also a heightened type of recitation which was declaimed against an instrumental accompaniment. There are unfortunately few texts which give direct evidence on the execution of this measured declamation. But the introduction into the plays of more varied rhythms—tetrameters and lyric systems into which iambics were inserted—would suggest that these were points of declamation, with musical accompaniment. The ancients designated this manner of recitation by the term *paracatalogê*. Plutarch *(De musica* 28) says: "Archilochus indeed discovered the rhythm of the iambic trimeters, the versification into heterogeneous rhythms, the alternation of song and recitation and the corresponding musical accompaniment." Aristotle *(Problems* 19.6) asks: "Why does recitative *(paracatalogê)*, intermingled with song, have a tragic element?"

Also suggesting recitative are anapestic systems which likewise appear at points of heightened dramatic tension, often in places where the dialogue shifts to song, before the entrance of the chorus, or sometimes intercalated between the strophes of a *canticum*. Aeschylus has anapests even before his *stasima (Agamemnon* 355–66; *Persians* 532–47, 623–32).[3] The typical use of these anapestic systems as a meter of transition and their frequent appearance in choral ensembles suggests a sung declamation approaching an actual melody. There is, however, no direct evidence on this question.[4]

The three elements described above, which we may here call speech, declamation and song, are exemplified in the dramas of Aeschylus, Sophocles and Euripides. The songs, in their turn, may be divided into three types: The stage songs *(apo skênês),* in which one or two actors took part; the lamentations *(commoi)* and threnodies *(threnoi),* in which one or two actors sang in conjunction with the chorus; and the episodic choruses, in which the chorus, divided into two groups, sang antiphonally, or in which the *coryphaeus* sang in dialogue with the chorus as a whole. The musical accompaniment to

---

3 However, Aristotle, *Poetics* 12, defines the *stasimon:* "a choral song which is not accompanied by a speech of anapests or trochees."

4 Cf. A. Pickard-Cambridge, *The Dramatic Festivals of Athens* (Oxford: Oxford University Press, 1953), 157–158.

these varied arrangements consisted usually of a single flute. From all
the music which must have been composed for these dramas, only one
scrap of evidence has come down to us—a fragment from the musical
setting of Euripides' *Orestes* 338–44. Other than this, we have no
direct access to the actual music which was composed and performed.

It will be necessary in this brief summary to omit certain considerations of Greek music *per se,* since the problems connected with
its structure are so complex that one meets at the outset countless
difficulties and scholarly controversies. We can, however, obtain some
notion of the music in Greek drama from a consideration of certain
references which appear scattered throughout Greek literature and
from the technical discussions of later Greek music theoreticians.

In addition to what we know about the variety of rhythms which
the Greek dramatists had at their disposal, we learn from these literary
and technical sources that the Greeks also had a number of musical
modes of distinctive interval structure. These modes could also be
modified by the enlargement and diminution of their larger and
smaller intervals, modifications effected by the requirements of the
genera—enharmonic, chromatic and diatonic. Moreover, these modes
and their genera could be played or sung in a variety of keys (*tonoi*).
Thus the possibilities for melodic variety were, it seems, very exten-
sive. Yet the Greeks themselves imposed severe limitations on such
melodic invention, these limitations deriving from their notions of
the suitability or appropriateness of the modes. They believed that
these modes possessed certain ethical powers, that they could directly
affect the character of those who listened to music constructed on
their foundations. Thus, some modes were considered suitable for certain types of composition, others were not. It was for this reason that
Plato excluded certain modes from his ideal state as being unsuited
to a vigorous and manly nature (cf. *Republic* 398E). It followed, then,
that for their tragic dramas only certain modes were considered appropriate by the Greeks.

Two modes characterized the choral music of ancient tragedy: the
Mixolydian, the mode of passionate lament, and the Dorian, the mode
of stoic heroism. Plutarch tells us (*De musica* 16): "The Mixolydian
is a pathetic mode suited to tragedy. Aristoxenus says that Sappho invented it and the tragic poets learned it from her." He goes on to say
that the use of these two modes is suited to the mixture in tragedy of
the two elements—the pathetic and the heroic.

Along with these two principal modes of the dramatic chorus, two
or three other modes appear to have occupied a secondary position.
There were, for example, the Hypodorian and the Hypophrygian—
modes which were used for the lyrics sung by the actors but not by
the chorus. According to Aristotle (*Problems* 19.48): "Both these modes
are inappropriate to the chorus and more suitable to actors on the
stage." Further, in the *Life of Sophocles* we learn that, according to

Aristoxenus, Sophocles was the first Athenian poet to introduce the Phrygian, the mode of the dithyramb, into his songs. It is worth noting that the one fragment of music we have, from the score of *Orestes*, is noted in this mode. The most remarkable feature of this fragment is that it has decided affinities not with the Phrygian mode as described by Aristoxenus, but with a more primitive Phrygian formation documented by Aristides Quintilianus (*De musica* 21–22M).[5]

In addition to modal limitations, there were restrictions on the use of the genera. It is known that the enharmonic genus was regarded with great veneration, while neither tragedy nor the choral lyric made use of the chromatic genus. Plutarch reports (*De musica* 1137E) that Phrynichus and Aeschylus, as well as Pindar and Simonides, abstained from the chromatic genus. After the Peloponnesian War, however, we find a gradual but steady breaking down of these modal and generic restrictions until "the dithyrambic composers, Philoxenus, Timotheus and Telestes passed frequently from one key to another, employing Dorian, Phrygian and Lydian modes in the same composition and intermingling all species of melodies, either enharmonic or chromatic."[6] Melanippides, Phrynis and Kinesias are also reported to have been guilty of taking great liberties with accepted musical standards and are accused of corrupting the classical purity of music with their elaborate and ornate arrangements.[7] In the same way, Aristophanes mocks Agathon and Euripides for admitting this florid style of music into their dramas.[8]

Independent or solo instrumental music was apparently not used in tragedy, the primary function of instrumental music having been that of accompaniment. There are, however, a few isolated reports of solo instrumental passages in comedy, although these were for special sound effects. For example, the scholiast on Aristophanes' *Birds* 222 explains that the flute is to imitate the song of the nightingale.

It may be seen, even from such a brief summation as this, that our knowledge about the actual music performed in Greek drama is drawn from evidence that is discouragingly fragmentary. More often than not, our sources assume in us the very knowledge that we are seeking to obtain. We are almost totally uninformed about musical practices in the 6th and 5th centuries—the periods of great lyric and tragic poetry; most of our speculations are dependent upon literary allusions which are often more suggestive than conclusive. The development of music from the classical period through the era of corrup-

---

5 Cf. J. F. Mountford, "Greek Music in the Papyri and Inscriptions," in *New Chapters in the History of Greek Literature*, 2nd ser., ed. J. U. Powell and E. A. Barber (Oxford: Oxford University Press, 1929), 168–169.

6 Dionysius of Halicarnassus, *De compositione verborum* 19.

7 Cf. Plutarch, *De musica* 30.

8 *Thesmophoriazusae* 100; *Frogs* 1301 ff.

tion and change, the latter era exemplified in the virtuosi Melanippides and Timotheus, can be only dimly ascertained. Nevertheless, significant advances have been made by dedicated scholars over the last hundred years in relating the available evidence and establishing important connections between theoretical data and literary references. It is, therefore, to these researchers that we are indebted for any information that exists in this area of classical studies.

OEDIPUS—THE MYTH AND THE PLAY

Homer

From *The Odyssey*, Book 11, lines 271–281.
Translated by Albert Cook.

I saw the mother of Oedipus, lovely Jocasta,
Who did a huge deed in the ignorance of her mind
And married her son. He slew his own father
And married her. The gods soon made it apparent to men.
But he suffered pains in his much-beloved Thebes,
And ruled the Cadmeians through the ruinous plans of the gods;
And she went to the place of the mighty gate-keeper Hades.
She hung up a high noose from the lofty roof-beam,
Possessed by her grief. For him she left many pains
Behind her, the kind a mother's Furies bring to pass.

Edwin Muir

"Oedipus." From *Collected Poems*. New
York: Grove Press, 1957. Reprinted by permission of the publisher.

I, Oedipus, the club-foot, made to stumble,
Who long in the light have walked the world in darkness,
And once in the darkness did that which the light

9

Found and disowned—too well I have loved the light,
Too dearly have rued the darkness. I am one
Who as in innocent play sought out his guilt,
And now through guilt seeks other innocence,
Beset by evil thoughts, led by the gods. [163]
There was a room, a bed of darkness, once
Known to me, now to all. Yet in that darkness,
Before the light struck, she and I who lay
There without thought of sin and knew each other
Too well, yet were to each other quite unknown
Though fastened mouth to mouth and breast to breast—
Strangers laid on one bed, as children blind,
Clear-eyed and blind as children—did we sin
Then on that bed before the light came on us,
Desiring good to each other, bringing, we thought,
Great good to each other? But neither guilt nor death.

Yet if that darkness had been darker yet,
Buried in endless dark past reach of light
Or eye of the gods, a kingdom of solid darkness
Impregnable and immortal, would we have sinned,
Or lived like the gods in deathless innocence?
For sin is born in the light; therefore we cower
Before the face of the light that none can meet
And all must seek. And when in memory now,
Woven of light and darkness, a stifling web,
I call her back, dear, dreaded, who lay with me,
I see guilt, only guilt, my nostrils choke
With the smell of guilt, and I can scarcely breathe
Here in the guiltless, guilt evoking sun.

And when young Oedipus—for it was Oedipus
And not another—on that long vanished night
Far in my night, at that predestined point
Where three paths like three fates crossed one another,
Tracing the evil figure—when I met
The stranger who menaced me, and flung the stone [164]
That brought him death and me this that I carry,
It was not him but fear I sought to kill,
Fear that, the wise men say, is father of evil,
And was my father in flesh and blood, yet fear,
Fear only, father and fear in one dense body,
So that there was no division, no way past:
Did I sin then, by the gods admonished to sin,
By men enjoined to sin? For it is duty
Of god and man to kill the shapes of fear.

These thoughts recur, vain thoughts. The gods see all,
And will what must be willed, which guards us here.
Their will in them was anger, in me was terror
Long since, but now is peace. For I am led

By them in darkness; light is all about me;
My way lies in the light; they know it; I
Am theirs to guide and hold. And I have learned,
Though blind, to see with something of their sight,
Can look into that other world and watch
King Oedipus the just, crowned and discrowned,
As one may see oneself rise in a dream,
Distant and strange. Even so I see
The meeting at the place where three roads crossed,
And who was there and why, and what was done
That had to be done and paid for. Innocent
The deed that brought the guilt of father-murder. Pure
The embrace on the bed of darkness. Innocent
And guilty. I have wrought and thought in darkness,
And stand here now, an innocent mark of shame,
That so men's guilt might be made manifest
In such a walking riddle—their guilt and mine,
For I've but acted out this fable. I have judged [165]
Myself, obedient to the gods' high judgment,
And seen myself with their pure eyes, have learnt
That all must bear a portion of the wrong
That is driven deep into our fathomless hearts
Past sight or thought; that bearing it we may ease
The immortal burden of the gods who keep
Our natural steps and the earth and skies from harm. [166]

Robert Graves

"Oedipus." From *The Greek Myths*, Vol. II.
Baltimore: Penguin Books, 1955. Reprinted
by permission of the author's agent, Willis
Kingsley Wing.

Laius, son of Labdacus, married Iocaste, and ruled over Thebes.
Grieved by his prolonged childlessness, he secretly consulted the Delphic Oracle, which informed him that this seeming misfortune was a
blessing, because any child born to Iocaste would become his murderer.

He therefore put Iocaste away, though without offering any reason for his decision, which caused her such vexation that, having made him drunk, she inveigled him into her arms again as soon as night fell. When, nine months later, Iocaste was brought to bed of a son, Laius snatched him from the nurse's arms, pierced his feet with a nail and, binding them together, exposed him on Mount Cithaeron.

b. Yet the Fates had ruled that this boy should reach a green old age. A Corinthian shepherd found him, named him Oedipus because his feet were deformed by the nail-wound, and brought him to Corinth, where King Polybus was reigning at the time.[1]

c. According to another version of the story, Laius did not expose Oedipus on the mountain, but locked him in a chest, which was lowered into the sea from a ship. This chest drifted ashore at Sicyon, where Periboea, Polybus's queen, happened to be on the beach, supervising her royal laundry-women. She picked up Oedipus, retired to a thicket and pretended to have been overcome by the pangs of labour. Since the laundry-women were too busy to notice what she was about, she deceived them all into thinking that he had only just been born. But Periboea told the truth to Polybus who, also being childless, was pleased to rear Oedipus as his own son.

One day, taunted by a Corinthian youth with not in the least resembling his supposed parents, Oedipus went to ask the Delphic Oracle what future lay in store for him. 'Away from the shrine, wretch!' the Pythoness cried in disgust. 'You will kill your father and marry your mother!'

d. Since Oedipus loved Polybus and Periboea, and shrank from bringing disaster upon them, he at once decided against returning to Corinth. But in the narrow defile between Delphi and Daulis he happened to meet Laius, who ordered him roughly to step off the road and make way for his betters; Laius, it should be explained, was in a chariot[9] and Oedipus on foot. Oedipus retorted that he acknowledged no betters except the gods and his own parents.

'So much the worse for you!' cried Laius, and ordered his charioteer Polyphontes to drive on.

One of the wheels bruised Oedipus's foot and, transported by rage, he killed Polyphontes with his spear. Then, flinging Laius on the road entangled in the reins, and whipping up the team, he made them drag him to death. It was left to the king of Plataeae to bury both corpses.[2]

e. Laius had been on his way to ask the Oracle how he might rid Thebes of the Sphinx. This monster was a daughter of Typhon and Echidne or, some say, of the dog Orthrus and the Chimaera, and had flown to Thebes from the uttermost part of Ethiopia. She was easily

---

[1] Apollodorus: iii. 5. 7.
[2] Hyginus: *Fabula* 66; Scholiast on Euripides's *Phoenician Women* 13 and 26; Apollodorus: *loc. cit.*; Pausanias: x. 5. 2.

recognized by her woman's head, lion's body, serpent's tail, and eagle's wings.[3] Hera had recently sent the Sphinx to punish Thebes for Laius's abduction of the boy Chrysippus from Pisa and, settling on Mount Phicium, close to the city, she now asked every Theban wayfarer a riddle taught her by the Three Muses: 'What being, with only one voice, has sometimes two feet, sometimes three, sometimes four, and is weakest when it has the most?' Those who could not solve the riddle she throttled and devoured on the spot, among which unfortunates was Iocaste's nephew Haemon, whom the Sphinx made *haimon,* or 'bloody', indeed.

Oedipus, approaching Thebes fresh from the murder of Laius, guessed the answer. 'Man,' he replied, 'because he crawls on all fours as an infant, stands firmly on his two feet in his youth, and leans upon a staff in his old age.' The mortified Sphinx leaped from Mount Phicium and dashed herself to pieces in the valley below. At this the grateful Thebans acclaimed Oedipus king, and he married Iocaste, unaware that she was his mother.

f. Plague then descended upon Thebes, and the Delphic Oracle, when consulted once more, replied: 'Expel the murderer of Laius!' Oedipus, not knowing whom he had met in the defile, pronounced a curse on Laius's murderer and sentenced him to exile.

g. Blind Teiresias, the most renowned seer in Greece at this time, now demanded an audience with Oedipus. Some say that Athene, who had blinded him for having inadvertently seen her bathing, was moved by his mother's plea and, taking the serpent Erichthonius from her aegis, gave the order: 'Cleanse Teiresias's ears with your tongue that he may understand the language of prophetic birds.'[10]

h. Others say that once, on Mount Cyllene, Teiresias had seen two serpents in the act of coupling. When both attacked him, he struck at them with his staff, killing the female. Immediately he was turned into a woman, and became a celebrated harlot; but seven years later he happened to see the same sight again at the same spot, and this time regained his manhood by killing the male serpent. Still others say that when Aphrodite and the three Charites, Pasithea, Cale, and Euphrosyne, disputed as to which of the four was most beautiful, Teiresias awarded Cale the prize; whereupon Aphrodite turned him into an old woman. But Cale took him with her to Crete and presented him with a lovely head of hair. Some days later Hera began reproaching Zeus for his numerous infidelities. He defended them by arguing that, at any rate, when he did share her couch, she had the more enjoyable time by far. 'Women, of course, derive infinitely greater pleasure from the sexual act than men,' he blustered.

3 Apollodorus: iii. 5. 8; Hesiod: *Theogony* 326; Sophocles: *Oedipus the Tyrant* 391; Scholiast on Aristophanes's *Frogs* 1287.

'What nonsense!' cried Hera. 'The exact contrary is the case, and well you know it.'

Teiresias, summoned to settle the dispute from his personal experience, answered:

> 'If the parts of love-pleasure be counted as ten,
> Thrice three go to women, one only to men.'

Hera was so exasperated by Zeus's triumphant grin that she blinded Teiresias; but Zeus compensated him with inward sight, and a life extended to seven generations.[4]

i. Teiresias now appeared at Oedipus's court, leaning on the cornel-wood staff given him by Athene, and revealed to Oedipus the will of the gods: that the plague would cease only if a Sown Man died for the sake of the city. Iocaste's father Menoeceus, one of those who had risen out of the earth when Cadmus sowed the serpent's teeth, at once leaped from the walls, and all Thebes praised his civic devotion.

Teiresias then announced further: 'Menoeceus did well, and the plague will now cease. Yet the gods had another of the Sown Men in mind, one of the third generation: for he has killed his father and married his mother. Know, Queen Iocaste, that it is your husband Oedipus!'

j. At first, none would believe Teiresias, but his words were soon confirmed by a letter from Periboea at Corinth. She wrote that the sudden death of King Polybus now allowed her to reveal the circumstances[11] of Oedipus's adoption; and this she did in damning detail. Iocaste then hanged herself for shame and grief, while Oedipus blinded himself with a pin taken from her garments.[5]

k. Some say that, although tormented by the Erinnyes, who accused him of having brought about his mother's death, Oedipus continued to reign over Thebes for a while, until he fell gloriously in battle.[6] According to others, however, Iocaste's brother Creon expelled him, but not before he had cursed Eteocles and Polyneices—who were at once his sons and his brothers—when they insolently sent him the inferior portion of the sacrificial beast, namely haunch instead of royal shoulder. They therefore watched dry-eyed as he left the city which he had delivered from the Sphinx's power. After wandering for many years through country after country, guided by his faithful daughter Antigone, Oedipus finally came to Colonus in Attica, where the Erinnyes, who have a grove there, hounded him to death, and Theseus

---

[4] Apollodorus: iii. 6. 7; Hyginus: *Fabula* 75; Ovid: *Metamorphoses* iii. 320; Pindar: *Nemean Odes* i. 91; Tzetzes: *On Lycophron* 682; Sosostratus, quoted by Eustathius: p. 1665.

[5] Apollodorus: iii. 5. 8; Sophocles: *Oedipus the Tyrant* 447, 713, 731, 774, 1285, etc.

[6] Homer: *Odyssey* xi. 270 and *Iliad* xxiii. 679.

buried his body in the precinct of the Solemn Ones at Athens, lamenting by Antigone's side.[7]

1. The story of Laius, Iocaste, and Oedipus has been deduced from a set of sacred icons by a deliberate perversion of their meaning. A myth which would explain Labdacus's name ('help with torches') has been lost; but it may refer to the torchlight arrival of a Divine Child, carried by cattlemen or shepherds at the New Year ceremony, and acclaimed as a son of the goddess Brimo ('raging'). This *eleusis,* or advent, was the most important incident in the Eleusinian Mysteries, and perhaps also in the Isthmian, which would explain the myth of Oedipus's[12] arrival at the court of Corinth. Shepherds fostered or paid homage to many other legendary or semi-legendary infant princes, such as Hippothous, Pelias, Amphion, Aegisthus, Moses, Romulus, and Cyrus, who were all either exposed on a mountain or else consigned to the waves in an ark, or both. Moses was found by Pharaoh's daughter when she went down to the water with her women. It is possible that *Oedipus,* 'swollen foot,' was originally *Oedipais,* 'son of the swelling sea,' which is the meaning of the name given to the corresponding Welsh hero, Dylan; and that the piercing of Oedipus's feet with a nail belongs to the end, not to the beginning, of history, as in the myth of Talus.

2. Laius's murder is a record of the solar king's ritual death at the hands of his successor: thrown from a chariot and dragged by the horses. His abduction of Chrysippus probably refers to the sacrifice of a surrogate when the first year of his reign ended.

3. The anecdote of the Sphinx has evidently been deduced from an icon showing the winged Moon-goddess of Thebes, whose composite body represents the two parts of the Theban year—lion for the waxing part, serpent for the waning part—and to whom the new king offers his devotions before marrying her priestess, the Queen. It seems also that the riddle which the Sphinx learned from the Muses has been invented to explain a picture of an infant, a warrior, and an old man, all worshipping the Triple-goddess: each pays his respects to a different person of the triad. But the Sphinx, overcome by Oedipus, killed herself, and so did her priestess Iocaste. Was Oedipus a thirteenth-century invader of Thebes, who suppressed the old Minoan cult of the goddess and reformed the calendar? Under the old system, the new king, though a foreigner, had theoretically been a son of the old king whom he killed and whose widow he married; a custom that the patriarchal invaders misrepresented as parricide and incest. The Freudian theory that the 'Oedipus complex' is an instinct common to all men was suggested by this perverted anecdote; and while Plutarch records (*On*

[7] Sophocles: *Oedipus at Colonus* 166 and scholiast on 1375; Euripides: *Phoenician Women, Proem;* Apollodorus: iii. 5. 9; Hyginus: *Fabula* 67; Pausanias: i. 20. 7.

Isis and Osiris 32) that the hippopotamus 'murdered his sire and forced his dam,' he would never have suggested that every man has a hippopotamus complex.

4. Though Theban patriots, loth to admit that Oedipus was a foreigner who took their city by storm, preferred to make him the lost heir to the kingdom, the truth is revealed by the death of Menoeceus, a member of the pre-Hellenic race that celebrated the Peloria festival in memory of Ophion the Demiurge, from whose teeth they claimed to have sprung. He leaped to his death in the desperate hope of placating the goddess, like Mettus Curtius, when a chasm opened in the Roman Forum (Livy: vii. 6); and the same sacrifice was offered during the War of the 'Seven Against Thebes'. However, he died in vain; otherwise the Sphinx, and her chief priestess, would not have been[13] obliged to commit suicide. The story of Iocaste's death by hanging is probably an error; Helen of the Olive-trees, like Erigone and Ariadne of the vine cult, was said to have died in this way—perhaps to account for figurines of the Moon-goddess which dangled from the boughs of orchard trees, as a fertility charm. Similar figurines were used at Thebes; and when Iocaste committed suicide, she doubtless leaped from a rock, as the Sphinx did.

5. The occurrence of 'Teiresias', a common title for soothsayers, throughout Greek legendary history suggested that Teiresias had been granted a remarkably long life by Zeus. To see snakes coupling is still considered unlucky in Southern India; the theory being that the witness will be punished with the 'female disease' (as Herodotus calls it), namely homosexuality; here the Greek fabulist has taken the tale a stage further in order to raise a laugh against women. Cornel, a divinatory tree sacred to Cronus, symbolized the fourth month, that of the Spring Equinox; Rome was founded at this season, on the spot where Romulus's cornel-wood javelin struck the ground. Hesiod turned the traditional two Charites into three, calling them Euphrosyne, Aglaia, and Thalia (*Theogony* 945). Sosostratus's account of the beauty contest makes poor sense, because *Pasithea Cale Euphrosyne*, 'the Goddess of Joy who is beautiful to all', seems to have been Aphrodite's own title. He may have borrowed it from the Judgement of Paris.

6. Two incompatible accounts of Oedipus's end survive. According to Homer, he died gloriously in battle. According to Apollodorus and Hyginus, he was banished by Iocaste's brother, a member of the Cadmean royal house, and wandered as a blind beggar through the cities of Greece until he came to Colonus in Attica, where the Furies hounded him to death. Oedipus's remorseful self-blinding has been interpreted by psychologists to mean castration; but though the blindness of Achilles's tutor Phoenix was said by Greek grammarians to be a euphemism for impotence, primitive myth is always downright, and the castration of Uranus and Attis continued to be recorded unblushingly in Classical text books. Oedipus's blinding, therefore, reads like

a theatrical invention, rather than original myth. Furies were personifications of conscience, but conscience in a very limited sense: aroused only by the breach of a maternal taboo.

7. According to the non-Homeric story, Oedipus's defiance of the City-goddess was punished by exile, and he eventually died a victim of his own superstitious fears. It is probable that his innovations were repudiated by a body of Theban conservatives; and, certainly, his sons' and brothers' unwillingness to award him the shoulder of the sacrificial victim amounted to a denial of his divine authority. The shoulder-blade was the priestly perquisite at Jerusalem (*Leviticus* vii. 32 and xi. 21, etc.) and[14] Tantalus set one before the goddess Demeter at a famous banquet of the gods.

Did Oedipus, like Sisyphus, try to substitute patrilineal for matrilineal laws of succession, but get banished by his subjects? It seems probable. Theseus of Athens, another patriarchal revolutionary from the Isthmus, who destroyed the ancient Athenian clan of Pallantids, is associated by the Athenian dramatists with Oedipus's burial, and was likewise banished at the close of his reign.

8. Teiresias here figures dramatically as the prophet of Oedipus's final disgrace, but the story, as it survives, seems to have been turned inside-out. It may once have run something like this:

Oedipus of Corinth conquered Thebes and became king by marrying Iocaste, a priestess of Hera. Afterwards he announced that the kingdom should henceforth be bequeathed from father to son in the male line, which is a Corinthian custom, instead of remaining the gift of Hera the Throttler. Oedipus confessed that he felt himself disgraced as having let chariot horses drag to death Laius, who was accounted his father, and as having married Iocaste, who had enroyalled him by a ceremony of rebirth. But when he tried to change these customs, Iocaste committed suicide in protest, and Thebes was visited by a plague. Upon the advice of an oracle, the Thebans then withheld from Oedipus the sacred shoulder-blade, and banished him. He died in a fruitless attempt to regain his throne by warfare.[15]

Sophocles

OEDIPUS REX

Translated by Albert Cook. Produced by the
Tributary Theatre of Boston (1948) and by
The Cleveland Playhouse (1958). Copyright
1948, 1957 by the translator.

CHARACTERS

OEDIPUS, *king of* Thebes
A PRIEST
CREON, *brother-in-law of Oedipus*
CHORUS *of* Theban *elders*
TEIRESIAS, *a prophet*
JOCASTA, *sister of Creon, wife of Oedipus*
MESSENGER
SERVANT *of Laius, father of Oedipus*
SECOND MESSENGER
(silent) ANTIGONE *and* ISMENE, *daughters of Oedipus*

SCENE. *Before the palace of Oedipus at Thebes. In front of the large
central doors, an altar; and an altar near each of the two side doors.
On the altar steps are seated supplicants—old men, youths, and young
boys—dressed in white tunics and cloaks, their hair bound with white
fillets. They have laid on the altars olive branches wreathed with
wool-fillets.*

The old PRIEST OF ZEUS *stands alone facing the central doors of the
palace. The doors open, and* OEDIPUS, *followed by two attendants who
stand at either door, enters and looks about.*

OEDIPUS: O children, last born stock of ancient Cadmus,
What petitions are these you bring to me
With garlands on your suppliant olive branches?
The whole city teems with incense fumes,
Teems with prayers for healing and with groans.

19

Thinking it best, children, to hear all this
Not from some messenger, I came myself,
The world renowned and glorious Oedipus.
But tell me, aged priest, since you are fit
To speak before these men, how stand you here,   10[1]
In fear or want? Tell me, as I desire
To do my all; hard hearted I would be
To feel no sympathy for such a prayer.

PRIEST: O Oedipus, ruler of my land, you see
How old we are who stand in supplication
Before your altars here, some not yet strong
For lengthy flight, some heavy with age,
Priests, as I of Zeus, and choice young men.
The rest of the tribe sits with wreathed branches,
In market places, at Pallas' two temples,   20
And at prophetic embers by the river.
The city, as you see, now shakes too greatly
And cannot raise her head out of the depths
Above the gory swell. She wastes in blight,
Blight on earth's fruitful blooms and grazing flocks,
And on the barren birth pangs of the women.
The fever god has fallen on the city,
And drives it, a most hated pestilence
Through whom the home of Cadmus is made empty.
Black Hades is enriched with wails and groans.   30
Not that we think you equal to the gods
These boys and I sit suppliant at your hearth,
But judging you first of men in the trials of life,
And in the human intercourse with spirits:—
You are the one who came to Cadmus' city
And freed us from the tribute which we paid
To the harsh-singing Sphinx. And that you did
Knowing nothing else, unschooled by us.
But people say and think it was some god
That helped you to set our life upright.
Now Oedipus, most powerful of all,   40
We all are turned here toward you, we beseech you,
Find us some strength, whether from one of the gods
You hear an omen, or know one from a man.
For the experienced I see will best
Make good plans grow from evil circumstance.
Come, best of mortal men, raise up the state.
Come, prove your fame, since now this land of ours
Calls you savior for your previous zeal.

---

[1] Numeration refers throughout to the line-numbers in the Greek text.

O never let our memory of your reign
Be that we first stood straight and later fell,   50
But to security raise up this state.
With favoring omen once you gave us luck;
Be now as good again; for if henceforth
You rule as now, you will be this country's king,
Better it is to rule men than a desert,
Since nothing is either ship or fortress tower
Bare of men who together dwell within.

OEDIPUS: O piteous children, I am not ignorant
Of what you come desiring. Well I know
You are all sick, and in your sickness none   60
There is among you as sick as I,
For your pain comes to one man alone,
To him and to none other, but my soul
Groans for the state, for myself, and for you.
You do not wake a man who is sunk in sleep;
Know that already I have shed many tears,
And travelled many wandering roads of thought.
Well have I sought, and found one remedy;
And this I did: the son of Menoeceus,
Creon, my brother-in-law, I sent away   70
Unto Apollo's Pythian halls to find
What I might do or say to save the state.
The days are measured out that he is gone;
It troubles me how he fares. Longer than usual
He has been away, more than the fitting time.
But when he comes, then evil I shall be,
If all the god reveals I fail to do.

PRIEST: You speak at the right time. These men just now
Signal to me that Creon is approaching.

OEDIPUS: O Lord Apollo, grant that he may come   80
In saving fortune shining as in eye.

PRIEST: Glad news he brings, it seems, or else his head
Would not be crowned with leafy, berried bay.

OEDIPUS: We will soon know. He is close enough to hear.—
Prince, my kinsman, son of Menoeceus,
What oracle do you bring us from the god?

CREON: A good one. For I say that even burdens
If they chance to turn out right, will all be well.

OEDIPUS: Yet what is the oracle? Your present word
Makes me neither bold nor apprehensive.   90

CREON: If you wish to hear in front of this crowd
I am ready to speak, or we can go within.

OEDIPUS: Speak forth to all. The sorrow that I bear
Is greater for these men than for my life.

CREON: May I tell you what I heard from the god?
  Lord Phoebus clearly bids us to drive out,
  And not to leave uncured within this country,
  A pollution we have nourished in our land.
OEDIPUS: With what purgation? What kind of misfortune?
CREON: Banish the man, or quit slaughter with slaughter   100
  In cleansing, since this blood rains on the state.
OEDIPUS: Who is this man whose fate the god reveals?
CREON: Laius, my lord, was formerly the guide
  Of this our land before you steered this city.
OEDIPUS: I know him by hearsay, but I never saw him.
CREON: Since he was slain, the god now plainly bids us
  To punish his murderers, whoever they may be.
OEDIPUS: Where are they on the earth? How shall we find
  This indiscernible track of ancient guilt?
CREON: In this land, said Apollo. What is sought   110
  Can be apprehended; the unobserved escapes.
OEDIPUS: Did Laius fall at home on this bloody end?
  Or in the fields, or in some foreign land?
CREON: As a pilgrim, the god said, he left his tribe
  And once away from home, returned no more.
OEDIPUS: Was there no messenger, no fellow wayfarer
  Who saw, from whom an inquirer might get aid?
CREON: They are all dead, save one, who fled in fear
  And he knows only one thing sure to tell.
OEDIPUS: What is that? We may learn many facts from one   120
  If we might take for hope a short beginning.
CREON: Robbers, Apollo said, met there and killed him
  Not by the strength of one, but many hands.
OEDIPUS: How did the robber, unless something from here
  Was at work with silver, reach this point of daring?
CREON: These facts are all conjecture. Laius dead,
  There rose in evils no avenger for him.
OEDIPUS: But when the king had fallen slain, what trouble
  Prevented you from finding all this out?
CREON: The subtle-singing Sphinx made us let go   130
  What was unclear to search at our own feet.
OEDIPUS: Well then, I will make this clear afresh
  From the start. Phoebus was right, you were right
  To take this present interest in the dead.
  Justly it is you see me as your ally
  Avenging alike this country and the god.
  Not for the sake of some distant friends,
  But for myself I will disperse this filth.
  Whoever it was who killed that man
  With the same hand may wish to do vengeance on me.   140

And so assisting Laius I aid myself.
But hurry quickly, children, stand up now
From the altar steps, raising these suppliant boughs.
Let someone gather Cadmus' people here
To learn that I will do all, whether at last
With Phoebus' help we are shown saved or fallen.

PRIEST: Come, children, let us stand. We came here
First for the sake of what this man proclaims.
Phoebus it was who sent these prophecies
And he will come to save us from the plague.   150

CHORUS:
        Strophe A
O sweet-tongued voice of Zeus, in what spirit do you come
From Pytho rich in gold
To glorious Thebes? I am torn on the rack, dread shakes my fearful
     mind,
Apollo of Delos, hail!
As I stand in awe of you, what need, either new
Do you bring to the full for me, or old in the turning times of the
     year?
Tell me, O child of golden Hope, undying Voice!

        Antistrophe A
First on you do I call, daughter of Zeus, undying Athene
And your sister who guards our land,   160
Artemis, seated upon the throne renowned of our circled Place,
And Phoebus who darts afar;
Shine forth to me, thrice warder-off of death;
If ever in time before when ruin rushed upon the state,
The flame of sorrow you drove beyond our bounds, come also now.

        Strophe B
O woe! Unnumbered that I bear
The sorrows are! My whole host is sick, nor is there a sword of
     thought
To ward off pain. The growing fruits   170
Of glorious earth wax not, nor women
Withstand in childbirth shrieking pangs.
Life on life you may see, which, like the well-winged bird,
Faster than stubborn fire, speed
To the strand of the evening god.

        Antistrophe B
Unnumbered of the city die.   180
Unpitied babies bearing death lie unmoaned on the ground.

Grey-haired mothers and young wives
From all sides at the altar's edge
Lift up a wail beseeching, for their mournful woes.
The prayer for healing shines blent with a grieving cry;
Wherefore, O golden daughter of Zeus,
Send us your succour with its beaming face.

Strophe C

Grant that fiery Ares, who now with no brazen shield   190
Flames round me in shouting attack
May turn his back in running flight from our land,
May be borne with fair wind
To Amphitrite's great chamber
Or to the hostile port
Of the Thracian surge.
For even if night leaves any ill undone
It is brought to pass and comes to be in the day.
O Zeus who bear the fire   200
And rule the lightning's might,
Strike him beneath your thunderbolt with death!

Antistrophe C

O lord Apollo, would that you might come and scatter forth
Untamed darts from your twirling golden bow;
Bring succour from the plague; may the flashing
Beams come of Artemis,
With which she glances through the Lycian hills.
Also on him I call whose hair is held in gold,
Who gives a name to this land,   210
Bacchus of winy face, whom maidens hail!
Draw near with your flaming Maenad band
And the aid of your gladsome torch
Against the plague, dishonoured among the gods.

OEDIPUS: You pray; if for what you pray you would be willing
To hear and take my words, to nurse the plague,
You may get succour and relief from evils.
A stranger to this tale I now speak forth,
A stranger to the deed, for not alone   220
Could I have tracked it far without some clue,
But now that I am enrolled a citizen
Latest among the citizens of Thebes
To all you sons of Cadmus I proclaim
Whoever of you knows at what man's hand
Laius, the son of Labdacus, met his death,
I order him to tell me all, and even

If he fears, to clear the charge and he will suffer
No injury, but leave the land unharmed.
If someone knows the murderer to be an alien   230
From foreign soil, let him not be silent;
I will give him a reward, my thanks besides.
But if you stay in silence and from fear
For self or friend thrust aside my command,
Hear now from me what I shall do for this;
I charge that none who dwell within this land
Whereof I hold the power and the throne
Give this man shelter whoever he may be,
Or speak to him, or share with him in prayer
Or sacrifice, or serve him lustral rites,   240
But drive him, all, out of your homes, for he
Is this pollution on us, as Apollo
Revealed to me just now in oracle.
I am therefore the ally of the god
And of the murdered man. And now I pray
That the murderer, whether he hides alone
Or with his partners, may, evil coward,
Wear out in luckless ills his wretched life.
I further pray, that, if at my own hearth
He dwells known to me in my own home,   250
I may suffer myself the curse I just now uttered.
And you I charge to bring all this to pass
For me, and for the god, and for our land
Which now lies fruitless, godless, and corrupt.
Even if Phoebus had not urged this affair,
Not rightly did you let it go unpurged
When one both noble and a king was murdered!
You should have sought it out. Since now I reign
Holding the power which he had held before me,
Having the selfsame wife and marriage bed—   260
And if his seed had not met barren fortune
We should be linked by offspring from one mother;
But as it was, fate leapt upon his head.
Therefore in this, as if for my own father
I fight for him, and shall attempt all
Searching to seize the hand which shed that blood,
For Labdacus' son, before him Polydorus,
And ancient Cadmus, and Agenor of old.
And those who fail to do this, I pray the gods
May give them neither harvest from their earth   270
Nor children from their wives, but may they be
Destroyed by a fate like this one, or a worse.
You other Thebans, who cherish these commands,

May Justice, the ally of a righteous cause,
And all the gods be always on your side.
CHORUS: By the oath you laid on me, my king, I speak.
I killed not Laius, nor can show who killed him.
Phoebus it was who sent this question to us,
And he should answer who has done the deed.
OEDIPUS: Your words are just, but to compel the gods   280
In what they do not wish, no man can do.
CHORUS: I would tell what seems to me our second course.
OEDIPUS: If there is a third, fail not to tell it too.
CHORUS: Lord Teiresias I know, who sees this best
Like lord Apollo; in surveying this,
One might, my lord, find out from him most clearly.
OEDIPUS: Even this I did not neglect; I have done it already.
At Creon's word I twice sent messengers.
It is a wonder he has been gone so long.
CHORUS: And also there are rumors, faint and old.   290
OEDIPUS: What are they? I must search out every tale.
CHORUS: They say there were some travellers who killed him.
OEDIPUS: So I have heard, but no one sees a witness.
CHORUS: If his mind knows a particle of fear
He will not long withstand such curse as yours.
OEDIPUS: He fears no speech who fears not such a deed.
CHORUS: But here is the man who will convict the guilty.
Here are these men leading the divine prophet
In whom alone of men the truth is born.
OEDIPUS: O you who ponder all, Teiresias,   300
Both what is taught and what cannot be spoken,
What is of heaven and what trod on the earth,
Even if you are blind, you know what plague
Clings to the state, and, master, you alone
We find as her protector and her saviour.
Apollo, if the messengers have not told you,
Answered our question, that release would come
From this disease only if we make sure
Of Laius' slayers and slay them in return
Or drive them out as exiles from the land.
But you now, grudge us neither voice of birds   310
Nor any way you have of prophecy.
Save yourself and the state; save me as well.
Save everything polluted by the dead.
We are in your hands; it is the noblest task
To help a man with all your means and powers.
TEIRESIAS: Alas! Alas! How terrible to be wise,
Where it does the seer no good. Too well I know
And have forgot this, or would not have come here.

OEDIPUS: What is this? How fainthearted you have come!

TEIRESIAS: Let me go home; it is best for you to bear   320
  Your burden, and I mine, if you will heed me.

OEDIPUS: You speak what is lawless, and hateful to the state
  Which raised you, when you deprive her of your answer.

TEIRESIAS: And I see that your speech does not proceed
  In season; I shall not undergo the same.

OEDIPUS: Don't by the gods turn back when you are wise,
  When all we suppliants lie prostrate before you.

TEIRESIAS: And all unwise; I never shall reveal
  My evils, so that I may not tell yours.

OEDIPUS: What do you say? You know, but will not speak?   330
  Would you betray us and destroy the state?

TEIRESIAS: I will not hurt you or me. Why in vain
  Do you probe this? You will not find out from me.

OEDIPUS: Worst of evil men, you would enrage
  A stone itself. Will you never speak,
  But stay so untouched and so inconclusive?

TEIRESIAS: You blame my anger and do not see that
  With which you live in common, but upbraid me.

OEDIPUS: Who would not be enraged to hear these words
  By which you now dishonor this our city?   340

TEIRESIAS: Of itself this will come, though I hide it in silence.

OEDIPUS: Then you should tell me what it is will come.

TEIRESIAS: I shall speak no more. If further you desire,
  Rage on in wildest anger of your soul.

OEDIPUS: I shall omit nothing I understand
  I am so angry. Know that you seem to me
  Creator of the deed and worker too
  In all short of the slaughter; if you were not blind,
  I would say this crime was your work alone.

TEIRESIAS: Really? Abide yourself by the decree   350
  You just proclaimed, I tell you! From this day
  Henceforth address neither these men nor me.
  You are the godless defiler of this land.

OEDIPUS: You push so bold and taunting in your speech;
  And how do you think to get away with this?

TEIRESIAS: I have got away. I nurse my strength in truth.

OEDIPUS: Who taught you this? Not from your art you got it.

TEIRESIAS: From you. You had me speak against my will.

OEDIPUS: What word? Say again, so I may better learn.

TEIRESIAS: Didn't you get it before? Or do you bait me?   360

OEDIPUS: I don't remember it. Speak forth again.

TEIRESIAS: You are the slayer whom you seek, I say.

OEDIPUS: Not twice you speak such bitter words unpunished.

TEIRESIAS: Shall I speak more to make you angrier still?

OEDIPUS: Do what you will, your words will be in vain.

TEIRESIAS: I say you have forgot that you are joined
  With those most dear to you in deepest shame
  And do not see where you are in sin.

OEDIPUS: Do you think you will always say such things in joy?

TEIRESIAS: Surely, if strength abides in what is true.

OEDIPUS: It does, for all but you, this not for you   370
  Because your ears and mind and eyes are blind.

TEIRESIAS: Wretched you are to make such taunts, for soon
  All men will cast the selfsame taunts on you.

OEDIPUS: You live in entire night, could do no harm
  To me or any man who sees the day.

TEIRESIAS: Not at your hands will it be my fate to fall.[2]
  Apollo suffices, whose concern it is to do this.

OEDIPUS: Are these devices yours, or are they Creon's?

TEIRESIAS: Creon is not your trouble; you are yourself.

OEDIPUS: O riches, empire, skill surpassing skill   380
  In all the numerous rivalries of life,
  How great a grudge there is stored up against you
  If for this kingship, which the city gave,
  Their gift, not my request, into my hands—
  For this, the trusted Creon, my friend from the start
  Desires to creep by stealth and cast me out
  Taking a seer like this, a weaver of wiles,
  A crooked swindler who has got his eyes
  On gain alone, but in his art is blind.
  Come, tell us, in what clearly are you a prophet?   390
  How is it, when the weave-songed bitch was here
  You uttered no salvation for these people?
  Surely the riddle then could not be solved
  By some chance comer; it needed prophecy.
  You did not clarify that with birds
  Or knowledge from a god; but when I came,
  The ignorant Oedipus, I silenced her,
  Not taught by birds, but winning by my wits,
  Whom you are now attempting to depose,
  Thinking to minister near Creon's throne.   400
  I think that to your woe you and that plotter
  Will purge the land, and if you were not old
  Punishment would teach you what you plot.

CHORUS: It seems to us, O Oedipus our king,
  Both this man's words and yours were said in anger.

---

[2] This reading is based on the interpretation of the papyrus text by Bernard Knox in *Oedipus at Thebes* (New Haven: Yale University Press, 1957), pp. 198–199. The usual reading is "Not at my hands will it be your fate to fall."

Such is not our need, but to find out
How best we shall discharge Apollo's orders.
TEIRESIAS: Even if you are king, the right to answer
  Should be free to all; of that I too am king.
  I live not as your slave, but as Apollo's.   410
  And not with Creon's wards shall I be counted.
  I say, since you have taunted even my blindness,
  You have eyes, but see not where in evil you are
  Nor where you dwell, nor whom you are living with.
  Do you know from whom you spring? And you forget
  You are an enemy to your own kin
  Both those beneath and those above the earth.
  Your mother's and father's curse, with double goad
  And dreaded foot shall drive you from this land.
  You who now see straight shall then be blind,
  And there shall be no harbour for your cry   420
  With which all Mount Cithaeron soon shall ring,
  When you have learned the wedding where you sailed
  At home, into no port, by voyage fair.
  A throng of other ills you do not know
  Shall equal you to yourself and to your children.
  Throw mud on this, on Creon, on my voice—
  Yet there shall never be a mortal man
  Eradicated more wretchedly than you.
OEDIPUS: Shall these unbearable words be heard from him?
  Go to perdition! Hurry! Off, away,   430
  Turn back again and from this house depart.
TEIRESIAS: If you had not called me, I should not have come.
OEDIPUS: I did not know that you would speak such folly
  Or I would not soon have brought you to my house.
TEIRESIAS: And such a fool I am, as it seems to you.
  But to the parents who bore you I seem wise.
OEDIPUS: What parents? Wait! What mortals gave me birth?
TEIRESIAS: This day shall be your birth and your destruction.
OEDIPUS: All things you say in riddles and unclear.
TEIRESIAS: Are you not he who best can search this out?   440
OEDIPUS: Mock, if you wish, the skill that made me great.
TEIRESIAS: This is the very fortune that destroyed you.
OEDIPUS: Well, if I saved the city, I do not care.
TEIRESIAS: I am going now. You, boy, be my guide.
OEDIPUS: Yes, let him guide you. Here you are in the way.
  When you are gone you will give no more trouble.
TEIRESIAS: I go when I have said what I came to say
  Without fear of your frown; you cannot destroy me.
  I say, the very man whom you long seek

With threats and announcements about Laius' murder—   450
This man is here. He seems an alien stranger,
But soon he shall be revealed of Theban birth,
Nor at this circumstance shall he be pleased.
He shall be blind who sees, shall be a beggar
Who now is rich, shall make his way abroad
Feeling the ground before him with a staff.
He shall be revealed at once as brother
And father to his own children, husband and son
To his mother, his father's kin and murderer.   460
Go in and ponder that. If I am wrong,
Say then that I know nothing of prophecy.

CHORUS:
   Strophe A
Who is the man the Delphic rock said with oracular voice
Unspeakable crimes performed with his gory hands?
It is time for him now to speed
His foot in flight, more strong
Than horses swift as the storm.
For girt in arms upon him springs,
With fire and lightning, Zeus' son   470
And behind him, terrible,
Come the unerring Fates.

   Antistrophe A
From snowy Parnassus just now the word flashed clear
To track the obscure man by every way,
For he wanders under the wild
Forest, and into caves
And cliff rocks, like a bull,
Reft on his way, with care on care
Trying to shun the prophecy
Come from the earth's mid-navel,   480
But about him flutters the ever living doom.

   Strophe B
Terrible, terrible things the wise bird-augur stirs.
I neither approve nor deny, at a loss for what to say,
I flutter in hopes and fears, see neither here nor ahead;
For what strife has lain
On Labdacus' sons or Polybus' that I have found ever before   490
Or now, whereby I may run for the sons of Labdacus
In sure proof against Oedipus' public fame
As avenger for dark death?

Antistrophe B
Zeus and Apollo surely understand and know
The affairs of mortal men, but that a mortal seer
Knows more than I, there is no proof. Though a man   500
May surpass a man in knowledge,
Never shall I agree, till I see the word true, when men blame
    Oedipus,
For there came upon him once clear the winged maiden
And wise he was seen, by sure test sweet for the state.   510
So never shall my mind judge him evil guilt.

CREON: Men of our city, I have heard dread words
    That Oedipus our king accuses me.
    I am here indignant. If in the present troubles
    He thinks that he has suffered at my hands
    One word or deed tending to injury
    I do not crave the long-spanned age of life
    To bear this rumor, for it is no simple wrong
    The damage of this accusation brings me;   520
    It brings the greatest, if I am called a traitor
    To you and my friends, a traitor to the state.
CHORUS: Come now, for this reproach perhaps was forced
    By anger, rather than considered thought.
CREON: And was the idea voiced that my advice
    Persuaded the prophet to give false accounts?
CHORUS: Such was said. I know not to what intent.
CREON: Was this accusation laid against me
    From straightforward eyes and straightforward mind?
CHORUS: I do not know. I see not what my masters do;   530
    But here he is now, coming from the house.
OEDIPUS: How dare you come here? Do you own a face
    So bold that you can come before my house
    When you are clearly the murderer of this man
    And manifestly pirate of my throne?
    Come, say before the gods, did you see in me
    A coward or a fool, that you plotted this?
    Or did you think I would not see your wiles
    Creeping upon me, or knowing, would not ward off?
    Surely your machination is absurd   540
    Without a crowd of friends to hunt a throne
    Which is captured only by wealth and many men.
CREON: Do you know what you do? Hear answer to your charges
    On the other side. Judge only what you know.
OEDIPUS: Your speech is clever, but I learn it ill
    Since I have found you harsh and grievous toward me.
CREON: This very matter hear me first explain.

OEDIPUS: Tell me not this one thing: you are not false.
CREON: If you think stubbornness a good possession
   Apart from judgment, you do not think right.   550
OEDIPUS: If you think you can do a kinsman evil
   Without the penalty, you have no sense.
CREON: I agree with you. What you have said is just.
   Tell me what you say you have suffered from me.
OEDIPUS: Did you, or did you not, advise my need
   Was summoning that prophet person here?
CREON: And still is. I hold still the same opinion.
OEDIPUS: How long a time now has it been since Laius—
CREON: Performed what deed? I do not understand.
OEDIPUS: —Disappeared to his ruin at deadly hands.   560
CREON: Far in the past the count of years would run.
OEDIPUS: Was this same seer at that time practising?
CREON: As wise as now, and equally respected.
OEDIPUS: At that time did he ever mention me?
CREON: Never when I stood near enough to hear.
OEDIPUS: But did you not make inquiry of the murder?
CREON: We did, of course, and got no information.
OEDIPUS: How is it that this seer did not utter this then?
CREON: When I don't know, as now, I would keep still.
OEDIPUS: This much you know full well, and so should speak:—   570
CREON: What is that? If I know, I will not refuse.
OEDIPUS: This: If he had not first conferred with you
   He never would have said that I killed Laius.
CREON: If he says this, you know yourself, I think;
   I learn as much from you as you from me.
OEDIPUS: Learn then: I never shall be found a slayer.
CREON: What then, are you the husband of my sister?
OEDIPUS: What you have asked is plain beyond denial.
CREON: Do you rule this land with her in equal sway?
OEDIPUS: All she desires she obtains from me.   580
CREON: Am I with you two not an equal third?
OEDIPUS: In just that do you prove a treacherous friend.
CREON: No, if, like me, you reason with yourself.
   Consider this fact first: would any man
   Choose, do you think, to have his rule in fear
   Rather than doze unharmed with the same power?
   For my part I have never been desirous
   Of being king instead of acting king.
   Nor any other man has, wise and prudent.
   For now I obtain all from you without fear.   590
   If I were king, I would do much unwilling.
   How then could kingship sweeter be for me
   Than rule and power devoid of any pain?

I am not yet so much deceived to want
Goods besides those I profitably enjoy.
Now I am hailed and gladdened by all men.
Now those who want from you speak out to me,
Since all their chances' outcome dwells therein.
How then would I relinquish what I have
To get those gains? My mind runs not so bad. 600
I am prudent yet, no lover of such plots,
Nor would I ever endure others' treason.
And first as proof of this go on to Pytho;
See if I told you truly the oracle.
Next proof: see if I plotted with the seer;
If you find so at all, put me to death
With my vote for my guilt as well as yours.
Do not convict me just on unclear conjecture.
It is not right to think capriciously
The good are bad, nor that the bad are good. 610
It is the same to cast out a noble friend,
I say, as one's own life, which best he loves.
The facts, though, you will safely know in time,
Since time alone can show the just man just,
But you can know a criminal in one day.
CHORUS: A cautious man would say he has spoken well.
O king, the quick to think are never sure.
OEDIPUS: When the plotter, swift, approaches me in stealth
I too in counterplot must be as swift.
If I wait in repose, the plotter's ends 620
Are brought to pass and mine will then have erred.
CREON: What do you want then? To cast me from the land?
OEDIPUS: Least of all that. My wish is you should die,
Not flee to exemplify what envy is.
CREON: Do you say this? Will you neither trust nor yield?
OEDIPUS: [No, for I think that you deserve no trust.]
CREON: You seem not wise to me
OEDIPUS: I am for me.
CREON: You should be for me too.
OEDIPUS: No, you are evil.
CREON: Yes, if you understand nothing.
OEDIPUS: Yet I must rule.
CREON: Not when you rule badly.
OEDIPUS: O city, city!
CREON: It is my city too, not yours alone. 630
CHORUS: Stop, princes. I see Jocasta coming
Out of the house at the right time for you.
With her you must settle the dispute at hand.
JOCASTA: O wretched men, what unconsidered feud

Of tongues have you aroused? Are you not ashamed,
The state so sick, to stir up private ills?
Are you not going home? And you as well?
Will you turn a small pain into a great?

CREON: My blood sister, Oedipus your husband
   Claims he will judge against me two dread ills: 640
   Thrust me from the fatherland or take and kill me.

OEDIPUS: I will, my wife; I caught him in the act
   Doing evil to my person with evil skill.

CREON: Now may I not rejoice but die accursed
   If ever I did any of what you accuse me.

JOCASTA: O, by the gods, believe him, Oedipus.
   First, in reverence for his oath to the gods,
   Next, for my sake and theirs who stand before you.

CHORUS: Hear my entreaty, lord. Consider and consent.

OEDIPUS: What wish should I then grant?   650

CHORUS: Respect the man, no fool before, who now in oath is strong.

OEDIPUS: You know what you desire?

CHORUS: I know.

OEDIPUS: Say what you mean.

CHORUS: Your friend who has sworn do not dishonour
   By casting guilt for dark report.

OEDIPUS: Know well that when you ask this grant from me,
   You ask my death or exile from the land.

CHORUS: No, by the god foremost among the gods,   660
   The Sun, may I perish by the utmost doom
   Godless and friendless, if I have this in mind.
   But ah, the withering earth wears down
   My wretched soul, if to these ills
   Of old are added ills from both of you.

OEDIPUS: Then let him go, though surely I must die
   Or be thrust dishonoured from this land by force.   670
   Your grievous voice I pity, not that man's;
   Wherever he may be, he will be hated.

CREON: Sullen you are to yield, as you are heavy
   When you exceed in wrath. Natures like these
   Are justly sorest for themselves to bear.

OEDIPUS: Will you not go and leave me?

CREON: I am on my way.
   You know me not, but these men see me just.

CHORUS: O queen, why do you delay to bring this man indoors?

JOCASTA: I want to learn what happened here.   680

CHORUS: Unknown suspicion rose from talk, and the unjust devours.

JOCASTA: In both of them?

CHORUS: Just so.

JOCASTA: What was the talk?

CHORUS: Enough, enough! When the land is pained
  It seems to me at this point we should stop.
OEDIPUS: Do you see where you have come? Though your intent
  Is good, you slacken off and blunt my heart.
CHORUS: O lord, I have said not once alone,
  Know that I clearly would be mad   690
  And wandering in mind, to turn away
  You who steered along the right,
  When she was torn with trouble, our beloved state.
  O may you now become in health her guide.
JOCASTA: By the gods, lord, tell me on what account
  You have set yourself in so great an anger.
OEDIPUS: I shall tell you, wife; I respect you more than these men.   700
  Because of Creon, since he has plotted against me.
JOCASTA: Say clearly, if you can; how started the quarrel?
OEDIPUS: He says that I stand as the murderer of Laius.
JOCASTA: He knows himself, or learned from someone else?
OEDIPUS: No, but he sent a rascal prophet here.
  He keeps his own mouth clean in what concerns him.
JOCASTA: Now free yourself of what you said, and listen.
  Learn from me, no mortal man exists
  Who knows prophetic art for your affairs,
  And I shall briefly show you proof of this: 710
  An oracle came once to Laius. I do not say
  From Phoebus himself, but from his ministers
  That his fate would be at his son's hand to die—
  A child, who would be born from him and me.
  And yet, as the rumor says, they were strangers,
  Robbers who killed him where three highways meet.
  But three days had not passed from the child's birth
  When Laius pierced and tied together his ankles,
  And cast him by others' hands on a pathless mountain.
  Therein Apollo did not bring to pass   720
  That the child murder his father, nor for Laius
  The dread he feared, to die at his son's hand.
  Such did prophetic oracles determine.
  Pay no attention to them. For the god
  Will easily make clear the need he seeks.
OEDIPUS: What wandering of soul, what stirring of mind
  Holds me, my wife, in what I have just heard!
JOCASTA: What care has turned you back that you say this?
OEDIPUS: I thought I heard you mention this, that Laius
  Was slaughtered at the place where three highways meet.   730
JOCASTA: That was the talk. The rumour has not ceased.
OEDIPUS: Where is this place where such a sorrow was?
JOCASTA: The country's name is Phocis. A split road

Leads to one place from Delphi and Daulia.

OEDIPUS: And how much time has passed since these events?

JOCASTA: The news was heralded in the city scarcely
A little while before you came to rule.

OEDIPUS: O Zeus, what have you planned to do to me?

JOCASTA: What passion is this in you, Oedipus?

OEDIPUS: Don't ask me that yet. Tell me about Laius.   740
What did he look like? How old was he when murdered?

JOCASTA: A tall man, with his hair just brushed with white.
His shape and form differed not far from yours.

OEDIPUS: Alas! Alas! I think unwittingly
I have just laid dread curses on my head.

JOCASTA: What are you saying? I shrink to behold you, lord.

OEDIPUS: I am terribly afraid the seer can see.
That will be clearer if you say one thing more.

JOCASTA: Though I shrink, if I know what you ask, I will answer.

OEDIPUS: Did he set forth with few attendants then,   750
Or many soldiers, since he was a king?

JOCASTA: They were five altogether among them.
One was a herald. One chariot bore Laius.

OEDIPUS: Alas! All this is clear now. Tell me, my wife,
Who was the man who told these stories to you?

JOCASTA: One servant, who alone escaped, returned.

OEDIPUS: Is he by chance now present in our house?

JOCASTA: Not now. Right from the time when he returned
To see you ruling and Laius dead,
Touching my hand in suppliance, he implored me   760
To send him to fields and to pastures of sheep
That he might be farthest from the sight of this city.
So I sent him away, since he was worthy
For a slave, to bear a greater grant than this.

OEDIPUS: How then could he return to us with speed?

JOCASTA: It can be done. But why would you order this?

OEDIPUS: O lady, I fear I have said too much.
On this account I now desire to see him.

JOCASTA: Then he shall come. But I myself deserve
To learn what it is that troubles you, my lord.   770

OEDIPUS: And you shall not be prevented, since my fears
Have come to such a point. For who is closer
That I may speak to in this fate than you?
Polybus of Corinth was my father,
My mother, Dorian Merope. I was held there
Chief citizen of all, till such a fate
Befell me—as it is, worthy of wonder,
But surely not deserving my excitement.
A man at a banquet overdrunk with wine

Said in drink I was a false son to my father.   780
The weight I held that day I scarcely bore,
But on the next day I went home and asked
My father and mother of it. In bitter anger
They took the reproach from him who had let it fly.
I was pleased at their actions; nevertheless
The rumour always rankled; and spread abroad.
In secret from mother and father I set out
Toward Delphi. Phoebus sent me away ungraced
In what I came for, but other wretched things
Terrible and grievous, he revealed in answer;   790
That I must wed my mother and produce
An unendurable race for men to see,
That I should kill the father who begot me.
When I heard this response, Corinth I fled
Henceforth to measure her land by stars alone.
I went where I should never see the disgrace
Of my evil oracles be brought to pass,
And on my journey to that place I came
At which you say this king had met his death.
My wife, I shall speak the truth to you. My way   800
Led to a place close by the triple road.
There a herald met me, and a man
Seated on colt-drawn chariot, as you said.
There both the guide and the old man himself
Thrust me with driving force out of the path.
And I in anger struck the one who pushed me,
The driver. Then the old man, when he saw me,
Watched when I passed, and from his chariot
Struck me full on the head with double goad.
I paid him back and more. From this very hand   810
A swift blow of my staff rolled him right out
Of the middle of his seat onto his back.
I killed them all. But if relationship
Existed between this stranger and Laius,
What man now is wretcheder than I?
What man is cursed by a more evil fate?
No stranger or citizen could now receive me
Within his home, or even speak to me,
But thrust me out; and no one but myself
Brought down these curses on my head.   820
The bed of the slain man I now defile
With hands that killed him. Am I evil by birth?
Am I not utterly vile if I must flee
And cannot see my family in my flight
Nor tread my homeland soil, or else be joined

In marriage to my mother, kill my father,
Polybus, who sired me and brought me up?
Would not a man judge right to say of me
That this was sent on me by some cruel spirit?
O never, holy reverence of the gods,   830
May I behold that day, but may I go
Away from mortal men, before I see
Such a stain of circumstance come to me.

CHORUS: My lord, for us these facts are full of dread.
Until you hear the witness, stay in hope.

OEDIPUS: And just so much is all I have of hope,
Only to wait until the shepherd comes.

JOCASTA: What, then, do you desire to hear him speak?

OEDIPUS: I will tell you, if his story is found to be
The same as yours, I would escape the sorrow.   840

JOCASTA: What unusual word did you hear from me?

OEDIPUS: You said he said that they were highway robbers
Who murdered him. Now, if he still says
The selfsame number, I could not have killed him,
Since one man does not equal many men.
But if he speaks of a single lonely traveller,
The scale of guilt now clearly falls to me.

JOCASTA: However, know the word was set forth thus
And it is not in him now to take it back;
This tale the city heard, not I alone.   850
But if he diverges from his previous story,
Even then, my lord, he could not show Laius' murder
To have been fulfilled properly. Apollo
Said he would die at the hands of my own son.
Surely that wretched child could not have killed him,
But he himself met death some time before.
Therefore, in any prophecy henceforth
I would not look to this side or to that.

OEDIPUS: Your thoughts ring true, but still let someone go
To summon the peasant. Do not neglect this.   860

JOCASTA: I shall send without delay. But let us enter.
I would do nothing that did not please you.

CHORUS:
    Strophe A
May fate come on me as I bear
Holy pureness in all word and deed,
For which the lofty striding laws were set down,
Born through the heavenly air
Whereof the Olympian sky alone the father was;
No mortal spawn of mankind gave them birth,

Nor may oblivion ever lull them down;   870
Mighty in them the god is, and he does not age.

   Antistrophe A
Pride breeds the tyrant.
Pride, once overfilled with many things in vain,
Neither in season nor fit for man,
Scaling the sheerest height
Hurls to a dire fate
Where no foothold is found.
I pray the god may never stop the rivalry   880
That works well for the state.
The god as my protector I shall never cease to hold.

   Strophe B
But if a man goes forth haughty in word or deed
With no fear of the Right
Nor pious to the spirits' shrines,
May evil doom seize him
For his ill-fated pride,
If he does not fairly win his gain
Or works unholy deeds,   890
Or, in bold folly lays on the sacred profane hands.
For when such acts occur, what man may boast
Ever to ward off from his life darts of the gods?
If practices like these are in respect,
Why then must I dance the sacred dance?

   Antistrophe B
Never again in worship shall I go
To Delphi, holy navel of the earth,
Nor to the temple at Abae,
Nor to Olympia,   900
If these prophecies do not become
Examples for all men.
O Zeus, our king, if so you are rightly called,
Ruler of all things, may then not escape
You and your forever deathless power.
Men now hold light the fading oracles
Told about Laius long ago
And nowhere is Apollo clearly honored;
Things divine are going down to ruin.   910

JOCASTA: Lords of this land, the thought has come to me
   To visit the spirits' shrines, bearing in hand
   These suppliant boughs and offerings of incense.

For Oedipus raises his soul too high
With all distresses; nor, as a sane man should,
Does he confirm the new by things of old,
But stands at the speaker's will if he speaks terrors.
And so, because my advice can do no more,
To you, Lycian Apollo—for you are nearest—
A suppliant, I have come here with these prayers,   920
That you may find some pure deliverance for us:
We all now shrink to see him struck in fear,
That man who is the pilot of our ship.

MESSENGER: Strangers, could I learn from one of you
Where is the house of Oedipus the king?
Or best, if you know, say where he is himself.

CHORUS: This is his house, stranger; he dwells inside;
This woman is the mother of his children.

MESSENGER: May she be always blessed among the blest,
Since she is the fruitful wife of Oedipus.   930

JOCASTA: So may you, stranger, also be. You deserve
As much for your graceful greeting. But tell me
What you have come to search for or to show.

MESSENGER: Good news for your house and your husband, lady.

JOCASTA: What is it then? And from whom have you come?

MESSENGER: From Corinth. And the message I will tell
Will surely gladden you—and vex you, perhaps.

JOCASTA: What is it? What is this double force it holds?

MESSENGER: The men who dwell in the Isthmian country
Have spoken to establish him their king.   940

JOCASTA: What is that? Is not old Polybus still ruling?

MESSENGER: Not he. For death now holds him in the tomb.

JOCASTA: What do you say, old man? Is Polybus dead?

MESSENGER: If I speak not the truth, I am ready to die.

JOCASTA: O handmaid, go right away and tell your master
The news. Where are you, prophecies of the gods?
For this man Oedipus has trembled long,
And shunned him lest he kill him. Now the man
Is killed by fate and not by Oedipus.

OEDIPUS: O Jocasta, my most beloved wife,   950
Why have you sent for me within the house?

JOCASTA: Listen to this man, and while you hear him, think
To what have come Apollo's holy prophecies.

OEDIPUS: Who is this man? Why would he speak to me?

JOCASTA: From Corinth he has come, to announce that your father
Polybus no longer lives, but is dead.

OEDIPUS: What do you say, stranger? Tell me this yourself.

MESSENGER: If I must first announce my message clearly,
Know surely that the man is dead and gone.

OEDIPUS: Did he die by treachery or chance disease? 960
MESSENGER: A slight scale tilt can lull the old to rest.
OEDIPUS: The poor man, it seems, died by disease.
MESSENGER: And by the full measure of lengthy time.
OEDIPUS: Alas, alas! Why then do any seek
    Pytho's prophetic art, my wife, or hear
    The shrieking birds on high, by whose report
    I was to slay my father? Now he lies
    Dead beneath the earth, and here am I
    Who have not touched the blade. Unless in longing
    For me he died, and in this sense was killed by me. 970
    Polybus has packed away these oracles
    In his rest in Hades. They are now worth nothing.
JOCASTA: Did I not tell you that some time ago?
OEDIPUS: You did, but I was led astray by fear.
JOCASTA: Henceforth put nothing of this on your heart.
OEDIPUS: Why must I not still shrink from my mother's bed?
JOCASTA: What should man fear, whose life is ruled by fate,
    For whom there is clear foreknowledge of nothing?
    It is best to live by chance, however you can.
    Be not afraid of marriage with your mother; 980
    Already many mortals in their dreams
    Have shared their mother's bed. But he who counts
    This dream as nothing, easiest bears his life.
OEDIPUS: All that you say would be indeed propitious,
    If my mother were not alive. But since she is,
    I still must shrink, however well you speak.
JOCASTA: And yet your father's tomb is a great eye.
OEDIPUS: A great eye indeed. But I fear her who lives.
MESSENGER: Who is this woman that you are afraid of?
OEDIPUS: Merope, old man, with whom Polybus lived. 990
MESSENGER: What is it in her that moves you to fear?
OEDIPUS: A dread oracle, stranger, sent by the god.
MESSENGER: Can it be told, or must no other know?
OEDIPUS: It surely can. Apollo told me once
    That I must join in intercourse with my mother
    And shed with my own hands my father's blood.
    Because of this, long since I have kept far
    Away from Corinth—and happily—but yet
    It would be most sweet to see my parents' faces.
MESSENGER: Was this your fear in shunning your own city? 1000
OEDIPUS: I wished, too, old man, not to slay my father.
MESSENGER: Why then have I not freed you from this fear,
    Since I have come with friendly mind, my lord?
OEDIPUS: Yes, and take thanks from me, which you deserve.

MESSENGER: And this is just the thing for which I came,
That when you got back home I might fare well.
OEDIPUS: Never shall I go where my parents are.
MESSENGER: My son, you clearly know not what you do—
OEDIPUS: How is that, old man? By the gods, let me know—
MESSENGER: If for these tales you shrink from going home.   1010
OEDIPUS: I tremble lest what Phoebus said comes true.
MESSENGER: Lest you incur pollution from your parents?
OEDIPUS: That is the thing, old man, that always haunts me.
MESSENGER: Well, do you know that surely you fear nothing?
OEDIPUS: How so? If I am the son of those who bore me.
MESSENGER: Since Polybus was no relation to you.
OEDIPUS: What do you say? Was Polybus not my father?
MESSENGER: No more than this man here but just so much.
OEDIPUS: How does he who begot me equal nothing?
MESSENGER: That man was not your father, any more than I am.
OEDIPUS: Well then, why was it he called me his son?   1021
MESSENGER: Long ago he got you as a gift from me.
OEDIPUS: Though from another's hand, yet so much he loved me!
MESSENGER: His previous childlessness led him to that.
OEDIPUS: Had you bought or found me when you gave me to him?
MESSENGER: I found you in Cithaeron's folds and glens.
OEDIPUS: Why were you travelling in those regions?
MESSENGER: I guarded there a flock of mountain sheep.
OEDIPUS: Were you a shepherd, wandering for pay?
MESSENGER: Yes, and your saviour too, child, at that time.   1030
OEDIPUS: What pain gripped me, that you took me in your arms?
MESSENGER: The ankles of your feet will tell you that.
OEDIPUS: Alas, why do you mention that old trouble?
MESSENGER: I freed you when your ankles were pierced together.
OEDIPUS: A terrible shame from my swaddling clothes I got.
MESSENGER: Your very name you got from this misfortune.
OEDIPUS: By the gods, did my mother or father do it? Speak.
MESSENGER: I know not. He who gave you knows better than I.
OEDIPUS: You didn't find me, but took me from another?
MESSENGER: That's right. Another shepherd gave you to me.   1040
OEDIPUS: Who was he? Can you tell me who he was?
MESSENGER: Surely. He belonged to the household of Laius.
OEDIPUS: The man who ruled this land once long ago?
MESSENGER: Just so. He was a herd in that man's service.
OEDIPUS: Is this man still alive, so I could see him?
MESSENGER: You dwellers in this country should know best.
OEDIPUS: Is there any one of you who stand before me
Who knows the shepherd of whom this man speaks?
If you have seen him in the fields or here,
Speak forth; the time has come to find this out.   1050

CHORUS: I think the man you seek is no one else
  Than the shepherd you were so eager to see before.
  Jocasta here might best inform us that.
OEDIPUS: My wife, do you know the man we just ordered
  To come here? Is it of him that this man speaks?
JOCASTA: Why ask of whom he spoke? Think nothing of it.
  Brood not in vain on what has just been said.
OEDIPUS: It could not be that when I have got such clues,
  I should not shed clear light upon my birth.
JOCASTA: Don't, by the gods, investigate this more   1060
  If you care for your own life. I am sick enough.
OEDIPUS: Take courage. Even if I am found a slave
  For three generations, your birth will not be base.
JOCASTA: Still, I beseech you, hear me. Don't do this.
OEDIPUS: I will hear of nothing but finding out the truth.
JOCASTA: I know full well and tell you what is best.
OEDIPUS: Well, then, this best, for some time now, has given me pain.
JOCASTA: O ill-fated man, may you never know who you are.
OEDIPUS: Will someone bring the shepherd to me here?
  And let this lady rejoice in her opulent birth.   1070
JOCASTA: Alas, alas, hapless man. I have this alone
  To tell you, and nothing else forevermore.
CHORUS: O Oedipus, where has the woman gone
  In the rush of her wild grief? I am afraid
  Evil will break forth out of this silence.
OEDIPUS: Let whatever will break forth. I plan to see
  The seed of my descent, however small.
  My wife, perhaps, because a noblewoman
  Looks down with shame upon my lowly birth.
  I would not be dishonoured to call myself
  The Son of Fortune, giver of the good.   1080
  She is my mother. The years, her other children,
  Have marked me sometimes small and sometimes great.
  Such was I born! I shall prove no other man,
  Nor shall I cease to search out my descent.

CHORUS:
    Strophe
  If I am a prophet and can know in mind,
  Cithaeron, by tomorrow's full moon   1090
  You shall not fail, by mount Olympus,
  To find that Oedipus, as a native of your land,
  Shall honour you for nurse and mother.
  And to you we dance in choral song because you bring
  Fair gifts to him our king.
  Hail, Phoebus, may all this please you.

Antistrophe

Who, child, who bore you in the lengthy span of years?
One close to Pan who roams the mountain woods,   1100
One of Apollo's bedfellows?
For all wild pastures in mountain glens to him are dear.
Was Hermes your father, who Cyllene sways,
Or did Bacchus, dwelling on the mountain peaks,
Take you a foundling from some nymph
Of those by springs of Helicon, with whom he sports the most?

OEDIPUS: If I may guess, although I never met him,   1110
I think, elders, I see that shepherd coming
Whom we have long sought, as in the measure
Of lengthy age he accords with him we wait for.
Besides, the men who lead him I recognize
As servants of my house. You may perhaps
Know better than I if you have seen him before.
CHORUS: Be assured, I know him as a shepherd
As trusted as any other in Laius' service.
OEDIPUS: Stranger from Corinth, I will ask you first,
Is this the man you said?
MESSENGER: You are looking at him.   1120
OEDIPUS: You there, old man, look here and answer me
What I shall ask you. Were you ever with Laius?
SERVANT: I was a slave, not bought but reared at home.
OEDIPUS: What work concerned you? What was your way of life?
SERVANT: Most of my life I spent among the flocks.
OEDIPUS: In what place most of all was your usual pasture?
SERVANT: Sometimes Cithaeron, or the ground nearby.
OEDIPUS: Do you know this man before you here at all?
SERVANT: Doing what? And of what man do you speak?
OEDIPUS: The one before you. Have you ever had congress with
him?   1130
SERVANT: Not to say so at once from memory.
MESSENGER: That is no wonder, master, but I shall remind him,
Clearly, who knows me not; yet well I know
That he knew once the region of Cithaeron.
He with a double flock and I with one
Dwelt there in company for three whole years
During the six months' time from spring to fall.
When winter came, I drove into my fold
My flock, and he drove his to Laius' pens.
Do I speak right, or did it not happen so?   1140
SERVANT: You speak the truth, though it was long ago.
MESSENGER: Come now, do you recall you gave me then
A child for me to rear as my own son?

SERVANT: What is that? Why do you ask me this?

MESSENGER: This is the man, my friend, who then was young.

SERVANT: Go to destruction! Will you not be quiet?

OEDIPUS: Come, scold him not, old man. These words of yours
  Deserve a scolding more than this man's do.

SERVANT: In what, most noble master, do I wrong?

OEDIPUS: Not to tell of the child he asks about.   1150

SERVANT: He speaks in ignorance, he toils in vain.

OEDIPUS: If you will not speak freely, you will under torture.

SERVANT: Don't, by the gods, outrage an old man like me.

OEDIPUS: Will someone quickly twist back this fellow's arms?

SERVANT: Alas, what for? What do you want to know?

OEDIPUS: Did you give this man the child of whom he asks?

SERVANT: I did. Would I had perished on that day!

OEDIPUS: You will come to that unless you tell the truth.

SERVANT: I come to far greater ruin if I speak.

OEDIPUS: This man, it seems, is trying to delay.   1160

SERVANT: Not I. I said before I gave it to him.

OEDIPUS: Where did you get it? At home or from someone else?

SERVANT: It was not mine. I got him from a man.

OEDIPUS: Which of these citizens? Where did he live?

SERVANT: O master, by the gods, ask me no more.

OEDIPUS: You are done for if I ask you this again.

SERVANT: Well then, he was born of the house of Laius.

OEDIPUS: One of his slaves, or born of his own race?

SERVANT: Alas, to speak I am on the brink of horror.

OEDIPUS: And I to hear. But still it must be heard.   1170

SERVANT: Well, then, they say it was his child. Your wife
  Who dwells within could best say how this stands.

OEDIPUS: Was it she who gave him to you?

SERVANT: Yes, my lord.

OEDIPUS: For what intent?

SERVANT: So I could put it away.

OEDIPUS: When she bore him, the wretch.

SERVANT: She feared bad oracles.

OEDIPUS: What were they?

SERVANT: They said he should kill his father.

OEDIPUS: Why did you give him up to this old man?

SERVANT: I pitied him, master, and thought he would take him away
  To another land, the one from which he came.
  But he saved him for greatest woe. If you are he   1180
  Whom this man speaks of, you were born curst by fate.

OEDIPUS: Alas, alas! All things are now come true.
  O light, for the last time now I look upon you;
  I am shown to be born from those I ought not to have been.

I married the woman I should not have married,
I killed the man whom I should not have killed.

CHORUS:
   Strophe A
   Alas, generations of mortal men!
   How equal to nothing do I number you in life!
   Who, O who, is the man
   Who bears more of bliss   1190
   Than just the seeming so,
   And then, like a waning sun, to fall away?
   When I know your example,
   Your guiding spirit, yours, wretched Oedipus,
   I call no mortal blest.

   Antistrophe A
   He is the one, O Zeus,
   Who peerless shot his bow and won well-fated bliss,
   Who destroyed the hook-clawed maiden,
   The oracle-singing Sphinx,   1200
   And stood a tower for our land from death;
   For this you are called our king,
   Oedipus, are highest-honoured here,
   And over great Thebes hold sway.

   Strophe B
   And now who is more wretched for men to hear,
   Who so lives in wild plagues, who dwells in pains,
   In utter change of life?
   Alas for glorious Oedipus!
   The selfsame port of rest
   Was gained by bridegroom father and his son,   1210
   How, O how did your father's furrows ever bear you, suffering man?
   How have they endured silence for so long?

   Antistrophe B
   You are found out, unwilling, by all-seeing Time.
   It judges your unmarried marriage where for long
   Begetter and begot have been the same.
   Alas, child of Laius,
   Would I had never seen you.
   As one who pours from his mouth a dirge I wail,
   To speak the truth, through you I breathed new life,   1220
   And now through you I lulled my eye to sleep.

SECOND MESSENGER: O men most honoured always of this land
   What deeds you shall hear, what shall you behold!

What grief shall stir you up, if by your kinship
You are still concerned for the house of Labdacus!
I think neither Danube nor any other river
Could wash this palace clean, so many ills
Lie hidden there which now will come to light.
They were done by will, not fate; and sorrows hurt   1230
The most when we ourselves appear to choose them.
CHORUS: What we heard before causes no little sorrow.
     What can you say which adds to that a burden?
SECOND MESSENGER: This is the fastest way to tell the tale;
     Hear it: Jocasta, your divine queen, is dead.
CHORUS: O sorrowful woman! From what cause did she die?
SECOND MESSENGER: By her own hand. The most painful of the action
     Occurred away, not for your eyes to see.
     But still, so far as I have memory
     You shall learn the sufferings of that wretched woman: 1240
     How she passed on through the door enraged
     And rushed straight forward to her nuptial bed,
     Clutching her hair's ends with both her hands.
     Once inside the doors she shut herself in
     And called on Laius, who has long been dead,
     Having remembrance of their seed of old
     By which he died himself and left her a mother
     To bear an evil brood to his own son.
     She moaned the bed on which by double curse
     She bore husband to husband, children to child.   1250
     How thereafter she perished I do not know,
     For Oedipus burst in on her with a shriek,
     And because of him we could not see her woe.
     We looked on him alone as he rushed around.
     Pacing about, he asked us to give him a sword,
     Asked where he might find the wife no wife,
     A mother whose plowfield bore him and his children.
     Some spirit was guiding him in his frenzy,
     For none of the men who are close at hand did so.
     With a horrible shout, as if led on by someone,   1260
     He leapt on the double doors, from their sockets
     Broke hollow bolts aside, and dashed within.
     There we beheld his wife hung by her neck
     From twisted cords, swinging to and fro.
     When he saw her, wretched man, he terribly groaned
     And slackened the hanging noose. When the poor woman
     Lay on the ground, what happened was dread to see.
     He tore the golden brooch pins from her clothes,
     And raised them up, and struck his own eyeballs,   1270
     Shouting such words as these: "No more shall you

Behold the evils I have suffered and done.
Be dark from now on, since you saw before
What you should not, and knew not what you should."
Moaning such cries, not once but many times
He raised and struck his eyes. The bloody pupils
Bedewed his beard. The gore oozed not in drops,
But poured in a black shower, a hail of blood.
From both of them these woes have broken out,   1280
Not for just one, but man and wife together.
The bliss of old that formerly prevailed
Was bliss indeed, but now upon this day
Lamentation, madness, death, and shame—
No evil that can be named is not at hand.

CHORUS: Is the wretched man in any rest now from pain?

SECOND MESSENGER: He shouts for someone to open up the doors
And show to all Cadmeans his father's slayer,
His mother's—I should not speak the unholy word.
He says he will hurl himself from the land, no more   1290
To dwell cursed in the house by his own curse.
Yet he needs strength and someone who will guide him.
His sickness is too great to bear. He will show it to you
For the fastenings of the doors are opening up,
And such a spectacle you will soon behold
As would make even one who abhors it take pity.

CHORUS: O terrible suffering for men to see,
Most terrible of all that I
Have ever come upon. O wretched man,
What madness overcame you, what springing daimon   1300
Greater than the greatest for men
Has caused your evil-daimoned fate?
Alas, alas, grievous one,
But I cannot bear to behold you, though I desire
To ask you much, much to find out,
Much to see,
You make me shudder so!

OEDIPUS: Alas, alas, I am grieved!
Where on earth, so wretched, shall I go?
Where does my voice fly through the air,   1310
O Fate, where have you bounded?

CHORUS: To dreadful end, not to be heard or seen.

    Strophe A
OEDIPUS: O cloud of dark
That shrouds me off, has come to pass, unspeakable,
Invincible, that blows no favoring blast.
Woe,

O woe again, the goad that pierces me,
Of the sting of evil now, and memory of before.
CHORUS: No wonder it is that among so many pains
You should both mourn and bear a double evil.   1320

Antistrophe A
OEDIPUS: Ah, friend,
You are my steadfast servant still,
You still remain to care for me, blind.
Alas! Alas!
You are not hid from me; I know you clearly,
And though in darkness, still I hear your voice.
CHORUS: O dreadful doer, how did you so endure
To quench your eyes? What daimon drove you on?

Strophe B
OEDIPUS: Apollo it was, Apollo, friends
Who brought to pass these evil, evil woes of mine.   1330
The hand of no one struck my eyes but wretched me.
For why should I see,
When nothing sweet there is to see with sight?
CHORUS: This is just as you say.
OEDIPUS: What more is there for me to see,
My friends, what to love,
What joy to hear a greeting?
Lead me at once away from here,   1340
Lead me away, friends, wretched as I am,
Accursed, and hated most
Of mortals to the gods.
CHORUS: Wretched alike in mind and in your fortune,
How I wish that I had never known you.

Antistrophe B
OEDIPUS: May he perish, whoever freed me
From fierce bonds on my feet,   1350
Snatched me from death and saved me, doing me no joy.
For if then I had died, I should not be
So great a grief to friends and to myself.
CHORUS: This also is my wish.
OEDIPUS: I would not have come to murder my father,
Nor have been called among men
The bridegroom of her from whom I was born.
But as it is I am godless, child of unholiness,   1360
Wretched sire in common with my father.
And if there is any evil older than evil left,
It is the lot of Oedipus.

CHORUS: I know not how I could give you good advice,
  For you would be better dead than living blind.

OEDIPUS: That how things are was not done for the best—
  Teach me not this, or give me more advice.   **1370**
  If I had sight, I know not with what eyes
  I could ever face my father among the dead,
  Or my wretched mother. What I have done to them
  Is too great for a noose to expiate.
  Do you think the sight of my children would be a joy
  For me to see, born as they were to me?
  No, never for these eyes of mine to see.
  Nor the city, nor the tower, nor the sacred
  Statues of gods; of these I deprive myself,
  Noblest among the Thebans, born and bred,   **1380**
  Now suffering everything. I tell you all
  To exile me as impious, shown by the gods
  Untouchable and of the race of Laius.
  When I uncovered such a stain on me,
  Could I look with steady eyes upon the people?
  No, No! And if there were a way to block
  The spring of hearing, I would not forbear
  To lock up wholly this my wretched body.
  I should be blind and deaf.—For it is sweet
  When thought can dwell outside our evils.   **1390**
  Alas, Cithaeron, why did you shelter me?
  Why did you not take and kill me at once, so I
  Might never reveal to men whence I was born?
  O Polybus, O Corinth, O my father's halls,
  Ancient in fable, what an outer fairness,
  A festering of evils, you raised in me.
  For now I am evil found, and born of evil.
  O the three paths! Alas the hidden glen,
  The grove of oak, the narrow triple roads
  That drank from my own hands my father's blood. **1400**
  Do you remember any of the deeds
  I did before you then on my way here
  And what I after did? O wedlock, wedlock!
  You gave me birth, and then spawned in return
  Issue from the selfsame seed; you revealed
  Father, brother, children, in blood relation,
  The bride both wife and mother, and whatever
  Actions are done most shameful among men.
  But it is wrong to speak what is not good to do.
  By the gods, hide me at once outside our land,   **1410**
  Or murder me, or hurl me in the sea

Where you shall never look on me again.
Come, venture to lay your hands on this wretched man.
Do it. Be not afraid. No mortal man
There is, except myself, to bear my evils.
CHORUS: Here is Creon, just in time for what you ask
To work and to advise, for he alone
Is left in place of you to guard the land.
OEDIPUS: Alas, what word, then, shall I tell this man?
What righteous ground of trust is clear in me,   1420
As in the past in all I have done him evil?
CREON: Oedipus, I have not come to laugh at you,
Nor to reproach you for your former wrongs.
     (*To the attendants*)
If you defer no longer to mortal offspring,
Respect at least the all-nourishing flame
Of Apollo, lord of the sun. Fear to display
So great a pestilence, which neither earth
Nor holy rain nor light will well receive.
But you, conduct him to the house at once.
It is most pious for the kin alone   1430
To hear and to behold the family sins.
OEDIPUS: By the gods, since you have plucked me from my fear,
Most noble, facing this most vile man,
Hear me one word—I will speak for you, not me.
CREON: What desire do you so persist to get?
OEDIPUS: As soon as you can, hurl me from this land
To where no mortal man will ever greet me.
CREON: I would do all this, be sure. But I want first
To find out from the god what must be done.
OEDIPUS: His oracle, at least, is wholly clear;   1440
Leave me to ruin, an impious parricide.
CREON: Thus spake the oracle. Still, as we stand
It is better to find out sure what we should do.
OEDIPUS: Will you inquire about so wretched a man?
CREON: Yes. You will surely put trust in the god.
OEDIPUS: I order you and beg you, give the woman
Now in the house such burial as you yourself
Would want. Do last rites justly for your kin.
But may this city never be condemned—
My father's realm—because I live within.   1450
Let me live in the mountains where Cithaeron
Yonder has fame of me, which father and mother
When they were alive established as my tomb.
There I may die by those who sought to kill me.
And yet this much I know, neither a sickness
Nor anything else can kill me. I would not

Be saved from death, except for some dread evil.
Well, let my fate go wherever it may.
As for my sons, Creon, assume no trouble;
They are men and will have no difficulty   1460
Of living wherever they may be.
O my poor grievous daughters, who never knew
Their dinner table set apart from me,
But always shared in everything I touched—
Take care of them for me, and first of all
Allow me to touch them and bemoan our ills.
Grant it, lord,
Grant it, noble. If with my hand I touch them
I would think I had them just as when I could see.   1470
        (*Cleon's attendants bring in* ANTIGONE *and* ISMENE.)
What's that?
By the gods, can it be I hear my dear ones weeping?
And have you taken pity on me, Creon?
Have you had my darling children sent to me?
Do I speak right?
CREON: You do. For it was I who brought them here,
        Knowing this present joy your joy of old.
OEDIPUS: May you fare well. For their coming may the spirit
        That watches over you be better than mine.
        My children, where are you? Come to me, come   1480
        Into your brother's hands, that brought about
        Your father's eyes, once bright, to see like this.
        Your father, children, who, seeing and knowing nothing,
        Became a father whence he was got himself.
        I weep also for you—I cannot see you—
        To think of the bitter life in days to come
        Which you will have to lead among mankind.
        What citizens' gatherings will you approach?
        What festivals attend, where you will not cry   1490
        When you go home, instead of gay rejoicing?
        And when you arrive at marriageable age,
        What man, my daughters, will there be to chance you,
        Incurring such reproaches on his head,
        Disgraceful to my children and to yours?
        What evil will be absent, when your father
        Killed his own father, sowed seed in her who bore him,
        From whom he was born himself, and equally
        Has fathered you whence he himself was born.
        Such will be the reproaches. Who then will wed you?   1500
        My children, there is no one for you. Clearly
        You must decay in barrenness, unwed.
        Son of Menoeceus—since you are alone

Left as a father to them, for we who produced them
Are both in ruin—see that you never let
These girls wander as beggars without husbands,
Let them not fall into such woes as mine.
But pity them, seeing how young they are
To be bereft of all except your aid.
Grant this, my noble friend, with a touch of your hand.   1510
My children, if your minds were now mature,
I would give you much advice. But, pray this for me,
To live as the time allows, to find a life
Better than that your siring father had.

CREON: You have wept enough here, come, and go inside the house.

OEDIPUS: I must obey, though nothing sweet.

CREON: All things are good in their time.

OEDIPUS: Do you know in what way I go?

CREON: Tell me, I'll know when I hear.

OEDIPUS: Send me outside the land.

CREON: You ask what the god will do.

OEDIPUS: But to the gods I am hated.

CREON: Still, it will soon be done.

OEDIPUS: Then you agree?

CREON: What I think not I would not say in vain. 1520

OEDIPUS: Now lead me away.

CREON: Come then, but let the children go.

OEDIPUS: Do not take them from me.

CREON: Wish not to govern all,
    For what you ruled will not follow you through life.

CHORUS: Dwellers in native Thebes, behold this Oedipus,
    Who solved the famous riddle, was your mightiest man.
    What citizen on his lot did not with envy gaze?
    See to how great a surge of dread fate he has come!
    So I would say a mortal man, while he is watching
    To see the final day, can have no happiness
    Till he pass the bound of life, nor be relieved of pain.   1530

Aristotle

THE POETICS

From *Aristotle's Theory of Poetry and Fine Art* by S. H. Butcher. London: Macmillan & Co., Ltd., 1911. Translated by S. H. Butcher.

I—I propose to treat of Poetry in itself and of its various kinds, noting the essential quality of each; to inquire into the structure of the plot as requisite to a good poem; into the number and nature of the parts of which a poem is composed; and similarly into whatever else falls within the same inquiry. Following, then, the order of nature, let us begin with the principles which come first.

Epic poetry and Tragedy, Comedy also and Dithyrambic poetry, and the music of the flute and of the lyre in most of their forms, are all in their general conception modes of imitation. They differ, however, from one another in three respects—the medium, the objects, the manner or mode of imitation, being in each case distinct.

For as there are persons who, by conscious art or mere habit, imitate and represent various objects through the medium of color and form, or again by the voice, so in the arts above mentioned, taken as a whole, the imitation is produced by rhythm, language, or "harmony," either singly or combined.[7] [1]

Thus in the music of the flute and of the lyre, "harmony" and rhythm alone are employed; also in other arts, such as that of the shepherd's pipe, which are essentially similar to these. In dancing

[1] No even-numbered pages are given because those pages in Butcher's edition contain the Greek text. [Ed.]

rhythm alone is used without "harmony"; for even dancing imitates character, emotion, and action, by rhythmical movement.

There is another art which imitates by means of language alone, and that either in prose or verse—which verse, again, may either combine different metres or consist of but one kind—but this has hitherto been without a name. For there is no common term we could apply to the mimes of Sophron and Xenarchus and the Socratic dialogues on the one hand; and, on the other, to poetic imitations in iambic, elegiac, or any similar metre. People do, indeed, add the word "maker" or "poet" to the name of the metre, and speak of elegiac poets, or epic (that is, hexameter) poets, as if it were not the imitation that makes the poet, but the verse that entitles them all indiscriminately to the name. Even when a treatise on medicine or natural science is brought out in verse, the name of poet is by custom given to the author; and yet Homer and Empedocles have nothing in common but the metre, so that it would be right to call the one poet, the other physicist rather than poet. On the same principle, even if a writer in his poetic imitation were to combine all metres, as Chaeremon did in his *Centaur*, which is a medley composed of metres[9] of all kinds, we should bring him, too, under the general term "poet." So much, then, for these distinctions.

There are, again, some arts which employ all the means above mentioned—namely, rhythm, tune, and metre. Such are Dithyrambic and Nomic poetry, and also Tragedy and Comedy; but between them the difference is that in the first two cases these means are all employed in combination, in the latter, now one means is employed, now another.

Such, then, are the differences of the arts with respect to the medium of imitation.

II—Since the objects of imitation are men in action, and these men must be either of a higher or a lower type (for moral character mainly answers to these divisions, goodness and badness being the distinguishing marks of moral differences), it follows that we must represent men either as better than in real life, or as worse, or as they are. It is the same in painting. Polygnotus depicted men as nobler than they are, Pauson as less noble, Dionysius drew them true to life.

Now it is evident that each of the modes of imitation above mentioned will exhibit these differences and become a distinct kind in imitating objects that are thus distinct. Such diversities may be found even in dancing, flute-playing, and lyre-playing. So again in language, whether prose or verse unaccompanied by music. Homer, for example, makes men better than they are; Cleophon as they are; Hegemon the Thasian, the inventor of parodies, and Nicochares, the author of the *Deiliad*, worse than they are. The same thing holds good of Dithyrambs and Nomes; here, too, one may portray different types, as[11]

Timotheus and Philoxenus differed in representing their Cyclopes. The same distinction marks off Tragedy from Comedy; for Comedy aims at representing men as worse, Tragedy as better than in actual life.

III—There is still a third difference—the manner in which each of these objects may be imitated. For the medium being the same, and the objects the same, the poet may imitate by narration—in which case he can either take another personality, as Homer does, or speak in his own person, unchanged—or he may present all his characters as living and moving before us.

These, then, as we said at the beginning, are the differences which distinguish artistic imitation—the medium, the objects, and the manner. So that from one point of view, Sophocles is an imitator of the same kind as Homer, for both imitate higher types of character; from another point of view, of the same kind as Aristophanes, for both imitate persons acting and doing. Hence some say the name of "drama" is given to such poems as representing action. For the same reason the Dorians claim the invention both of Tragedy and Comedy. The claim to Comedy is put forward by the Megarians—not only by those of Greece proper, who allege that it originated under their democracy, but also by the Megarians of Sicily, for the poet Epicharmus, who is much earlier than Chionides and Magnes, belonged to that country. Tragedy, too, is claimed by certain Dorians of the Peloponnese. In each case they appeal to the evidence of language. The outlying villages, they say, are by them called *comae*, by the Athenians *demes*: and they assume that Comedians were so named, not from *komazein*, "to[13] revel," but because they wandered from village to village, being excluded contemptuously from the city. They add also that the Dorian word for "doing" is *dran*, and the Athenian, *prattein*.

This may suffice as to the number and nature of the various modes of imitation.

IV—Poetry in general seems to have sprung from two causes, both natural ones. First, the instinct of imitation is implanted in man from childhood, one difference between him and other animals being that he is the most imitative of living creatures, and through imitation learns his earliest lessons; and it is also natural to delight in imitations. We have evidence of this in the facts of experience. Objects which in themselves we view with pain, we delight to contemplate when reproduced with minute fidelity: such as the forms of the lowest animals and of dead bodies. The cause of this again is that to learn gives the liveliest pleasure, not only to philosophers, but to men in general; whose capacity, however, of learning is more limited. Thus the reason why men enjoy seeing a likeness is that in contemplating it they find themselves learning or inferring, and saying perhaps, "Ah, that is he."

For if you happen not to have seen the original, the pleasure will be due not to the imitation as such, but to the execution, the coloring, or some such other cause.

Imitation and harmony and rhythm being natural to us, metres are manifestly sections of rhythm. Persons, therefore, starting with this natural gift, developed by degrees their[15] special aptitudes till their rude improvisations gave birth to Poetry.

Poetry now diverged in two directions, according to the individual character of the writers. The graver spirits imitated noble actions and the actions of good men. The more trivial sort imitated the actions of meaner persons, at first composing satires, as the former did hymns to the gods and the praises of famous men. A poem of the satirical kind cannot indeed be put down to any author earlier than Homer, though many such writers probably there were. But from Homer onward, instances can be cited—his own *Margites,* for example, and other similar compositions. The appropriate metre was also here introduced; hence the measure is still called the iambic or lampooning measure, being that in which people lampooned one another. Thus the older poets were distinguished as writers of heroic or of lampooning verse.

As, in the serious style, Homer is pre-eminent among poets, for he alone combined dramatic form with excellence of imitation, so he, too, first laid down the main lines of Comedy, by dramatizing the ludicrous instead of writing personal satire. His *Margites* bears the same relation to Comedy that the *Iliad* and *Odyssey* do to Tragedy. But when Tragedy and Comedy came to light, the two classes of poets still followed their natural bent: the lampooners became writers of Comedy, and the Epic poets were succeeded by Tragedians, since the drama was a larger and higher form of art.

Whether Tragedy has as yet perfected its proper[17] types or not, and whether it is to be judged in itself or in relation also to the audience—this raises another question. Be that as it may, Tragedy—as also Comedy—was at first mere improvisation. The one originated with the authors of the Dithyramb, the other with those of the phallic songs, which are still in use in many of our cities. Tragedy advanced by slow degrees; each new element that showed itself was in turn developed. Having passed through many changes, it found its natural form, and there it stopped.

Aeschylus first introduced a second actor; he diminished the importance of the Chorus and assigned the leading part to the dialogue. Sophocles raised the number of actors to three and added scene-painting. Moreover, it was not till late that the short plot was discarded for one of greater compass, and the grotesque diction of the earlier satyric form for the stately manner of Tragedy. This iambic measure then replaced the trochaic tetrameter, which was originally employed when the poetry was of the satyric order and had greater affinities with dancing. Once dialogue had come in, Nature herself discovered the appropriate measure. For the iambic is, of all measures, the most colloquial: we see it in the fact that conversational speech runs into iambic lines more frequently than into any other kind of verse, rarely into hexameters, and only when we drop the colloquial intonation. The additions to the number of Episodes or acts, and the other accessories of which tradition[19] tells, must be taken as already described; for to discuss them in detail would doubtless be a large undertaking.

V—Comedy is, as we have said, an imitation of persons inferior—not, however, in the full sense of the word bad, the Ludicrous being merely a subdivision of the ugly. It consists in some defect or ugliness which is not painful or destructive. To take an obvious example, the comic mask is ugly and distorted, but does not imply pain.

The successive changes through which Tragedy passed, and the authors of these changes, are well known, whereas Comedy has had no history because it was not at first treated seriously. It was late before the Archon granted a comic chorus to a poet; the performers were till then voluntary. Comedy had already taken definite shape when comic poets, distinctively so called, are heard of. Who furnished it with masks, or prologues, or increased the number of actors—these and other similar details remain unknown. As for the plot, it came originally from Sicily; but of Athenian writers, Crates was the first who, abandoning the "iambic" or lampooning form, generalized his themes and plots.

Epic poetry agrees with Tragedy in so far as it is an imitation in verse of characters of a higher type. They differ in that Epic poetry admits but one kind of metre, and is narrative in form. They differ again[21] in their length; for Tragedy endeavors, as far as possible, to confine itself to a single revolution of the sun, or but slightly to exceed this limit, whereas the Epic action has no limits of time. This, then, is a second point of difference, though at first the same freedom was admitted in Tragedy as in Epic poetry.

Of their constituent parts some are common to both, some peculiar to Tragedy: whoever, therefore, knows what is good or bad Tragedy knows also about Epic poetry. All the elements of an Epic poem are found in Tragedy, but the elements of a Tragedy are not all found in the Epic poem.

VI—Of the poetry which imitates in hexameter verse, and of Comedy, we will speak hereafter. Let us now discuss Tragedy, resuming its formal definition as resulting from what has been already said.

Tragedy, then, is an imitation of an action that is serious, complete, and of a certain magnitude; in language embellished with each kind of artistic ornament, the several kinds being found in separate parts of the play; in the form of action, not of narrative; with incidents arousing pity and fear, wherewith to accomplish its katharsis of such emotions. By "language embellished," I mean language into which rhythm, "harmony," and song enter. By "the several kinds in separate parts," I mean that some parts are rendered through the medium of verse alone, others again with the aid of song.

Now as tragic imitation implies persons acting, it necessarily follows, in the first place, that Spectacular equipment will be a part of Tragedy. Next, Song and Diction, for these are the media of imitation. By Diction,[23] I mean the mere metrical arrangement of the words; as for "Song," it is a term whose sense everyone understands.

Again, Tragedy is the imitation of an action; and an action implies personal agents who necessarily possess certain distinctive qualities both of character and thought; for it is by these that we qualify actions themselves, and these—thought and character—are the two natural causes from which actions spring, and on actions again all success or failure depends. Hence the Plot is the imitation of the action—for by Plot I here mean the arrangement of the incidents. By Character, I mean that in virtue of which we ascribe certain qualities to the agents. Thought is required wherever a statement is proved or, it may be, a general truth enunciated. Every Tragedy, therefore, must have six parts, which parts determine its quality—namely, Plot, Characters, Diction, Thought, Spectacle, Melody. Two of the parts constitute the medium of imitation, one the manner, and three the objects of imitation. And these complete the list. These elements have been employed, we may say, by the poets to a man; in fact, every play contains Spectacular elements as well as Character, Plot, Diction, Melody, and Thought.

But most important of all is the structure of the[25] incidents. For Tragedy is an imitation, not of men, but of action and of life, and life consists in action, and its end is a mode of action, not a quality. Now character determines men's qualities, but it is by their actions that they are happy or the reverse. Dramatic action, therefore, is not with a view to the representation of character: character comes in as subsidiary to the actions. Hence the incidents and the plot are the end of a tragedy; and the end is the chief thing of all. Again, without action there cannot be a tragedy; there may be without character. The tragedies of most of our modern poets fail in the rendering of character; and of poets in general this is often true. It is the same in painting; and here lies the difference between Zeuxis and Polygnotus. Polygnotus delineates character well; the style of Zeuxis is devoid of ethical quality. Again, if you string together a set of speeches expressive of character, and well finished in point of diction and thought, you will not produce the essential tragic effect nearly so well as with a play, which, however deficient in these respects, yet has a plot and artistically constructed incidents. Besides which the most powerful elements of emotional interest in Tragedy—*peripeteia* or "reversal of the situation," and "recognition" scenes—are parts of the plot. A further proof is that novices in the art attain to finish of diction and precision of portraiture before they can construct the plot. It is the same with almost all the early poets.

The Plot, then, is the first principle and, as it were,[27] the soul of a tragedy; Character holds the second place. A similar fact is seen in painting. The most beautiful colors, laid on confusedly, will not give as much pleasure as the chalk outline of a portrait. Thus Tragedy is the imitation of an action, and of the agents mainly with a view to the action.

Third in order is Thought—that is, the faculty of saying what is possible and pertinent in given circumstances. In the case of oratory, this is the function of the political art and of the art of rhetoric; and so indeed the older poets make their characters speak the language of civic life; the poets of our time, the language of the rhetoricians. Character is that which reveals moral purpose, showing what kind of things a man chooses or avoids. Speeches, therefore, which do not make this manifest, or in which the speaker does not choose or avoid anything whatever, are not expressive of character. Thought, on the other hand, is found where something is proved to be or not to be, or a general maxim is enunciated.

Fourth among the elements enumerated comes Diction—by which I mean, as has been already said, the expression of the meaning in words, and its essence is the same both in verse and prose.

Of the remaining elements, Melody holds the chief place among the embellishments.

The Spectacle has, indeed, an emotional attraction of its own, but, of all the parts, it is the least artistic and connected least with the art of poetry. For the power of Tragedy, we may be sure, is felt even apart from representation and actors. Besides,[29] the production of spectacular effects depends more on the art of the stage machinist than on that of the poet.

VII—These principles being established, let us now discuss the proper structure of the Plot, since this is the first and most important thing in Tragedy.

Now, according to our definition, Tragedy is an imitation of an action that is complete and whole and of a certain magnitude; for there may be a whole that is wanting in magnitude. A whole is that which has a beginning, a middle, and an end. A beginning is that which does not itself follow anything by causal necessity, but after which something naturally is or comes to be. An end, on the contrary, is that which itself naturally follows some other thing, either by necessity or as a rule, but has nothing following it. A middle is that which follows something as some other thing follows it. A well-constructed plot, therefore, must neither begin nor end at haphazard but conform to these principles.

Again, a beautiful object, whether it be a living organism or any whole composed of parts, must not only have an orderly arrangement of parts, but must also be of a certain magnitude; for beauty depends on magnitude and order. Hence a very small animal organism cannot be beautiful, for the view of it is confused, the object being seen in an almost imperceptible moment of time. Nor, again, can one of vast size be beautiful; for as the eye cannot take it all in at once, the unity and sense of the whole is lost for the spectator, as, for instance, if there were one a thousand miles long. As, therefore, in the case of animate bodies and organisms a certain magnitude is necessary, and a magnitude[31] which may be easily embraced in one view, so in the plot a certain length is necessary, and a length which can be easily embraced by the memory. The limit of length in relation to dramatic competition and sensuous presentment is no part of artistic theory. For had it been the rule for a hundred tragedies to compete together, the performance would have been regulated by the waterclock—as indeed we are told was formerly done. But the limit as fixed by the nature of the drama itself is this: the greater the length, the more beautiful will the piece be by reason of its size, provided that the whole be perspicuous. And to define the matter roughly, we may say that the proper magnitude is comprised within such limits that the sequence of events, according to the law of probability or necessity, will admit of a change from bad fortune to good, or from good fortune to bad.

VIII—Unity of plot does not, as some persons think, consist in the unity of the hero. For infinitely various are the incidents in one man's life which cannot be reduced to unity; and so, too, there are many actions of one man out of which we cannot make one action. Hence the error, as it appears, of all poets who have composed a *Heracleid,* a *Theseid,* or other poems of the kind. They imagine that as Heracles was one man, the story of Heracles must also be a unity. But Homer, as in all else he is of surpassing merit, here too—whether from art or natural genius—seems to have happily discerned the truth. In composing the *Odyssey* he did not include all the adventures of Odysseus—such as his wound on Parnassus, or his feigned madness at the mustering of[33] the host—incidents between which there was no necessary or probable connection; but he made the *Odyssey,* and likewise the *Iliad,* to center around an action that in our sense of the word is one. As, therefore, in the other imitative arts, the imitation is one when the object imitated is one, so the plot, being an imitation of an action, must imitate one action and that a whole, the structural union of the parts being such that, if any one of them is displaced or removed, the whole will be disjointed and disturbed. For a thing whose presence or absence makes no visible difference is not an organic part of the whole.

IX—It is, moreover, evident from what has been said that it is not the function of the poet to relate what has happened, but what may happen—what is possible according to the law of probability or necessity. The poet and the historian differ not by writing in verse or in prose. The work of Herodotus might be put into verse, and it would still be a species of history, with metre no less than without it. The true difference is that one relates what has happened, the other what may happen. Poetry, therefore, is a more philosophical and a higher thing than history, for poetry tends to express the universal, history the particular. By the universal, I mean how a person of a certain type will on occasion speak or act, according to the law of probability or necessity; and it is this universality at which poetry aims in the names she attaches to the personages. The particular is, for example, what Alcibiades did or suffered. In Comedy this is already apparent, for here the poet first constructs the plot on the lines of probability,[35] and then inserts characteristic names—unlike the lampooners who write about particular individuals. But tragedians still keep to real names, the reason being that what is possible is credible; what has not happened we do not at once feel sure to be possible, but what has happened is manifestly possible, otherwise it would not have happened. Still there are even some tragedies in which there are only one or two well-known names, the rest being fictitious. In others, none are well known—as in Agathon's *Antheus,* where incidents and names alike are fictitious, and yet they give none the less pleasure. We must not, therefore, at all costs keep to the received legends, which are the usual subjects of Tragedy. Indeed it would be absurd to attempt it; for even subjects that are known are known only to a few, and yet give pleasure to all. It clearly follows that the poet or "maker" should be the maker of plots rather than of verses, since he is a poet because he imitates, and what he imitates are actions. And even if he chances to take a historical subject, he is none the less a poet; for there is no reason why some events that have actually happened should not conform to the law of the probable and possible, and in virtue of that quality in them he is their poet or maker.

Of all plots and actions the episodic are the worst.[37] I call a plot "episodic" in which the episodes or acts succeed one another without probable or necessary sequence. Bad poets compose such pieces by their own fault, good poets, to please the players; for, as they write show pieces for competition, they stretch the plot beyond its capacity, and are often forced to break the natural continuity.

But again, Tragedy is an imitation not only of a complete action, but of events inspiring fear and pity. Such an effect is best produced when the events come on us by surprise; and the effect is heightened when, at the same time, they follow as cause and effect. The tragic wonder will then be greater than if they happened of themselves or by accident; for even coincidences are most striking when they have an air of design. We may instance the statue of Mitys at Argos, which fell upon his murderer while he was a spectator at a festival, and killed him. Such events seem not to be due to mere chance. Plots, therefore, constructed on these principles are necessarily the best.

X—Plots are either simple or complex, for the actions in real life, of which the plots are an imitation, obviously show a similar distinction. An action which is one and continuous in the sense above defined I call simple when the change of fortune takes place without reversal of the situation and without recognition.

A complex action is one in which the change is accompanied by such reversal or by recognition, or by both. These last should arise from the internal structure of the Plot, so that what follows should be the[39] necessary or probable result of the preceding action. It makes all the difference whether any given event is a case of *propter hoc* or *post hoc.*

XI—"Reversal of the situation" is a change by which the action veers round to its opposite, subject always to our rule of probability or necessity. Thus in the *Oedipus,* the messenger comes to cheer Oedipus and free him from his alarms about his mother, but by revealing who he is he produces the opposite effect. Again in the *Lynceus,* Lynceus is being led away to his death, and Danaus goes with him, meaning to slay him; but the outcome of the preceding incidents is that Danaus is killed and Lynceus saved.

"Recognition," as the name indicates, is a change from ignorance to knowledge, producing love or hate between the persons destined by the poet for good or bad fortune. The best form of recognition is co-incident with a reversal of the situation, as in the *Oedipus.* There are indeed other forms. Even inanimate things of the most trivial kind may in a sense be objects of recognition. Again, we may recognize or discover whether a person has done a thing or not. But the recognition which is most intimately connected with the plot and action is, as we have said, the recognition of persons. This recognition, combined with reversal, will produce either pity or fear; and actions producing these effects are those which, by our definition, Tragedy represents. Moreover, it is upon such situations that the issues of good or bad fortune will depend.[41] Recognition then being between persons, it may happen that one person only is recognized by the other—when the latter is already known—or it may be necessary that the recognition should be on both sides. Thus Iphigenia is revealed to Orestes by the sending of the letter; but another act of recognition is required to make Orestes known to Iphigenia.

Two parts, then, of the Plot—reversal of the situation and recognition—turn upon surprises. A third part is the "scene of suffering." The scene of suffering is a destructive or painful action, such as death on the stage, bodily agony, wounds, and the like.

XII—The parts of Tragedy which must be treated as elements of the whole have been already mentioned. We now come to the quantitative parts—the separate parts into which Tragedy is divided—namely, Prologue, Episode, Exode, Choric song; this last being divided into Parode and Stasimon. These are common to all plays; peculiar to some are the songs of actors from the stage and the *Commoe.*

The Prologue is that entire part of a tragedy which precedes the Parode of the Chorus. The Episode is that entire part of a tragedy which is between complete choric songs. The Exode is that entire part of a tragedy which has no Choric song after it. Of the Choric part, the Parode is the first undivided utterance of the Chorus; the Stasimon is a Choric ode without anapaests or trochaic tetrameters: the *commos* is a joint lamentation of Chorus and actors. The parts of Tragedy which must be treated as elements of the whole have been[43] already mentioned. The quantitative parts—the separate parts into which it is divided—are here enumerated.

XIII—As the sequel to what has already been said, we must proceed to consider what the poet should aim at, and what he should avoid, in constructing his plots; and by what means the specific effect of Tragedy will be produced.

A perfect tragedy should, as we have seen, be arranged not on the simple but on the complex plan. It should, moreover, imitate actions which excite pity and fear, this being the distinctive function of tragic imitation. It follows plainly, in the first place, that the change of fortune presented must not be the spectacle of a virtuous man brought from prosperity to adversity, for this moves neither pity nor fear; it merely shocks us. Nor, again, that of a bad man passing from adversity to prosperity, for nothing can be more alien to the spirit of Tragedy; it possesses no single tragic quality; it neither satisfies the moral sense nor calls forth pity or fear. Nor, again, should the downfall of the utter villain be exhibited. A plot of this kind would doubtless satisfy the moral sense, but it would inspire neither pity nor fear; for pity is aroused by unmerited misfortune, fear by the misfortune of a man like ourselves. Such an event, therefore, will be neither pitiful nor terrible. There remains, then, the character between these two extremes—that of a man who is not eminently good and just, yet whose misfortune is brought about not by vice or depravity, but by some error or frailty. He must be one who is highly renowned and prosperous—a[45] personage like Oedipus, Thyestes, or other illustrious men of such families.

A well-constructed Plot should, therefore, be single in its issue rather than double, as some maintain. The change of fortune should be not from bad to good, but, on the contrary, from good to bad. It should come about as the result, not of vice, but of some great error or frailty in a character, either such as we have described or better rather than worse. The practice of the stage bears out our view. At first the poets recounted any legend that came in their way. Now the best tragedies are founded on the story of a few houses—on the fortunes of Alcmaeon, Oedipus, Orestes, Meleager, Thyestes, Telephus, and those others who have done or suffered something terrible. A Tragedy, then, to be perfect according to the rules of art should be of this construction. Hence they are in error who censure Euripides just because he follows this principle in his plays, many of which end unhappily. It is, as we have said, the right ending. The best proof is that, on the stage and in dramatic competition, such plays, if well worked out, are the most tragic in effect; and Euripides, faulty though he may be in the general management of his subject, yet is felt to be the most tragic of the poets.

In the second rank comes the kind of Tragedy which some place first. Like the *Odyssey*, it has a double thread of Plot, and also an opposite catastrophe for the good and for the bad. It is accounted the best because of the weakness of the spectators; for the poet is guided in what he writes by the wishes of his audience. The pleasure, however, thence derived is not the true tragic[47] pleasure. It is proper rather to Comedy, where those who, in the piece, are the deadliest enemies—like Orestes and Aegisthus—quit the stage as friends at the close, and no one slays or is slain.

XIV—Fear and pity may be aroused by means of the Spectacle; but they may also result from the inner structure of the piece, which is the better way and indicates a superior poet. For the plot ought to be so constructed that, even without the aid of the eye, he who hears the tale told will thrill with horror and melt to pity at what takes place. This is the impression we should receive from hearing the story of the *Oedipus*. But to produce this effect by the mere spectacle is a less artistic method, and dependent on extraneous aids. Those who use the Spectacle to create a sense, not of the terrible, but only of the monstrous are strangers to the purpose of Tragedy; for we must not demand of Tragedy any and every kind of pleasure, but only that which is proper to it. And since the pleasure which the poet should afford is that which comes from pity and fear through imitation, it is evident that this quality must be impressed upon the incidents.

Let us then determine what are the circumstances which strike us as terrible or pitiful.

Actions capable of this effect must happen between persons who are either friends or enemies or indifferent to one another. If an enemy kills an enemy, there is nothing to excite pity either in the act or the intention—except so far as the suffering in itself is pitiful. So again with indifferent persons. But when the tragic incident occurs between those who are near or dear to[49] one another—if, for example, a brother kills, or intends to kill, a brother, a son his father, a mother her son, a son his mother, or any other deed of the kind is done—these are the situations to be looked for by the poet. He may not indeed destroy the framework of the received legends—the fact, for instance, that Clytemnestra was slain by Orestes and Eriphyle by Alcmaeon—but he ought to show invention of his own and skilfully handle the traditional material. Let us explain more clearly what is meant by skilful handling.

The action may be done consciously and with knowledge of the persons, in the manner of the older poets. It is thus, too, that Euripides makes Medea slay her children. Or, again, the deed of horror may be done, but done in ignorance, and the tie of kinship or friendship be discovered afterwards. The *Oedipus* of Sophocles is an example. Here, indeed, the incident is outside the drama proper; but cases occur where it falls within the action of the play: one may cite the *Alcmaeon* of Astydamas, or Telegonus in the *Wounded Odysseus*. Again, there is a third case—[to be about to act with knowledge of the persons and then not to act. The fourth case is] when someone is about to do an irreparable deed through ignorance and makes the discovery before it is done. These are the only possible ways. For the deed must either be done or not done—and that wittingly or unwittingly. But of all these ways, to be about to act knowing the persons, and then not to act, is the worst. It is shocking without being tragic, for no disaster follows. It is, therefore, never or very rarely found in poetry. One instance, however, is in the *Antigone,* where Haemon threatens to kill Creon. The next and better way is that the deed[51] should be perpetrated. Still better, that it should be perpetrated in ignorance and the discovery made afterwards. There is then nothing to shock us, while the discovery produces a startling effect. The last case is the best, as when in the *Cresphontes* Merope is about to slay her son, but, recognizing who he is, spares his life. So in the *Iphigenia,* the sister recognizes the brother just in time. Again in the *Helle,* the son recognizes the mother when on the point of giving her up. This, then, is why a few families only, as has been already observed, furnish the subjects of tragedy. It was not art, but happy chance, that led the poets in search of subjects to impress the tragic quality upon their plots. They are compelled, therefore, to have recourse to those houses whose history contains moving incidents like these.

Enough has now been said concerning the structure of the incidents, and the right kind of plot.

XV—In respect of Character there are four things to be aimed at. First, and most important, it must be good. Now any speech or action that manifests moral purpose of any kind will be expressive of character: the character will be good if the purpose is good. This rule is relative to each class. Even a woman may be good, and also a slave, though the woman may be said to be an inferior being, and the slave quite worthless. The second thing to aim at is fitness of character. There is a type of manly valor; but valor in a woman, or unscrupulous cleverness, is inappropriate. Thirdly, character must be true to life; for[53] this is a distinct thing from goodness and fitness, as here described. The fourth point is consistency: for though the subject of the imitation, who suggested the type, be inconsistent, still he must be consistently inconsistent. As an example of motiveless degradation of character, we have Menelaus in the *Orestes;* of character indecorous and inappropriate, the lament of Odysseus in the *Scylla,* and the speech of Melanippe; of inconsistency, the *Iphigenia at Aulis*—for Iphigenia the suppliant in no way resembles her later self.

As in the structure of the Plot, so, too, in the portraiture of character, the poet should always aim either at the necessary or the probable. Thus a person of a given character should speak or act in a given way, by the rule either of necessity or of probability, just as this event should follow that by necessary or probable sequence. It is therefore evident that the unravelling of the Plot, no less than the complication, must arise out of the Plot itself; it must not be brought about by the *Deus ex Machina*—as in the *Medea,* or in the return of the Greeks in the *Iliad.* The *Deus ex Machina* should be employed only for events external to the drama—for antecedent or subsequent events which lie beyond the range of human knowledge and which require to be[55] reported or foretold; for to the gods we ascribe the power of seeing all things. Within the action there must be nothing irrational. If the irrational cannot be excluded, it should be outside the scope of the Tragedy. Such is the irrational element in the *Oedipus* of Sophocles.

Again, since Tragedy is an imitation of persons who are above the common level, the example of good portrait-painters should be followed. They, while reproducing the distinctive form of the original, make a likeness which is true to life and yet more beautiful. So, too, the poet, in representing men who are irascible or indolent, or have other defects of character, should preserve the type and yet ennoble it. In this way Achilles is portrayed by Agathon and Homer.

These then are rules the poet should observe. Nor should he neglect those impressions which, though not among the essentials, accompany poetry; for here, too, there is much room for error. But of this enough has been said in our published treatises.

XVI—What recognition is has been already explained. We will now enumerate its kinds.

First, the least artistic form, which, from poverty of wit, is most commonly employed—recognition by signs. Of these some are congenital—such as "the spear which the earth-born race bear on their bodies," or the stars introduced by Carcinus in his *Thyestes*. Others are acquired after birth; and of these some are bodily marks, as scars; some external tokens, as necklaces or the little ark in the Tyro by which the discovery is affected. Even these admit of more or less skilful treatment. Thus, in the recognition of Odysseus by his scar, the discovery is[57] made in one way by the nurse, in another by the swineherds. The use of tokens for the express purpose of proof—and, indeed, any former proof with or without token—is a less artistic mode of recognition. A better kind is that which comes about by a turn of incidents, as in the bath scene in the *Odyssey*.

Next come the recognitions invented at will by the poet, and on that account wanting in art. For example, Orestes in the *Iphigenia* reveals the fact that he is Orestes. She, indeed, makes herself known by the letter; but he by speaking himself and saying what the poet, not what the Plot, requires. This, therefore, is nearly allied to the fault above mentioned; for Orestes might as well have brought tokens with him. Another similar instance is the "voice of the shuttle" in the *Tereus* of Sophocles.

The third kind depends on memory when the sight of some object awakens a feeling, as in the *Cyprians* of Dicaeogenes, where the hero breaks into tears on seeing the picture; or again in the *Lay of Alcinous*, where Odysseus, hearing the minstrel play the lyre, recalls the past and weeps; and hence the recognition.

The fourth kind is by process of reasoning. Thus in the *Choëphori*: "Someone resembling me has come; no one resembles me but Orestes, therefore Orestes has come." Such, too, is the discovery made by Iphigenia in the play of Polyidus the Sophist. It was a natural reflection for Orestes to make, "So I, too, must die at the altar, like my sister." So, again, in the *Tydeus* of Theodectes, the father says, "I came to find my son, and I lose my own life." So, too, in the *Phineidae* —the women, on seeing the place, inferred their fate—"Here[59] we are doomed to die, for here we were cast forth." Again, there is a composite kind of recognition involving false inference on the part of one of the characters, as in the *Odysseus Disguised as a Messenger*. A said that no one else was able to bend the bow; . . . hence B (the disguised Odysseus) imagined that A would recognize the bow which, in fact, he had not seen; and to bring about a recognition by this means— the expectation that A would recognize the bow—is false inference.

But, of all recognitions, the best is that which arises from the incidents themselves, where the startling discovery is made by natural means. Such is that in the *Oedipus* of Sophocles, and in the *Iphigenia;*

for it was natural that Iphigenia should wish to dispatch a letter. These recognitions alone dispense with the artificial aid of tokens or amulets. Next come the recognitions by process of reasoning.

XVII—In constructing the Plot and working it out with the proper diction, the poet should place the scene, as far as possible, before his eyes. In this way, seeing everything with the utmost vividness, as if he were a spectator of the action, he will discover what is in keeping with it and be most unlikely to overlook inconsistencies. The need of such a rule is shown by the fault found in Carcinus. Amphiaraus was on his way from the temple. This fact escaped the observation of one who did not see the situation. On the stage, however, the piece failed, because the audience was offended at the oversight.

Again, the poet should work out his play to the best of his power, with appropriate gestures; for[61] those who feel emotion are most convincing through natural sympathy with the characters they represent; and one who is agitated storms, one who is angry rages, with the most life-like reality. Hence poetry implies either a happy gift of nature or a strain of madness. In the one case a man can take the mold of any character; in the other, he is lifted out of his proper self.

As for the story, whether the poet takes it ready-made or constructs it for himself, he should first sketch its general outline, and then fill in the episodes and amplify in detail. The general plan may be illustrated by the *Iphigenia*. A young girl is sacrificed; she disappears mysteriously from the eyes of those who sacrificed her; she is transported to another country where the custom is to offer up all strangers to the goddess. To this ministry she is appointed. Some time later her own brother chances to arrive. The fact that the oracle for some reason ordered him to go there is outside the general plan of the play. The purpose, again, of his coming is outside the action proper. However, he comes, he is seized, and, when on the point of being sacrificed, reveals who he is. The mode of recognition may be either that of Euripides or of Polyidus, in whose play he exclaims very naturally: "So it was not my sister only, but I too, who was doomed to be sacrificed"; and by that remark he is saved.

After this, the names being once given, it remains to fill in the episodes. We must see that they are relevant to the action. In the case of Orestes, for example, there is the madness which led to his capture and his deliverance by means of the purificatory rite. In the drama, the Episodes are short, but it is these that[63] give extension to Epic poetry. Thus the story of the *Odyssey* can be stated briefly. A certain man is absent from home for many years; he is jealously watched by Poseidon, and left desolate. Meanwhile, his home is in a wretched plight—suitors are wasting his substance and plotting against his son. At length, tempest-tost, he himself arrives; he makes certain persons acquainted with him; he attacks the suitors with his own hand and is himself preserved while he destroys them. This is the essence of the Plot; the rest is Episode.

XVIII—Every Tragedy falls into two parts—complication and unravelling or *dénouement*. Incidents extraneous to the action are frequently combined with a portion of the action proper, to form the complication; the rest is the unravelling. By the complication I mean all that extends from the beginning of the action to the part which marks the turning point to good or bad fortune. The unravelling is that which extends from the beginning of the change to the end. Thus, in the *Lynceus* of Theodectes, the complication consists of the incidents presupposed in the drama, the seizure of the child, and then again . . . [the unravelling] extends from the accusation of murder to the end.

There are four kinds of Tragedy: the complex, depending entirely on "reversal of the situation" and "recognition";[65] the pathetic (where the motive is passion)—such as the tragedies on Ajax and Ixion; the ethical (where the motives are ethical)—such as the *Phthiotides* and, the *Peleus*. The fourth kind is the simple. We here exclude the purely spectacular element, exemplified by the *Phorcides,* the *Prometheus,* and scenes laid in Hades. The poet should endeavor, if possible, to combine all poetic elements or, failing that, the greatest number and those the most important: the more so in face of the cavilling criticism of the day. For whereas there have hitherto been good poets, each in his own branch, the critics now expect one man to surpass all others in their several lines of excellence.

In speaking of a tragedy as the same or different, the best test to take is the Plot. Identity exists where the complication and unravelling are the same. Many poets tie the knot well, but unravel it ill. Both arts, however, should always be mastered.

Again, the poet should remember what has been often said and not make an Epic structure into a Tragedy—by an Epic structure, I mean one with a multiplicity of Plots—as if, for instance, you were to make a Tragedy out of the entire story of the *Iliad.* In the Epic poem, owing to its length, each part assumes its proper magnitude. In the drama the result is far from answering to the poet's expectation. The proof is that the poets who have dramatized the whole story of the fall of Troy, instead of selecting portions, like Euripides, or who have taken the whole tale of Niobe, and not a part of her story, like Aeschylus, either fail utterly or meet with poor success on the stage. Even Agathon[67] has been known to fail from this one defect. In his "reversals of the situation," however, he shows a marvellous skill in the effort to hit the popular taste—to produce a tragic effect that satisfies the moral sense. This effect is produced when the clever rogue, like Sisyphus, is outwitted or the brave villain defeated. Such an event is probable in Agathon's sense of the word: "it is probable," he says, "that many things should happen contrary to probability."

The Chorus, too, should be regarded as one of the actors; it should be an integral part of the whole and share in the action, in the manner not of Euripides but of Sophocles. As for the later poets, their choral songs pertain as little to the subject of the piece as to that of any other tragedy. They are, therefore, sung as mere interludes—a practice first begun by Agathon. Yet what difference is there between introducing such choral interludes and transferring a speech or even a whole act from one play to another?

XIX—It remains to speak of Diction and Thought, the other parts of Tragedy having been already discussed. Concerning Thought, we may assume what is said in the *Rhetoric*, to which inquiry the subject more strictly belongs. Under Thought is included every effect which has to be produced by speech, the subdivisions being proof and refutation; the arousing of emotions, such as pity, fear, anger, and the like; the suggestion of[69] importance or its opposite. Now it is evident that the dramatic incidents must be treated from the same points of view as the dramatic speeches when the object is to evoke the sense of pity, fear, importance, or probability. The only difference is that the incidents should speak for themselves, without verbal exposition, while the effects aimed at in speech should be produced by the speaker and as a result of the speech. For what were the business of a speaker if the Thought were revealed quite apart from what he says?

Next, as regards Diction: one branch of the inquiry treats of the "modes of utterance." But this province of knowledge belongs to the art of "delivery" and to the masters of that science. It includes, for instance, what is a command, a prayer, a statement, a threat, a question, an answer, and so forth. To know or not to know these things involves no serious censure upon the poet's art. For who can admit the fault imputed to Homer by Protagoras—that in the words "Sing, goddess, of the wrath," he gives a command under the idea that he utters a prayer? For to tell someone to do a thing or not to do it is, he says, a command. We may, therefore, pass this over as an inquiry that belongs to another art, not to poetry.

XX—Language in general includes the following parts: letter, syllable, connecting word, noun, verb, inflection or case, sentence or phrase.

A letter is an indivisible sound, yet not every such sound, but only one which can form part of a group of[71] sounds. For even brutes utter indivisible sounds, none of which I call a letter. The sound I mean may be either a vowel, a semi-vowel, or a mute. A vowel is that which without impact of tongue or lip has an audible sound.

A semi-vowel, that which with such impact has an audible sound, as S and R. A mute, that which with such impact has by itself no sound, but joined to a vowel sound becomes audible, as G and D. These are distinguished according to the form assumed by the mouth and the place where they are produced; according as they are aspirated or smooth, long or short; as they are acute, grave, or of an intermediate tone; which inquiry belongs in detail to the writers on metre.

A syllable is a non-significant sound, composed of a mute and a vowel: for GR without A is a syllable, as also with A—GRA. But the investigation of these differences belongs also to metrical science.

A "connecting word" is a non-significant sound which neither causes nor hinders the union of many sounds into one significant sound; it may be placed at either[73] end or in the middle of a sentence. Or, a non-significant sound which out of several sounds, each of them significant, is capable of forming one significant sound. Or, a non-significant sound, which marks the beginning, end, or division of a sentence; such, however, that it cannot correctly stand by itself at the beginning of a sentence.

A noun is a composite significant sound, not marking time, of which no part is in itself significant; for in double or compound words we do not employ the separate parts as if each were in itself significant. Thus in Theodorus, "god-given," the *dorow* or "gift" is not in itself significant.

A verb is a composite significant sound, marking time, in which, as in the noun, no part is in itself significant. For "man" or "white" does not express the idea of "when"; but "he walks" or "he has walked" does connote time, present or past.

Inflection belongs both to the noun and verb, and expresses either the relation "of," "to," or the like; or that of number, whether one or many, as "man" or "men"; or the modes or tones in actual delivery, e.g. a question or a command. "Did he go?" and "go" are verbal inflections of this kind.

A sentence or phrase is a composite significant sound, some at least of whose parts are in themselves significant; for not every such group of words consists of verbs and nouns—"the definition of man," for example—but it may dispense even with the verb. Still it will[75] always have some significant part, as "in walking," or "Cleon son of Cleon." A sentence or phrase may form a unity in two ways—either as signifying one thing or as consisting of several parts linked together. Thus the *Iliad* is one by the linking together of parts, the definition of man by the unity of the thing signified.

XXI—Words are of two kinds, simple and double. By simple, I mean those composed of non-significant elements, such as *ge;* by double or compound, those composed either of a significant and non-significant element (though within the whole word no element is significant), or of elements that are both significant. A word may likewise be triple, quadruple, or multiple in form, like so many Massilian expressions, e.g. "Hermo-caico-xanthus [who prayed to Father Zeus]."

Every word is either current, or strange, or metaphorical, or ornamental, or newly-coined, or lengthened, or contracted, or altered.

By a current or proper word, I mean one which is in general use among a people; by a strange word, one which is in use in another country. Plainly, therefore, the same word may be at once strange and current, but not in relation to the same people. The word "lance" is to the Cyprians a current term, but to us a strange one.

Metaphor is the application of an alien name by transference either from genus to species, or from species to genus, or from species to species, or by analogy, that is,[77] proportion. Thus from genus to species, as: "There lies my ship"; for lying at anchor is a species of lying. From species to genus, as: "Verily ten thousand noble deeds hath Odysseus wrought"; for ten thousand is a species of large number and is here used for a large number generally. From species to species, as: "With blade of bronze drew away the life," and "Cleft the water with the vessel of unyielding bronze." Here "to draw away" is used for "to cleave," and "to cleave" again for "draw away"—each being a species of "taking away." Analogy or proportion is when the second term is to the first as the fourth to the third. We may then use the fourth for the second, or the second for the fourth. Sometimes, too, we qualify the metaphor by adding the term to which the proper word is relative. Thus the cup is to Dionysus as the shield to Ares. The cup may, therefore, be called "the shield of Dionysus," and the shield "the cup of Ares." Or, again, as old age is to life, so is evening to day. Evening may therefore be called "the old age of the day," and old age, "the evening of life," or, in the phrase of Empedocles, "life's setting sun." For some of the terms of the proportion there is at times no word in existence; still the metaphor may be used. For instance, to scatter seed is called sowing; but the action of the sun in scattering his rays is nameless. Still this process bears to the sun the same relation as sowing to the seed. Hence the expression of the poet "sowing the god-created light." There is another way in which this kind of metaphor may be employed. We may apply an alien term, and then deny of that term one of its[79] proper attributes, as if we were to call the shield, not "the cup of Ares," but "the wineless cup."

[An ornamental word . . .]

A newly-coined word is one which has never been even in local use, but is adopted by the poet himself. Some such words there appear to be: as "sprouters" for "horns" and "supplicator" for "priest."

A word is lengthened when its own vowel is exchanged for a longer one, or when a syllable is inserted. A word is contracted when some part of it is removed.

An altered word is one in which part of the ordinary form is left unchanged, and part is re-cast . . .

XXII—The perfection of style is to be clear without being mean. The clearest style is that which uses only current or proper words; at the same time it is mean—witness the poetry of Cleophon and of Sthenelus. That diction,[81] on the other hand, is lofty and raised above the commonplace which employs unusual words. By unusual, I mean strange (or rare) words, metaphorical, lengthened—anything, in short, that differs from the normal idiom. Yet a style wholly composed of such words is either a riddle or a jargon; a riddle, if it consists of metaphors; a jargon, if it consists of strange (or rare) words. For the essence of a riddle is to express true fact under impossible combinations. Now this cannot be done by any arrangement of ordinary words, but by the use of metaphor it can. Such is the riddle: "A man I saw who on another man had glued the bronze by aid of fire," and others of the same kind. A diction that is made up of strange (or rare) terms is a jargon. A certain infusion, therefore, of these elements is necessary to style; for the strange (or rare) word, the metaphorical, the ornamental, and the other kinds above mentioned, will raise it above the commonplace and mean, while the use of proper words will make it perspicuous. But nothing contributes more to produce a clearness of diction that is remote from commonness than the lengthening, contraction, and alteration of words. For by deviating in exceptional cases from the normal idiom, the language will gain distinction; while, at the same time, the partial conformity with usage will give perspicuity. The critics, therefore, are in error who censure these licenses of speech and hold the author up to ridicule. Thus Eucleides the elder declared that it would be an easy matter to be a poet if you might lengthen syllables at will. He caricatured the practice in the very form of his diction . . .[83] To employ such license at all obtrusively is, no doubt, grotesque; but in any mode of poetic diction there must be moderation. Even metaphors, strange (or rare) words, or any similar forms of speech, would produce the like effect if used without propriety and with the express purpose of being ludicrous. How great a difference is made by the appropriate use of lengthening may be seen in Epic poetry by the insertion of ordinary forms in the verse. So, again, if we take a strange (or rare) word, a metaphor, or any similar mode of expression, and replace it by the current or proper term, the truth of our observation will be manifest. For example, Aeschylus and Euripides each composed the same iambic line. But the alteration of a single word by Euripides, who employed the rarer term instead of the ordinary one, makes one verse appear beautiful and the other trivial.[85] . . .

Again, Ariphrades ridiculed the tragedians for using phrases which no one would employ in ordinary speech . . . It is precisely because such phrases are not part of the current idiom that they give distinction to the style. This, however, he failed to see.

It is a great matter to observe propriety in these several modes of expression, as also in compound words, strange (or rare) words, and so forth. But the greatest thing by far is to have a command of metaphor. This alone cannot be imparted by another; it is the mark of genius, for to make good metaphors implies an eye for resemblances.

Of the various kinds of words, the compound are best adapted to dithyrambs, rare words to heroic poetry, metaphors to iambic. In heroic poetry, indeed, all these varieties are serviceable. But in iambic verse, which reproduces, as far as may be, familiar speech, the most appropriate words are those which are found even in prose. These are the current or proper, the metaphorical, the ornamental.

Concerning Tragedy and imitation by means of action this may suffice.[87]

XXIII—As to that poetry which is merely narrative in form or imitates by means of a single metre (without action), the plot manifestly ought, as in a tragedy, to be constructed on dramatic principles. It should have for its subject a single action, whole and complete, with a beginning, a middle, and an end. It will thus resemble a living organism in all its unity and produce the pleasure proper to it. It will differ in structure from historical compositions, which of necessity present not a single action, but a single period and all that happened within that period to one person or to many, little connected together as the events may be. For as the sea-fight at Salamis and the battle with the Carthaginians in Sicily took place at the same time, but did not tend to any one result, so in the sequence of events one thing sometimes follows another, and yet no single result is thereby produced. Such is the practice, we may say, of most poets. Here again, then, as has been already observed, the transcendent excellence of Homer is manifest. He never attempts to make the whole war of Troy the subject of his poem, though that war had a beginning and an end. It would have been too vast a theme, and not easily embraced in a single view. If, again, he had kept it within moderate limits, it must have been overcomplicated by the variety of the incidents. As it is, he detaches a single portion and admits as episodes many events from the general story of the war—such as the Catalogue of the ships and others —thus diversifying the poem. All other poets take a single hero, a single period, or an action single indeed, but with a multiplicity of parts. Thus did the[89] author of the *Cypria* and of the *Little Iliad*. For this reason the *Iliad* and the *Odyssey* each furnish the subject of one tragedy, or, at most, of two; while the *Cypria* supplies materials for many, and the *Little Iliad* for eight—the *Award of the Arms*, the *Philoctetes*, the *Neoptolemus*, the *Eurypylus*, the *Mendicant Odys-*

seus, the *Laconian Women,* the *Fall of Ilium,* the *Departure of the Fleet.*

XXIV—Again, Epic poetry must have as many kinds as Tragedy: it must be simple, or complex, or "ethical," or "pathetic." The parts also, with the exception of song and spectacle, are the same, for it requires reversals of the situation, recognitions, and scenes of suffering. Moreover, the Thoughts and the Diction must be artistic. In all these respects Homer is our earliest and sufficient model. Indeed, each of his poems has a twofold character. The *Iliad* is at once simple and "pathetic," and the *Odyssey* complex (for "recognition" scenes run through it), and at the same time "ethical." Moreover, in Diction and Thought they are supreme.

Epic poetry differs from Tragedy in the scale on which it is constructed and in its metre. As regards scale or length, we have already laid down an adequate limit—the beginning and the end must be capable of being brought within a single view. This condition will be satisfied by poems on a smaller scale than the old epics, and answering in length to the group of tragedies presented at a single sitting.

Epic poetry has, however, a great—a special—capacity for enlarging its dimensions, and we can see the reason. In Tragedy we cannot imitate several lines of[91] actions carried on at one and the same time; we must confine ourselves to the action on the stage and the part taken by the players. But in Epic poetry, owing to the narrative form, many events simultaneously transacted can be presented; and these, if relevant to the subject, add mass and dignity to the poem. The Epic has here an advantage, and one that conduces to grandeur of effect, to diverting the mind of the hearer, and relieving the story with varying episodes. For sameness of incident soon produces satiety, and makes tragedies fail on the stage.

As for the metre, the heroic measure has proved its fitness by the test of experience. If a narrative poem in any other metre or in many metres were now composed, it would be found incongruous. For of all measures the heroic is the stateliest and the most massive; and hence it most readily admits rare words and metaphors, which is another point in which the narrative form of imitation stands alone. On the other hand, the iambic and the trochaic tetrameter are stirring measures, the latter being akin to dancing, the former expressive of action. Still more absurd would it be to mix together different metres, as was done by Chaeremon. Hence no one has ever composed a poem on a great scale in any other than heroic verse. Nature herself, as we have said, teaches the choice of the proper measure.

Homer, admirable in all respects, has the special merit of being the only poet who rightly appreciates the part he should take himself. The poet should speak as little as possible in his own person, for it is not this that makes him an imitator. Other poets appear themselves upon[93] the scene throughout, and imitate but little and rarely. Homer, after a few prefatory words, at once brings in a man, or woman, or other personage; none of them wanting in characteristic qualities, but each with a character of his own.

The element of the wonderful is required in Tragedy. The irrational, on which the wonderful depends for its chief effects, has wider scope in Epic poetry because there the person acting is not seen. Thus the pursuit of Hector would be ludicrous if placed upon the stage— the Greeks standing still and not joining in the pursuit, and Achilles waving them back. But in the Epic poem the absurdity passes unnoticed. Now the wonderful is pleasing, as may be inferred from the fact that everyone tells a story with some addition of his own, knowing that his hearers like it. It is Homer who has chiefly taught other poets the art of telling lies skilfully. The secret of it lies in a fallacy (i.e. paralogism). For, assuming that if one thing is or becomes, a second is or becomes, men imagine that, if the second is, the first likewise is or becomes. But this is a false inference. Hence, where the first thing is untrue, it is quite unnecessary, provided the second be true, to add that the first is or has become. For the mind, knowing the second to be true, falsely infers the truth of the first. There is an example of this in the bath scene of the Odyssey.

Accordingly, the poet should prefer probable impossibilities to improbable possibilities. The tragic plot must not be composed of irrational parts. Everything[95] irrational should, if possible, be excluded; or, at all events, it should lie outside the action of the play (as, in the Oedipus, the hero's ignorance as to the manner of Laius' death); not within the drama—as, in the Electra, the messenger's account of the Pythian games; or, as in the Mysians, the man who has come from Tegea to Mysia and is still speechless. The plea that otherwise the Plot would have been ruined is ridiculous; such a Plot should not in the first instance be constructed. But once the irrational has been introduced and an air of likelihood imparted to it, we must accept it in spite of the absurdity. Take even the irrational incidents in the Odyssey, where Odysseus is left upon the shore of Ithaca. How intolerable even these might have been would be apparent if an inferior poet were to treat the subject. As it is, the absurdity is veiled by the poetic charm with which the poet invests it.

The Diction should be elaborated in the pauses of the action, where there is no expression of Character or Thought. For, conversely, Character and Thought are merely obscured by a Diction that is overbrilliant.

XXV—With respect to problems and their solutions, the number and nature of the sources from which they may be drawn may be thus exhibited.

The poet, being an imitator, like a painter or any other artist, must of necessity imitate one of three objects—things as they were or are, things as they are said or thought to be, or things as they ought to be. The vehicle of expression is language—either current terms or, it may be, rare words or metaphors. There are also many modifications of language which we[97] concede to the poets. Add to this that the standard correctness is not the same in poetry and politics, any more than in poetry and any other art. Within the art of poetry itself there are two kinds of faults—those which touch its essence, and those which are accidental. If a poet has chosen to imitate something [but has imitated it incorrectly], through want of capacity, the error is inherent in the poetry. But if the failure is due to a wrong choice—if he has represented a horse as throwing out both his off legs at once, or introduced technical inaccuracies in medicine, for example, or in any other art—the error is not essential to the poetry. These are the points of view from which we should consider and answer the objections raised by the critics.

First, as to matters which concern the poet's own art. If he describes the impossible, he is guilty of an error; but the error may be justified if the end of the art be thereby attained (the end being that already mentioned)—if, that is, the effect of this or any other part of the poem is thus rendered more striking. A case in point is the pursuit of Hector. If, however, the end might have been as well or better attained without violating the special rules of the poetic art, the error is not justified; for every kind of error should, if possible, be avoided.

Again, does the error touch the essentials of the poetic art, or some accident of it? For example, not to know that a hind has no horns is a less serious matter than to paint it inartistically.

Further, if it be objected that the description is not[99] true to fact, the poet may perhaps reply, "But the objects are as they ought to be"; just as Sophocles said that he drew men as they ought to be; Euripides, as they are. In this way the objection may be met. If, however, the representation be of neither kind, the poet may answer, "This is how men say the thing is." This applies to tales about the gods. It may well be that these stories are not higher than fact nor yet true to fact; they are, very possibly, what Xenophanes says of them. But anyhow, "this is what is said." Again, a description may be no better than the fact: "still, it was the fact"; as in the passage about the arms: "Upright upon their butt-ends stood the spears." This was the custom then, as it now is among the Illyrians.

Again, in examining whether what has been said or done by someone is poetically right or not, we must not look merely to the particular act or saying, and ask whether it is poetically good or bad. We must also consider by whom it is said or done, to whom, when, by what means, or for what ends; whether, for instance, it be to secure a greater good or avert a greater evil.

Other difficulties may be resolved by due regard to the usage of language. We may note a rare word . . . So, again, of Dolon: "ill-favored indeed he was to look upon." It is not meant that his body was ill-shaped but that his face was ugly; for the Cretans use the word "well-favored" to denote a fair race. Again, "mix the drink livelier" does not mean "mix it stronger" as for hard drinkers, but "mix it quicker."[101]

Sometimes an expression is metaphorical, as "Now all gods and men were sleeping through the night,"—while at the same time the poet says: "Often indeed, as he turned his gaze to the Trojan plain, he marvelled at the sound of flutes and pipes." "All" is here used metaphorically for "many," all being a species of many. So in the verse—"alone she hath no part . . .," "alone" is metaphorical; for the best known may be called the only one.

Again, the solution may depend upon accent or breathing. . . .

Or again, the question may be solved by punctuation, as in Empedocles—"Of a sudden things became mortal that before had learnt to be immortal, and things unmixed before mixed."

Or again, by ambiguity of meaning . . .

Or by the usage of language. Thus any mixed drink is called "wine." Hence Ganymede is said[103] "to pour the wine to Zeus," though the gods do not drink wine. So, too, one calls workers in iron "workers in bronze." This, however, may also be taken as a metaphor.

Again, when a word seems to involve some inconsistency of meaning, we should consider how many senses it may bear in the particular passage. For example: "there was stayed the spear of bronze"—we should ask in how many ways we may take "being checked there." The true mode of interpretation is the precise opposite of what Glaucon mentions. Critics, he says, jump at certain groundless conclusions; they pass adverse judgment and then proceed to reason on it; and, assuming that the poet has said whatever they happen to think, find fault if a thing is inconsistent with their own fancy. The question about Icarius has been treated in this fashion. The critics imagine he was a Lacedaemonian. They think it strange, therefore, that Telemachus should not have met him when he went to Lacedaemon. But the Cephallenian story may perhaps be the true one. They allege that Odysseus took a wife from among themselves, and that her father was Icadius, not Icarius. It is merely a mistake, then, that gives plausibility to the objection.

In general, the impossible must be justified by reference to artistic requirements, or to the higher[105] reality, or to received opinion. With respect to the requirements of art, a probable impossibility is to be preferred to a thing improbable and yet possible. Again, it may be impossible that there should be men such as Zeuxis painted. "Yes," we say, "but the impossible is the higher thing; for the ideal type must surpass the reality." To justify the irrational, we appeal to what is commonly said to be. In addition to which, we urge that the irrational sometimes does not violate reason; just as "it is probable that a thing may happen contrary to probability."

Things that sound contradictory should be examined by the same rules as in dialectical refutation—whether the same thing is meant in the same relation and in the same sense. We should therefore solve the question by reference to what the poet says himself, or to what is tacitly assumed by a person of intelligence.

The element of the irrational and, similarly, depravity of character are justly censured when there is no inner necessity for introducing them. Such is the irrational element in the introduction of Aegeus by Euripides and the badness of Menelaus in the *Orestes*.

Thus there are five sources from which critical objections are drawn. Things are censured either as impossible, or irrational, or morally hurtful, or contradictory, or contrary to artistic correctness. The answers should be sought under the twelve heads above mentioned.

XXVI—The question may be raised whether the Epic or Tragic mode of imitation is the higher. If the more refined art is the higher, and the more refined in every case is that which appeals to the better sort of audience,[107] the art which imitates anything and everything is manifestly most unrefined. The audience is supposed to be too dull to comprehend unless something of their own is thrown in by the performers, who therefore indulge in restless movements. Bad flute-players twist and twirl, if they have to represent "the quoit-throw," or hustle the coryphaeus when they perform the "Scylla." Tragedy, it is said, has this same defect. We may compare the opinion that the older actors entertained of their successors. Mynniscus used to call Callippides "ape" on account of the extravagance of his action, and the same view was held of Pindarus. Tragic art, then, as a whole, stands to Epic in the same relation as the younger to the elder actors. So we are told that Epic poetry is addressed to a cultivated audience, who do not need gesture; Tragedy, to an inferior public. Being then unrefined, it is evidently the lower of the two.

Now, in the first place, this censure attaches not to the poetic but to the histrionic art; for gesticulation may be equally overdone in epic recitation, as by Sosistratus, or in lyrical competition, as by Mnasitheus the Opuntian. Next, all action is not to be condemned—any more than all dancing—but only that of bad performers. Such was the fault found in Callippides, as also in others of our own day who are censured for representing degraded women. Again, Tragedy, like Epic poetry, produces its effect even without action; it reveals its power by mere reading. If, then, in all other respects it is superior, this fault, we say, is not inherent in it.

And superior it is, because it has all the epic elements—it may even use the epic metre—with the[109] music and spectacle as important accessories; and these produce the most vivid of pleasures. Further, it has vividness of impression in reading as well as in representation. Moreover, the art attains its end within narrower limits; for the concentrated effect is more pleasurable than one which is spread over a long time and so diluted. What, for example, would be the effect of the *Oedipus* of Sophocles if it were cast into a form as long as the *Iliad*? Once more, the Epic imitation has less unity, as is shown by this, that any Epic poem will furnish subjects for several tragedies. Thus, if the story adopted by the poet has a strict unity, it must either be concisely told and appear truncated; or, if it conform to the Epic canon of length, it must seem weak and watery. [Such length implies some loss of unity] if, I mean, the poem is constructed out of several actions, like the *Iliad* and the *Odyssey*, which have many such parts, each with a certain magnitude of its own. Yet these poems are as perfect as possible in structure; each is, in the highest degree attainable, an imitation of a single action.

If, then, Tragedy is superior to Epic poetry in all these respects and, moreover, fulfils its specific function better as an art—for each ought to produce, not any chance pleasure, but the pleasure proper to it, as already stated—it plainly follows that Tragedy is the higher art, as attaining its end more perfectly.

Thus much may suffice concerning Tragic and Epic poetry in general; their several kinds and parts, with the number of each and their differences; the causes that make a poem good or bad; the objections of the critics and the answers to these objections.[111]

Ancient Scholia

From *Scholia in Sophoclis Tragoedias Vetera,*
edited by Petrus N. Papageorgius. Leipzig:
Teubner, 1888. Translated by Albert Cook.

On line 34: "And in the [human] intercourse with spirits": and,
in the community and friendship toward the divine, to guess at the
thought of the gods. By this he makes the tragedy more pathetic,
when a man who is considered to be so great is shown subject to
strange defilements.[164]

On line 873: "Pride breeds the tyrant." Through pride [*hybris*]
the tyrant is born and emerges—and when, the writer says, he ac-
complishes much, then he falls into great evils, aroused by pride.
These he says about Jocasta, in that she speaks harsh things about the
divine laws, and they [the chorus] make the statement about the tyrant
so that they may not seem to reproach her openly. The sense: pride
breeds the tyrant whenever there comes to be a vain superabundance
for a person of things which are not opportune or fitting for him.
[The poet] said it without a particular reference. Pride, he says, does
nothing in season; and once it has climbed the difficult mountain
ridge, it dashes down those who employ it; or else it rushes a person
precipitously into necessity, and brings him to the necessity of being
mastered by other men.[196]

Voltaire

From "Lettres sur Oedipe," 1719. In *Oeuvres Complètes,* Vol. II, edited by Beuchot. Paris: Garnier, 1877. Translated by Albert Cook.

It is already contrary to verisimilitude that Oedipus, who has been reigning so long, should not know how his predecessor died. But that he does not even know whether it was in the fields or the city that this murder was committed, and that he gives not the least reason or excuse for his ignorance—I confess that I know no words to express such an absurdity.[19]

It is a fault of the subject, one might say, and not of the author; as though it was not the author's job to correct his subject when it is so defective! . . .

One could blame the Thebans even more if the riddle of the Sphinx had not been easier to guess than all these contradictions. . . .[20]

So much ignorance in Oedipus and Jocasta is only a clumsy artifice on the part of the poet, who, to give his play the proper length, has drawn out to the fifth act a recognition which is already manifest in the second, and which violates the rules of common sense so as not to appear to fail the rules of the theatre. . . .[24]

I am not astonished that, in spite of so many imperfections, Sophocles took the admiration of his age by surprise: the harmony of his verses and the pathos which reigns in his style could have won over the Athenians, who, with all their intelligence and refinement, could not have had a clear idea of perfection in an art which was still in its infancy.[26]

Samuel Johnson

From Preface (unsigned) to *Poems and Miscellaneous Pieces* by Thomas Maurice. London: 1779.

Had Sophocles presented to our view a character less debased by vice, or more exalted by virtue, the end of his performance would have been frustrated; instead of agonizing compassion, he would have raised in us indignation unmixed, and horror unabated. . . . our indignation would have been transferred from Oedipus to the gods themselves . . . By making him criminal in a small degree, and miserable in a very great one, by investing him with some excellent qualities, and some imperfections, he at once inclines us to pity and to condemn . . . This . . . shows Sophocles to have had an intimate knowledge of the human heart, and the springs by which it is actuated. That his crimes and punishment still seem disproportionate is not to be imputed as a fault to Sophocles, who proceeded only on the ancient and popular notion of Destiny; which we know to have been the basis of Pagan theology.[151]

Friedrich von Schiller

From a Letter to Goethe, October 2, 1797.
In *The Correspondence between Schiller and
Goethe,* Vol. I. London: George Bell, 1877.
Translated by L. Dora Schmitz.

I have during these last days been occupying myself a good deal in finding a subject for a tragedy in the style of the *Oedipus Rex,* and one that will afford the same advantages to the poet. These advantages are inestimable, to mention but the one, that the most involved action —such as altogether resists the form of tragedy—may be taken as the foundation, inasmuch as this action has, of course, already happened, and consequently falls wholly beyond the domain of tragedy. In addition to this, that which has happened, in being unalterable, is naturally far more terrible, and the fear that something *might have happened* affects the mind quite differently from the fear that something may happen.

The Oedipus is, as it were, only a tragic analysis. Everything is already in existence, and has only to be unravelled. This can be done by the simplest action, and within a very limited period of time, be the incidents ever so complicated and dependent upon circumstances. How favorable this is to the poet!

But I fear that the Oedipus is its own genus, and that there is no second species of it; and least of all would one be able to find a *pendent* to it in less fabulous times. The oracle occupies a place in the tragedy which it would simply be impossible to replace by anything else; and should one attempt to retain the substance of the story itself while changing the characters and the times, then that which is now terrible, would become ludicrous.[411]

Thomas De Quincey

From "The Theban Sphinx." In *Collected Writings*, Vol. VI, edited by Masson. London: A & C Black, 1897.

The riddle proposed by the Sphinx ran in these terms: "What creature is that which moves on four feet in the morning, on two feet at noon-day, and on three towards the[144] going down of the sun?" Oedipus, after some consideration, answered that the creature was MAN, who creeps on the ground with hands and feet when an infant, walks upright in the vigour of manhood, and leans upon a staff in old age. . . .[145]

And now . . . in what respect is it that we object to the solution of the Sphinx's Riddle? We do not object to it as *a* solution of the riddle, and the only one possible at the moment. It is really *a* solution; and for the moment a satisfactory solution;[146] but what we contend is that it is not *the* solution. All great prophecies, all great mysteries, are likely to involve double, triple, or even quadruple interpretations; each rising in dignity, each cryptically involving another. . . .

. . . in our opinion the full and *final* answer to the Sphinx's riddle lay in the word OEDIPUS. Oedipus himself it was that fulfilled the conditions of the enigma. He it was, in the most pathetic sense, that went upon four feet when an infant; for the general condition of helplessness attached to all mankind in the period of infancy, and which is expressed symbolically by this image of creeping, applied to Oedipus in a far more[147] significant manner, as one abandoned by all his natural protectors, thrown upon the chances of a wilderness, and upon the mercies of a slave. The allusion to this general helplessness had, besides, a special propriety in the case of Oedipus, who drew his very name (viz. *Swollen Foot*) from the injury done to his infant feet. He again it was that, in a more emphatic sense than usual, asserted that majestic self-sufficingness and independence of all alien aid which is typified by the act of walking upright at noonday upon his own natural basis. Throwing off all the power and splendour borrowed from his royal protectors at Corinth, trusting exclusively to his native powers as a man, he had fought his way through insult and outrage to the presence of the dreadful Sphinx; her he had confounded and vanquished; he had leaped into a throne, the throne of him who had insulted him, without other resources than such as he drew from himself; and he had in the same way obtained a royal bride. With good right, therefore, he was foreshadowed in the riddle as one who walked upright by his own masculine vigour, and relied upon no gifts but those of nature. Lastly, by a sad and a pitying image, Oedipus is described as supporting himself at nightfall on three feet: for Oedipus it was that by his cruel sons would have been rejected from Thebes with no means of motion or support beyond his own languishing powers: blind and broken-hearted, he must have wandered into snares and ruin; his own feet must have been supplanted immediately; but then came to his aid another foot, the holy Antigone. She it was that guided and cheered him when all the world had forsaken him; she it was that already, in the vision of the cruel Sphinx, had been prefigured dimly as the staff upon which Oedipus should lean, as the *third* foot that should support his steps when the deep shadows of his sunset were gathering and settling about his grave.[148]

R. C. Jebb

From *Oedipus Tyrannus*. Cambridge: Cambridge University Press, 1883. Reprinted by permission of the publishers.

The *Oedipus Tyrannus* is in one sense the masterpiece of Attic Tragedy. No other shows an equal degree of art in the development of the plot; and this excellence depends on the powerful and subtle drawing of the characters. Modern drama, where minor parts can be multiplied and scene changed at will, can more easily divorce the two kinds of merit. Some of Voltaire's plays, for instance, not firstrate in other ways, are models of ingenious construction. The conditions of the Greek stage left less room for such a result. In the *Oedipus*

Tyrannus the highest constructive skill is seen to be intimately and necessarily allied with the vivid delineation of a few persons.

Here it is peculiarly interesting to recover, so far as we can, the form in which the story of Oedipus came to Sophocles; to remark what he has altered or added; and to see how the same subject has been handled by other dramatists.

The essence of the myth is the son slaying his unknown father, and thereby fulfilling a decree of fate. The subsequent marriage, if not an original part of the story, seems to have been an early addition. The central ideas are, (1) the irresistible power of destiny, and (2) the sacredness of the primary natural ties, as measured by the horror of an unconscious sin against it. The direct and simple form in which these ideas are embodied gives the legend an impress of high antiquity. This might be illustrated by a comparison with the story of Sohrab and Rustum as told in Mr. Matthew Arnold's beautiful poem. The slaying of the unknown son by the father is there surrounded with a pathos and a chivalrous tenderness which[xiii] have no counterpart in the grim simplicity of the Oedipus myth as it appears in its earliest known shape.

The *Iliad*, which knows the war of Polyneices and his allies against Thebes (4.378), once glances at the tale of Oedipus . . .

With regard to [the] outline in the *Odyssey*, it is to be noted that it ignores (a) the deliverance of Thebes from the Sphinx—though this may be implied in the marriage with Epicastè: (b) the self-blinding of Oedipus: (c) the expulsion of Oedipus from Thebes—herein agreeing with the indication in the *Iliad*. It further seems to exclude the notion of Epicastè having borne children to Oedipus, since the discovery followed 'presently' on the union.

Lost poems of Hesiod may have touched on the story of Oedipus; but in his extant work there is only a passing reference to the war at Thebes (between Polyneices and Eteocles), in which heroes fell, 'fighting for the flocks of Oedipus.' Hesiod knows the Sphinx as the daughter of Echidna and as the pest of Thebes.

But the story of Oedipus was fully treated in some of those lost epics which dealt with the Theban cycle of myths. One of these was the *'Oedipodeia.'* According to this, the four children of Oedipus were not born by Iocasta, but by a second wife, Euryganeia. Pausanias, who follows this account, does not know the author of the poem. It will be observed that this epic agrees with the *Odyssey* in not making Iocasta bear issue to Oedipus. It is by Attic writers, so far as we know, that she was first described as doing so. Poets or logographers who desired to preserve the favour of Dorians had a reason for avoiding that version. There were houses which traced their line from the children of Oedipus,—as Theron, tyrant of Acragas,[xv] claimed descent from Thersandros, son of Polyneices. To represent these children as the offspring of an incestuous union would have been to declare the stream polluted at its source.

We learn from Proclus that in the epic called the *Cyprian Lays,* which included the preparations for the Trojan war, Nestor related 'the story of Oedipus' in the course of a digression which comprised also the madness of Heracles, as well as the story of Theseus and Ariadne. This was probably one of the sources used by the Attic dramatists. Another source, doubtless more fertile in detail, was the epic entitled the *Thebaid,* and now usually designated as the 'Cyclic Thebaid,' to distinguish it from a later epic of the same name by Antimachus of Colophon, the contemporary of Euripides. Only about 20 verses remain from it. The chief fragment relates to the curse pronounced by Oedipus on his sons. They had broken his strict command by setting on his table the wine-cups used by Laïus; and he invoked a curse upon them:—

And straightway, while his two sons were by, he uttered dire curses,—and the Avenging goddess failed not to hear them,—that they should divide their heritage in no kindly spirit, but that war and strife should be ever between them.

This *Thebaid*—tracing the operation of a curse through the whole history of the house—must have had an important share in moulding the conception of the Aeschylean trilogy.

Pindar touches on the story of Oedipus in *Ol.*2.35ff. Destiny has often brought evil fortune after good,—[xvi]

—from the day when his doomed son met Laïus and killed him, and accomplished the word given aforetime at Pytho. But the swift Erinnys beheld it, and slew his warlike sons, each by the other's sword.

Here the Fury is represented as destroying the sons in direct retribution for the parricide, not in answer to the imprecation of Oedipus. A fragment of Pindar alludes to the riddle of the Sphinx, and he uses 'the wisdom of Oedipus' to denote counsel wrapped in dark sayings,—since the skill which solves riddling speech can weave it.

The logographers could not omit the story of Oedipus in a systematic treatment of the Theban myths. Hellanicus of Mitylene (circ. 450 B.C.) is mentioned by the scholiast on the Phoenissae (61) as agreeing with Euripides in regard to the self-blinding of Oedipus. The contemporary Pherecydes of Leros (usually called 'Athenian' since Athens was his home) treated the legends of Thebes in the fifth of ten books forming a comprehensive survey of Greek tradition. According to him, Iocasta bore two sons to Oedipus, who were slain by the Minyae: but, as in the *Oedipodeia,* his second wife Euryganeia bore Eteocles and Polyneices, Antigone and Ismene. This seems to be the earliest known version which ascribes issue to the marriage of Iocasta with Oedipus.

However incomplete this sketch may be relatively to the materials which existed in the early part of the fifth century B.C., it may at least serve to suggest the general conditions under which Tragedy entered on the treatment of the subject. The story of Oedipus, defined in its main features by a tradition older than the *Odyssey,* had been elaborated in the epics of later poets[xvii] and the prose of chroniclers. There were versions differing in detail, and allowing scope for selection. While the great outlines were constant, minor circumstances might be adapted to the dramatist's chosen view.

Aeschylus, Sophocles, and Euripides agree in a trait which does not belong to any extant version before theirs. Iocasta, not Euryganeia, is the mother of Eteocles and Polyneices, Antigone and Ismene. They agree also in connecting the doom of the two brothers with a curse pronounced by Oedipus. Neither the scanty fragments which alone represent the *Oedipus* of Euripides, nor the hints in the *Phoenissae,* enable us to determine the distinctive features of his treatment. With regard to Aeschylus, though our knowledge is very meagre, it suffices at least to show the broad difference between his plan and that of Sophocles.

Aeschylus treated the story of Oedipus as he treated the story of Agamemnon. Oedipus became the foremost figure of a trilogy which traced the action of an inherited curse in the house of Labdacus, even as the Orestia traced the action of such a curse in the house of Pelops. That trilogy consisted of the[xviii] *Laïus,* the *Oedipus,* and the extant *Seven against Thebes;* the satyric drama being the Sphinx. From the *Laïus* only a few words remain; from the *Oedipus,* three verses; but some general idea of the *Oedipus* may be gathered from a passage in the *Seven against Thebes* (772–791). Oedipus had been pictured by Aeschylus, as he is pictured by Sophocles, at the height of fame and power. He who had delivered Thebes from 'the devouring pest' was admired by all Thebans as the first of men. 'But when, hapless one, he came to knowledge of his ill-starred marriage, impatient of his pain, with frenzied heart he wrought a twofold ill': he blinded himself, and called down on his sons this curse, that one day they should divide their heritage with the sword. 'And now I tremble lest the swift Erinnys bring it to pass.'

Hence we see that the Oedipus of Aeschylus included the imprecation of Oedipus upon his sons. This was essential to the poet's main purpose, which was to exhibit the continuous action of the Erinnys in the house. Similarly the *Laïus* doubtless included the curse called down on Laïus by Pelops, when bereft by him of his son Chrysippus. The true climax of the Aeschylean *Oedipus* would thus have consisted, not in the discovery alone, but in the discovery followed by the curse. And we may safely infer that the process of discovery indicated in the *Seven against Thebes* was not comparable with that in the play of Sophocles. It was probably much more abrupt, and due to some of those more mechanical devices which were ordinarily employed to bring about a 'recognition' on the stage. The *Oedipus* of Aeschylus, however brilliant, was only a link in a chain which derived its essential unity from 'the mindful Erinnys.'

The *Oedipus Tyrannus* of Sophocles was not part of a trilogy, but a work complete in itself. The proper climax of such a work was the discovery, considered in its immediate effects, not in its ulterior consequences. Here the constructive art of the dramatist would be successful in proportion as the discovery was naturally prepared, approached by a process of rising interest, and attended in the moment of fulfilment with the most[xix] astounding reversal of a previous situation. In regard to the structure of the plot, this is what Sophocles has achieved. Before giving an analysis of his plot, we must notice two features of it which are due to his own invention.

(1) According to previous accounts, the infant Oedipus, when exposed on Mount Cithaeron, had been found by herdsmen, and reared either in Southern Boeotia, or at Sicyon, a place associated with the worship of the Eumenides. Sophocles makes the Theban herd of Laïus give the babe to the herd of Polybus, king of Corinth, who rears it as his own. Thus are prepared the two convergent threads of evidence which meet in the final discovery. And thus, too, the belief of Oedipus concerning his own parentage becomes to him a source, first of anxiety, then of dread, then of hope—in contrast, at successive moments, with that reality which the spectators know.

(2) The only verses remaining from the *Oedipus* of Aeschylus show that in that drama Oedipus encountered and slew Laïus at a meeting of three roads near Potniae, a place in Boeotia, on the road leading from Thebes to Plataea. At the ruins of this place Pausanias saw 'a grove of Demeter and Persephone.' It appears to have been sacred also to those other and more terrible goddesses who shared with these the epithet of ladies,—the Eumenides. For the purpose of Aeschylus, no choice of a scene could have been more fitting. The father and son, doomed by the curse in their house, are brought together at a spot sacred to the Erinnyes:—

'We were coming in our journey to the spot from which three high-roads part, where we must pass by the junction of triple ways at Potniae.'

But for Sophocles this local fitness did not exist. For him, the supernatural agency which dominates the drama is not that of the Furies, but of Apollo. He transfers the scene of the encounter from the 'three roads' at Potniae to the 'three roads'[xx] near Daulia in Phocis. The 'branching ways' of Potniae can no longer be traced. But in the Phocian pass a visitor can still feel how the aspect of nature is in unison with the deed of which Sophocles has made it the theatre.

This change of locality has something more than the significance of a detail. It symbolises the removal of the action from the control of the dark Avenging Powers to a region within the influence of that Delphian god who is able to disclose and to punish impurity, but who will also give final rest to the wanderer, final absolution to the weary mourner of unconscious sin.

The events which had preceded the action of the *Oedipus Tyrannus* are not set forth, after the fashion of Euripides, in a formal prologue. They have to be gathered from incidental hints in the play itself. . . .

The drama falls into six main divisions or chapters. The following analysis exhibits in outline the mechanism of the plot, which deserves study.

I. *Prologue:* 1–150. Oedipus appears as the great prince whom the Thebans rank second only to the gods. He pledges[xxiii] himself to relieve his afflicted people by seeking the murderer of Laïus.

Parodos: 151–215. The Chorus bewail the pestilence and invoke the gods.

II. *First Episode:* 216–462. Oedipus publicly invokes a solemn curse upon the unknown murderer of Laïus. At Creon's suggestion he sends for the seer Teiresias, who refuses to speak, but finally, stung by taunts, denounces Oedipus himself as the slayer.

First Stasimon: 463–512. The Chorus forebode that the unknown murderer is doomed; they refuse to believe the unproved charge brought by the seer.

III. *Second Episode:* 513–862. Creon protests against the suspicion that he has suborned Teiresias to accuse Oedipus. Oedipus is unconvinced. Iocasta stops the quarrel, and Creon departs. Oedipus then tells her that he has been charged with the murder of Laïus. She replies that he need feel no disquietude. Laïus, according to an oracle, was to have been slain by his own son; but the babe was exposed on the hills; and Laïus was actually slain by *robbers, at the meeting of three roads.*

This mention of three roads (v. 716) strikes the first note of alarm in the mind of Oedipus.

He questions her as to (1) the place, (2) the time, (3) the person and the company of Laïus. All confirm his fear that *he* has unwittingly done the deed.

He tells her his whole story—the taunt at Corinth—the visit to Delphi—the encounter in Phocis. But he has still one hope. The attendant of Laïus who escaped spoke of *robbers,* not of one robber.

Let this survivor—now a herdsman—be summoned and questioned.

Second Stasimon: 863–910. The Chorus utter a prayer against arrogance—such as the king's towards Creon; and impiety—such as they find in Iocasta's mistrust of oracles.

IV. *Third Episode:* 911–1085. A messenger from Corinth announces that Polybus is dead, and that Oedipus is now king[xxiv]

designate. Iocasta and Oedipus exult in the refutation of the oracle
which had destined Oedipus to slay his sire.

But Oedipus still dreads the other predicted horror—union with
his mother.

The messenger, on learning this, discloses that Polybus and Meropè
were not the parents of Oedipus. The messenger himself, when a herdsman in the service of Polybus, had found the infant Oedipus on
Cithaeron, and had brought him to Corinth. Yet no—not *found* him;
had *received* him *from another herdsman* (1040).

Who was this other herdsman? The Corinthian replies:—He was
said to be one of the people of Laïus.

Iocasta implores Oedipus to search no further. He answers that he
cares not how lowly his birth may prove to be—he will search to the
end. With a cry of despair, Iocasta rushes away.

Third Stasimon: 1086–1109. The Chorus joyously foretell that
Oedipus will prove to be a native of the land—perchance of seed divine.

V. *Fourth Episode:* 1110–1185. The Theban herdsman is brought in.
'There,' says the Corinthian, 'is the man who gave me the child.'
Bit by bit, the whole truth is wrung from the Theban. 'The babe was
the son of Laïus; the wife of Laïus gave her to me.' Oedipus knows all,
and with a shriek of misery he rushes away.

Fourth Stasimon: 1186–1222. The Chorus bewail the great king's
fall.

VI. *Exodus:* 1223–1530. A messenger from the house announces
that Iocasta has hanged herself, and that Oedipus has put out his eyes.
Presently Oedipus is led forth. With passionate lamentation he be-
seeches the Chorus of Theban Elders to banish or slay him.

Creon comes to lead him into the house. Oedipus obtains[xxv]
from him a promise of care for his young daughters; they are presently
brought to their father, who takes what he intends to be a last farewell.
For he craves to be sent out of the land; but Creon replies that Apollo
must pronounce.

As Creon leads Oedipus within, the Chorus speak the closing words:

> No mortal must be called happy on this side death.

With reference to the general structure of the plot, the first point
to observe is the skill with which Sophocles has managed those two
threads of proof which he created by his invention of the second
herdsman.

We have:—

(1) The thread of evidence from the reported statement of the
Theban herdsman as to the *place* of the murder, in connection with
Iocasta's statement as to the time, the person of Laïus, and the retinue.
This tends to show that Oedipus has slain Laïus—being presumably in
no wise his kinsman. The proof of Oedipus having slain Laïus is so far

completed at 754 as to leave no longer any moral doubt on the mind
of Oedipus himself.

(2) The thread of evidence from the Corinthian, showing, in the
first instance, that Oedipus is *not* the son of Polybus and Meropè, and
so relieving him from the fear of parricide and incest. Hence the confident tone of Oedipus (1076 ff.), which so powerfully contrasts with the
despair of Iocasta: *she* has known the worst from v. 1044.

(3) The convergence of these two threads, when the Theban herdsman is confronted with the Corinthian. This immediately follows the
moment of relief just noticed. It now appears that the slayer of Laïus
has *also* committed parricide and incest.

The frequent references of Aristotle to the *Oedipus Tyrannus*
indicate its value for him as a typical masterpiece, though the points
for which he commends it concern general analysis of form, not the
essence of its distinctive excellence. The points are these:—

1. The 'recognition' is contrived in the best way; *i.e.*, it is coinci-
dent with a reversal of fortunes.[xxvi]

2. This reversal is peculiarly impressive, because the Corinthian
messenger had come to bring tidings of the honour in store for Oedipus.

3. Oedipus is the most effective kind of subject for such a reversal,
because he had been (a) great and glorious, (b) *not* preeminently virtuous or just, (c) and, again, one whose reverses are not due to crime, but
only to unconscious error.

4. The story is told in such a manner as to excite pity and terror
by hearing without seeing (as in regard to the exposure of the child, the
killing of Laïus, the death of Iocasta).

5. If there is any improbability in the story, this is not in the plot
itself, but in the supposed antecedents.

In this last comment, Aristotle indicates a trait which is certainly
open to criticism—the ignorance of Oedipus as to the story of Laïus. He
knows, indeed, the name of his predecessor—though Creon does not
think it unnecessary to remind him of the name (103). He also knows
that Laïus had met a violent death: but he does not know whether this
had befallen at Thebes, or in its neighbourhood, or abroad (109–113).
Nor does he know that Laïus was reported to have been slain by
robbers, and that only one of his followers had escaped (116–123): and
he asks if no search had been made at the time (128, 566). Iocasta, who
has now been his wife for many years, tells him, as if for the first time,
the story of the oracle given to Laïus, and he tells her the story of his
own early fortunes—though here we need not press the fact that he even
names to her his Corinthian parents: that may be regarded as merely
a formal preface to a connected narrative. It may be conceded that the
matters of which Oedipus is supposed ignorant were themes of which
Iocasta, and all the persons about the new king, might well have been
reluctant to speak. Still it is evident that the measure of past reticence
imagined, both on their part and on his, exceeds the limit of verisimili-

tude. The true defence of this improbability consists in frankly recognising it. Exquisite as was the dramatic art exercised within the scope of the action, this art was still so far naïve as to feel no offence at some degree of freedom in the treatment of that[xxvii] which did not come within the framework,—of that which, in Aristotle's phrase, lay 'outside the piece.' It is as if a sculptor neglected to remove some roughness of support or environment which, he felt, would not come into account against the effect of a highly finished group. . . .

Plainly, it would be a mis-reading to construe the fate of Oedipus as a dramatic nemesis of impiety; but the case of Iocasta is at first sight less clear. She, at least, is one who openly avows scorn for oracles, and urges her lord to share it. It may often be noticed—where the dramatist has known how to draw from life—that the true key-note of a dominant mood is struck by a short utterance on which no special emphasis is thrown, just as, in life itself, the sayings most truly significant of character are not always long or marked. For Iocasta, such a key-note is given in the passage where she is telling Oedipus that a response from the Delphian temple had warned Laïus that he was destined to be slain by the child whom she bore to him. 'An oracle came to Laïus once—I will not say from Phoebus himself, but from his ministers' (v. 712). Iocasta thoroughly believes in the power of the gods to effect their will (1724),—to punish or to save (921). But she does not believe that any mortal—be he priest or prophet—is permitted by them to read the future. Had not the Delphian priests doomed her to sacrifice her first-born child,—and this, without saving the life of her husband, Laïus? The iron which years ago had entered into the soul of the wife and mother has wrought in her a result similar to that which pride of intellect has produced in Oedipus. Like Oedipus, she still believes in the wise omnipotence of the gods; like him also, she is no longer prepared to accept any mortal interpreter of their decrees. Thus are the two foremost persons of this tragedy separated from the offices of human intercession, and directly confronted in spirit—one by his self-reliance, the other by her remembered anguish—with[xxx] the inscrutable powers which control their fate. It is as a study of the human heart, true for every age, not as a protest against tendencies of the poet's own, that the *Oedipus Tyrannus* illustrates the relation of faith to reason.

The central figure of the drama is brought into clearer relief by the characters of Teiresias and Creon. Teiresias exists only for the god whom he serves. Through him Apollo speaks. As opposed to Oedipus, he *is* the divine knowledge of Apollo, opposed to human ignorance and blindness. While 'the servant of Loxias' thus stands above the king of Thebes, Creon stands below him, on the humbler but safer ground of ordinary humanity. Creon is shrewd, cautious, practical, not sentimental or demonstrative, yet of a fervid self-respect, and with a strong and manly kindliness which comes out in the hour of need. It might be said that the Creon of the *Oedipus Tyrannus* embodies a good type

of Scottish character, as the Creon of the *Antigone*—an earlier sketch—
is rather of the Prussian type, as it is popularly idealised by some of its
neighbours. Teiresias is the gauge of human insight matched against
divine; Creon, of fortune's heights and depths, compared with the less
brilliant but more stable lot of commoner men. 'Crave not to be master
in all things; for the mastery which thou didst win hath not followed
thee through life'—are his words to Oedipus at the end; and his own
position at the moment exemplifies the sense in which 'the god ever
gives the mastery to the middle state.'[xxxi]

Karl Reinhardt

From *Sophokles*. Frankfurt: Klostermann
Verlag, 1933. Translated by Carol R. Cook
and Albert Cook. Reprinted by permission
of the publishers.

But what sustains the oft-remarked tension of this play is by no
means merely the breathlessness and inexorability of the approaching
revelation as it gathers momentum, and not merely the cat-and-mouse
game played by a lurking fate with a victim who does not yet suspect
it. And it is not a game of deceptions like those that come up under
examination in the course of an inquest—not, in short, what has filled
so many subsequent dramas of revelation. Schiller, in his oft-quoted
statement [to Goethe, Oct. 2, 1797], has designated *Oedipus* as a "tragic
analysis"—"everything is already there, and it is only unravelled. . . .
Added to that is the fact that what happens, as inevitable, is in its
nature much more horrible." Yet he has at the same time, as a result
of his own work on Wallenstein,[109] stressed the practical structure
all too much and the essential all too little. For Sophocles, as for the
Greeks of an older time, fate in general is never a determinism but
rather a spontaneous development of the power of the daemonic, even
when it is prophesied and even when it is fulfilled through an order
immanent in what happens in the world's course. There is no predeter-

mined fate before Stoicism and the victory of astrology. The essential in *Oedipus* is not the unchangeability of a past as it unfolds itself. "Were it possible, I could no more do what I wanted": this has no place in *Oedipus*. Rather, it presents an active battle waged for deliverance, self-assertion, and the defense of an apparent human makeup that is threatened, one which is indeed fused with a great humanity. This makeup, out of its own order, for the sake of "truth" and survival, must set the limits of appearance and reality in a contrary sense. *Oedipus,* as distinct from other Greek tragedies, is by no means a tragedy of human fate, for which it has so long served as a pattern, and in which, to the idea of fate, as the German classical age understood it, the ideas of freedom and even of elevated freedom were always added. It is rather, as distinct from other Greek tragedies, the tragedy of human appearance, to which the idea of reality is added, as Parmenides adds "Seeming" to "Truth." It might already have occurred to someone that in all its choruses not a single one (as happens often enough elsewhere) sings about fate; one chorus, however, set in a prominent position, does sing of human appearance (1189):

> Who is the man, who
> Snatched from all luck
> More than appearance, so as hardly in appearance
> Even still to sink down? . . .

This battle, and this defense against appearance, begin first of all imperceptibly; it is already under way at the beginning of the inquiry the god orders them to undertake. It begins with an anomaly, a strange[110] one, which was pertinently noticed by Voltaire, as a logician, but not pertinently criticized. As soon as an inquest over the state of affairs appears to be planned and the question is asked, "Is there a witness?"; as soon as this is affirmed (118); then suddenly a suspicion fastens itself on the explicit word "robbers." And this supplants the concerns of the inquest: how had robbers dared, unless they were bribed "from here," that is, from a place in Thebes? The question, it is understood, put by a king himself, is about the murder of a king. The question is directed at Creon. Creon appears to exonerate himself from it: the suspicion which had to be raised could not have come up right after the deed. Why not? The Sphinx came. . . . After that, indeed, suspicion appears to be quieted for a while. But attention, henceforth, is directed no longer onto the scene of the crime, its circumstances, or the instrument, but rather onto the perpetrator, and onto Thebes. Then, suddenly, after the quarrel with the unruly and obviously ill-willed seer, once the suspicion is confirmed, the connection between Creon and Tiresias is established and a whole hostile intrigue is set down as a certainty. . . .[111]

The great tragedy of Sophocles develops only in the face of what is not tragic. By this token Odysseus and his generals are set against[123]

Ajax, Ismene against Antigone, the world of guardians, which preserves itself, against self-sacrifice. And so also is Creon set against Oedipus. Against the leader, the ruler, the man of highest pretensions who is first in all things, is set the man of spotless reputation who extricates himself from every risk and every abandonment of his person, securing himself, intriguing, satisfying himself with usefulness instead of with power. He is a man who is cheap by an average standard, born to be second in all things. It is not hard to recognize who remains the victor: it is Creon, to whose lot falls the first half of the verse divisions and who has the last word before Jocasta steps between the disputants. Oedipus is secretly wounded; he is bleeding internally, more because of the consequences of his own blind collision with an unmoving world than because a specific statement has injured him. At first he is struggling just within his own circle still; he can scarcely see whether he is coming upon anything, and what it is.[124]

John A. Moore

From *Sophocles and Arete*. Cambridge: Harvard University Press, 1938. Reprinted by permission of the publisher and the author.

[Sophocles'] greatest hero, probably, is Oedipus the King; the play is a parable of the dangerousness of life. There are mistakes through ignorance, and mistakes through excess of temper, and miasma through the disposition of the gods.

Of these dangers that of miasma is perhaps the most difficult for the modern mind to grasp. Miasma[52] is recognized as being of divine origin; but it has no moral connotations whatever; nor is it, strictly speaking, that which incites a feeling of physical revulsion. It may be defined as a ritualistic impurity. Absent in the main from the Homeric poems, the conception was fostered during the Greek Dark Ages by the oracle at Delphi; for the Pythian Apollo would tolerate no defilement.

At the opening of the *Oedipus* a group of suppliants is gathered round the altar, praying relief from a defilement which is on the land. Its consequences are blight and plague. Its origin is as yet unknown, but upon the return of Creon from the oracle of Apollo, its cause is discovered to be bloodguiltiness for the long-past murder of Laius. The Chorus enters in trepidation, and sings of it, so:

Woe that I bear unnumbered griefs. My folk is all afflicted, and there is no sword of thought whereby one may defend. For there is no increase from the splendid earth, nor by any birth of children do women desist from mournful shrieks. But another upon another mightst thou behold, sped like a well-winged bird stronger than irresistible fire, to the shore of the western god.

More awful still is the miasma which Oedipus fears himself and from which he prays deliverance. He calls it a "stain." The entire play is the story of how he sought and hoped to escape miasma, but how after all it overtook him, being all the while nearer him[53] than he thought. And when at last he sees himself stained, the most tragic thing of all is that he knows no good with which to seek reconciliation: to him his fate is caused by the disposition of heaven, and the oracle of Phoebus Apollo, and from these lies no appeal.

As if the mere presence of miasma in the world were not a sufficiently great danger to men, the poet believes also that human intelligence is not enough to cope with it. One of the most ironical motifs of the play is that of Oedipus' foresight. The suppliants come to Oedipus for counsel in their trials deeming him "wisest alike in the ordinary chances of life, and in the vicissitudes sent by heaven." Yet this is the very man who, fleeing the great curse he heard at Pytho, fell upon it as he fled; who, cursing an impious murderer, cursed himself; and asking to find him found his own great stains. As the Chorus pass from the stage they lament his fall, "For he knew the famous riddles, and he was a mighty man."[54]

Albert Cook

From *The Dark Voyage and the Golden Mean*. Cambridge: Harvard University Press, 1949. Copyright 1961 by Albert Cook.

Tragedy's subject is wonderful-as-probable: man, death, tribulations of the soul. In the action of the individual, its ethics presents on the conceptual level the pattern of paradox: the disease/health of the searcher, the prosperity/adversity of the saint, the good/evil, altruism/egotism, pride/modesty of man's search for God. Especially in "classical" tragedians, such as Sophocles and Racine, the antithesis of paradox is elaborated over and over, and back again into itself. Blacks merge with whites; whites become blacks, and the motives of the protagonist are always antithetically ambiguous. Oedipus is king/polluted pariah; he hides/reveals his guilt, which is fated/willed; he is infinitely wise/utterly ignorant; he sees/is blind, whereas Tiresias is blind/sees. At the end of the play he is made whole by a great wound. Pity-terror, the tragic spectator's emotion according to Aristotle, holds the ambiguity of the religious man's motivation; it might be transposed as "altruistic-egotistic sorrow." The paradox of Kierkegaard or Heraclitus says, not "Man cannot know" (though partly that), but "Man must probe deeper, into the level of symbolic truth, for his ethics to gain religious meaning."

Tragedy, as John Finley points out, is born after the advent of conceptualism; and conceptualism deepens tragedy by ordering it within the tensions of a logical pattern. Yet tragedy is not allegory, concepts clothed in metaphor. It is symbol; the probable concepts of paradox are stretched tight over the symbolic wonderful. The penultimate stage of the soul's journey is always ambiguous; in the ultimate state, light-darkness, guilt-innocence, free will-fate, all resolve themselves into the pure light of symbol. The elaborate paradoxes of *Oedipus Rex* melt into symbolic glow in *Oedipus at Colonus*, when the soul, purified and on the threshold of death, finds its ultimate destination.[32]

J. H. Letters

From *The Life and Work of Sophocles*. New York: Sheed and Ward, 1953. Reprinted by permission of the publisher.

The *Oedipus Tyrannus* (King Oedipus) is the best-known and best-built of classic tragedies. Yet in its treatment of inherent improbabilities . . . it is also the best illustration of the difference between ancient and modern views. . . .[201]

. . . the compactness and ingenuity of the plot depends on an unusual number of improbabilities. Those rooted in the antecedents and preambles of the drama may plead the Aristotelian canon permitting improbabilities "outside the play". Such are—there is no need of an exhaustive list—Oedipus' ignorance of and unconcern for the facts of Laius' death until at least some sixteen years later, and his unawareness even of the current rumours.

. . . it is obvious that the hero's very name should have hastened his identification: it points so directly to his early disability. That Iocasta never takes this into account is already strange enough. But that even the unusual mutilation, the scars of which must have lasted all his life, should never have aroused her suspicions, is more than improbable. It is incredible.

. . . the time comes for his avowal to her of those twin oracles—one of them a replica of the prophecy about her own son she had heard so long[215] ago herself. Surely the identical prophecies, the lingering scars, the tell-tale name must at last clamour their fearful implications to Iocasta's conscience and memory. They do not. They leave her no whit the wiser. Still, so many commentators have lodged no protest here either, that perhaps the "improbability" is dramatically not so unjustifiable after all! . . .[216]

. . . Sophocles deliberately shut out such Aeschylean elements as might suggest that the hero is expiating the sins of his line. Only once, and hesitatingly, does the chorus of elders offer that solution. But the play refutes, and the moral finally and unhesitatingly drawn by the same elders [in the closing lines] ignores the earlier suggestion. Oedipus, they now declare, warns us against putting trust in the stability of fortune. Beyond this they do not venture.

. . . it is so natural to look for at least a plain ethical judgment
on the facts, that most critics have been driven to hold that Oedipus
sinned and was justly punished. Their arguments purport to disclose
important faults in his intellect, if not his temperament: . . [Oedipus,
knowing the oracle, should never have attacked any man sufficiently far
in years to be his father. For the same reason he should never have
married a woman old enough to be his mother. Least of all should he
have taken both risks—especially, no doubt, in that order.] Oedipus was
arrogant, impulsive and not without a streak of the "tyrant" in the
modern, that is, in what was already becoming the Periclean sense of
the word. On one occasion he abused a prophet universally revered,
and even sneered at the whole prophetic order and tradition.

Now each of these charges may be answered in detail. In the first
place, none is laid by actors or chorus. And we may be sure the audience would not have laid them. Practised jurymen,[217] familiar to a
man with legal process and argument, . . . know that Oedipus had
not "attacked" Laius, but merely struck back in self-defence. And
when anyone has had his head almost split open he can hardly be
expected to weigh the possibilities of the assailant proving his unknown
father. . . .

I shall not examine the remaining heads of the indictment. Most
of them could be laid before no responsible court, whether temporal or
spiritual. . . . whatever were Oedipus' defects, they did not justify his
fate. A perfect man he is not, but within the scope of the play he is
certainly an innocent one. Do what he might to escape (and he tried
hard enough!) his fate is sure of him.

. . . Kitto's suggestion that a man of intellect like Oedipus should
have resolved never to kill a man older than himself, merely re-urges
what had been said long before. But since it has been resurrected by so
acute a critic, it is worth repeating that a man savagely struck on the
head with a two-pronged goad is not for the moment required to act
as a man of intellect. And if he did—that is, in this case, if he abstained
from retaliating[218] in kind—not only Aristotle, but Sophocles and
Pericles' Athens would have thought meekness so extreme not only un-
heroic, but a positive offence against that *mansuetudo,* that genuine
meekness which not only moderates anger but forbids excessive submis-
sion to "external" evils.

. . . in a sense Oedipus' tragedy is his character, or rather, as we
shall see, his intellectual gifts. Even so we must protest against the
insinuation that his case suggests no real question. The question is
there. But does Sophocles answer it? If he does not, are we for once to
agree with those who hold that the tragic conception of Sophocles
is vitally concerned with man, only conventionally with the gods and
religion? Has he blandly ignored the problem of evil staring at us
through this play? Or has he, in effect, at least, implied "God's ways are
not ours"? Yet trust Him we must, even in His ways with Oedipus?

It is the last question, I believe, that shows the deepest understanding of Sophocles, and I should answer it with a simple affirmative. . . . The conclusion is no more than fair inference from Sophocles' attitude elsewhere. Doubtless his silence here is largely due to the character of the myth as he received it. . . .[219]

. . . in Greek religion a cosmological sometimes appears to challenge a moral or a spiritual law.[220]

Gerald F. Else

From *Aristotle's Poetics: The Argument.*
Cambridge: Harvard University Press, 1957.
Reprinted by permission of the publisher.

What we require is an interpretation which will (a) do justice to the facts of the play, and (b) square with Aristotle's concept of peripety as a sudden and unexpected yet logical reversal in *our* expectations. In lines 994–999 of the drama Oedipus reveals the reason for his self-imposed exile from Corinth, viz., the oracle's prediction that he would slay his father and marry his mother. The Corinthian messenger asks for confirmation that that is indeed the reason (1000), . . . and Aristotle's remark is an echo of [his] words. The messenger's good will, which he had when he came to Thebes, *now* expresses itself in a wish to cheer up Oedipus and relieve him of his fears about his (father and) mother. The new decision is a logical and natural consequence of the good will. Yet it leads straight towards *un*happiness for Oedipus; and it does so contrary to our expectation. For although the intent which forms the premise is the messenger's, the judgment whether its consequence is logical yet 'paradoxical' belongs to us. (The messenger's surprise is of no[347] importance: he is present at the final revelation, 1185, but makes no further comment after he has identified the Theban, 1145, and we give no further thought to him.)

The case is still clearer with the *Lynceus,* little as we know about the play. The crucial point is not Lynceus' expectation that he will be executed, but ours.

There is still another apparent anomaly about the reference to the *Oedipus*, which I think gives strong support to this interpretation. So far as Oedipus himself is concerned, the peripety and climax of the action come not in the scene with the Corinthian messenger but in that with the Theban Shepherd, line 1110 ff. Here is the moment (line 1180) when the final revelation passes the old man's lips and Oedipus rushes offstage, only to discover Jocasta's body and blind himself. Thus Aristotle's location of the peripety seems to antedate the true one by a whole scene. But then chapter 18, 55b26, comes to our aid, where Aristotle (again with an illustration from the *Lynceus*, so that he is clearly thinking of the same kind of structure) defines the "tying of the knot", the *lusis* as "the part of the play which extends from the beginning as far as that 'part' (scene) which is the last *from which the shift takes place to happiness or unhappiness,*" and the "untying", *desis* as "the part from the beginning of the shift to the end (of the play)." In these terms, the peripety is the "beginning of the shift." And in fact in the *Oedipus*, although the final and official revelation does not come until line 1180, it begins with the fact supplied by the Corinthian, which 'naturally and probably' force Oedipus to the last discovery. The sign *to us* that the secret is out, that the dreadful 'change to unhappiness' is beginning, is Jocasta's exit at line 1072; it takes Oedipus himself another hundred lines to fill in the last link. The fact is that Sophocles, by an astonishing *tour de force*, has produced two successive climaxes, one for Jocasta and us, another (a second and redoubled one for us) for Oedipus. Aristotle's designation of the first one as the peripety is, it seems to me, the best confirmation that peripety is measured by *our* expectation and falls at the point where that expectation shifts to its opposite. The second climax is not a 'peripety' but a 'recognition.' . . .[348]

As we said, the attenuation of the *pathos* can take two forms. It can be placed outside the drama proper, in which case it figures as the *premise* of the action: so in the *Oedipus Rex*. Here, through a feat of virtuosity which was not likely to be duplicated, the poet has managed to sublimate his plot-structure into a *pure nexus of recognition*. Was Aristotle conscious of this fact? Whether he was or not, it must have been a principal reason for his almost unqualified admiration for the play; for the formulation we have arrived at just above through analysis of his theory (sublimation of the *pathos*) corresponds very closely to Sophocles' most striking achievement. The play is, above all other Greek tragedies we know anything about, a play of ideas (where by 'ideas' we mean, of course, not abstract or metaphysical ideas but pure[420] essences of tragic human relationship). But we should notice that the other mode of attenuation of the *pathos*, although it necessarily averts a tragic outcome and thereby makes a drastic difference in the total posture and effect of the play, achieves a similar end by another route. Here too the tragic emotions are involved and brought to a climax without the necessity of bringing the tragic act itself into the drama.[421]

Richmond Lattimore

From *The Poetry of Greek Tragedy*. Baltimore: The Johns Hopkins Press, 1957. Reprinted by permission of the publisher.

But let it never be thought right that I should stay
in the city of my father, and be part of it,
but let me go to the mountains and live there, where stands
Cithaeron, called *my* mountain, which, when they still lived,
my mother and my father gave me, for my final tomb.
So let them kill me at last, for they destroyed my life.

Such lines, spoken near the end[1] of *Oedipus Tyrannus* (hereafter simply *Oedipus*) after the catastrophe has taken place and all is out, are a kind of Sophoclean *anōmalia*. They are scarcely led to by the action; they lead nowhere, for the drama does not even tell us whether or not Oedipus got his wish, and there is no story we know of Oedipus dying on the mountain wilderness.[2] Thus the lines do not tie[81] the action to the establishment of a cult, or annual ceremony, in the manner of Euripides. They frame no moral precept. They seem, so taken, to escape from the structure of a play which is fastened together with a special coherence that leaves few loose ends, and none that are important. The most popular modern acting version practically wipes

1 Lines 1449–54.
2 On the origin, grave, and cult of Oedipus, see Robert, *Oidipus*, pp. 1–47. Robert finds his original home at Eteonus below Mount Cithaeron. See also Pickard-Cambridge, *Dithyramb, Tragedy, and Comedy*, p. 201.

the passage out.[3] But it will be seen to be, after all, a part of the larger action of the tragedy.

The plot of *Oedipus,* beginning with the prologue and continuing through the next to the last episode, or act, concerns itself with the investigation of events which have already happened. It consists essentially in the joining together of pieces of information (*symbola* or "clues") until the last piece has been put in, the pattern completed, the puzzle solved. There are two principal problems: the detection of the murderer of Laius and the discovery of the identity of Oedipus himself; a manhunt combined with what might be called a rescue party. But both searches turn out to be after the same game, and the solution—discovery—is complete when the two are identified.

Thus, the drama belongs to the general story pattern of the lost one found. The lost one may be a lost husband, wife, brother, sister, or any close *philos,* thought dead far away but discovered to be present, unknown. A particularly popular variant has been the one that makes the lost one the lost baby or the foundling: the type to which *Oedipus* belongs. Whichever variant happens to be followed, the pattern of itself seems to generate certain features that are required, or almost required. For the foundling story, we may note the following: the child is noble; the child is unwanted and is put away (usually for destruction) and[82] thought dead; but the method is always indirect (in Greek versions, a servant is usually delegated to do the dirty work) and the child is rescued, sometimes miraculously nursed by animals. The child grows up in the wilds, and is thought to be plebeian, but is at last recognized by infallible tests or unmistakable tokens and restored to its proper station. Thus the story is in part a story of the triumph of truth over rumor or opinion, and the triumph is pretty likely to come after the darkest moment, when error is on the point of prevailing.

A brief consideration of *Oedipus* will show that it follows the pattern almost perfectly. The tokens are not used by Sophocles toward the solution—he has another use for them—but they are there in the form of those otherwise so superfluously cruel pins stuck through the baby's ankles. It is also true that Oedipus is believed to be noble, though of the wrong noble stock: instead of being raised as the peasant's son, he is adopted by the great. In this, Oedipus resembles Ernest Moncrieff, alias Jack Worthing, in his black handbag deposited in the cloak room of Charing Cross Station. The resemblance is important. From the stories of Iamus, the young Cyrus, and Romulus, to the stories of Ernest and Ralph Rackstraw, the foundling story is a success story, a theme for what we call comedy or romantic comedy. But *Oedipus* is a true tragedy.

The tragically fulfilled story, mounted on so articulate a scheme

---

3 This is the version of W. B. Yeats, *Oedipus the King* (London, 1928). I have seen it acted only in the form of the motion picture directed by Tyrone Guthrie.

for comedy, accounts for much of the essential nature of *Oedipus*. No extant tragedy so bristles with tragic irony. It opposes Oedipus—possessed of rumor, opinion, or, that is, error—against those who know—Tiresias, the Theban Shepherd—the latter two pulling back against revelation, because they know it is bad, as insistently as Oedipus, armed with his native wit (*gnōmē*), goes plunging forward. Where characters themselves are not omniscient, the audience[83] is. They know the gist of the story and can be surprised only in the means by which the necessary ends are achieved. They know, for instance, that when Oedipus says (219–20):

> I shall speak, as a stranger to the whole question
> and stranger to the action

he is, in all sincerity, speaking falsehood, though the falsehood is qualified in the term stranger (*xenos*, outlander): the stranger who met and killed the king, the stranger who met and married the queen, who was no true stranger at all. Or when, at the outset, he says (59–61):

> For I know well
> that all of you are sick, but though you are sick, there's none
> of you who is so sick as I

he is, indeed, speaking the truth, but more truth than he knows, since he is using sickness metaphorically to describe the mental distress of a leader, himself sound, in a stricken kingdom. Oedipus keeps circling back on the truth and brushing against it, as if he subconsciously knew where it was; the omniscient audience can only wonder when the shock of contact will come.

In addition to this irony of detail, there is a larger irony in the inversion of the whole action. Tragic themes may mock the comic by matching them in reverse. Bassanio's three caskets are Lear's three daughters. Bassanio, marked for fortune, chooses the precious lead; Lear rejects it because he must suffer. The triumph of truth and virtue in the foundling play is the joyful recognition: "Our Perdita is found!" But to Oedipus, Tiresias says (449–54):

> I tell you: that man whom you have long been searching for
> with threats and proclamations for the murderer
> of Laius: that man is here.
> Supposed a stranger come to live with us, he shall[84]
> be shown to be a genuine Theban, and will not
> be pleased with this solution.
>   Blind, who once saw clear,
> beggared, who once was rich, he shall feel out his way
> into a foreign country, with a stick.

The homeless wanderer by delivering the land from the monster and marrying the princess became prince in fact and then was shown to be prince by right, but this revelation turned him once more into a homeless wanderer. But the wanderer, who had once gone bright-eyed with his strong traveler's staff, now uses the staff to tap out the way before him, because he is now old, and eyeless.

The reversed pattern shows again in the fact that the malignant oracles have their darkest moment just before they come clear, with Jocasta's (946–47)

> O prophesyings of the gods,
> where are you now?

echoed and amplified in Oedipus' typical tyrant-speech of scepticism. Or consider the design of the helpers. The pattern story of the foundling requires a helper or rescuer: the merciful forester or herdsman who refuses to kill the baby outright, or who finds it and saves it from exposure (sometimes this is a wild animal). Sophocles provides at least one helper, or rescuer, for every act. The appeal in the prologue is to Oedipus, himself a rescuer (*sōtēr*) in the past; and Oedipus appeals to Creon, who comes from and represents Apollo and Delphi. It is as rescuer that Tiresias is called, Jocasta intervenes to help, so does the Corinthian Herdsman, and the last helper, the Theban Herdsman, is the true and original rescuer. Those who do not know are eager to help, those who know are reluctant, but all helpers alike push Oedipus over the edge into disaster. Again, it is the story as design which seems to dictate the actual ceremony[85] of the blinding. The Greek word *arthron*, which means a socket, means also a piece which moves within a socket. The infant Oedipus was pinned through the ankles, the joints (*arthra*) of his feet, and while we would not speak of the joints of the eyes, *arthra* serves again for the eyeballs through which Oedipus sticks his wife's pins. Thus the foundling-property of the pinned feet is ignored for its original purpose as means of recognition and transposed into a means of dramatic justice in Oedipus' self-vengeance, by which the strong man renders himself helpless as the baby was rendered helpless.

The fundamental story pattern demands precision in all detail where repeated words are positive, not suggestive, and nowhere else in tragedy is language so precise as here. Consider this piece in Jocasta's résumé (715–19):

> But Laius, so the report goes, was murdered
> by foreign brigands at a place where three roads meet.
> And for his son, only three days had passed since birth
> when Laius, pinning his feet together at the joints,
> gave him to other hands, and these abandoned him
> upon the mountain wilderness.

The lines are stiff with clues, which though they involve material facts (the three roads, the pinned feet, the mountain side), yet have holes in them (the reported brigands, the second-hand casting away), and they are arranged so that the clue of the three roads forces Oedipus to fix on the fight with the king, and ignore the still more glaring clue that should lead to his own identification with the castaway baby.[86]

The plausibility of this, if it stands, is a case of the probable-impossible, or drama more perfect than actual life. The pattern story demands tailoring; and if this were a true report of real action, we could ask some awkward questions. For example: Why did the servant of Laius (Theban Shepherd) give the false report of *a body of brigands?* Why did he say nothing when he saw Oedipus in Thebes, but ask to go to the country? Why was he treated so well, when he had run away and left his master and fellow-servants dead on the road? One may answer these: he suspected the truth all the time, beginning with the encounter on the road, for he knew that the son of Laius had not died, and recognized him in this young man who looked like Laius;[4] he was loyal to his protégé, and perhaps disliked Laius, of whom no good has ever been told, here or elsewhere; the story of a body of brigands protected both him and Oedipus. These answers are plausible, but are we intended to work them out, or is there even time to consider them in the rapid progress of the action? This is not the tragedy of the Theban Shepherd. He is an agent, not a principal. There are other points of verisimilitude it would be possible but tedious to raise.[5]

But Sophocles himself raised a couple of questions which he did not answer. Why, if Tiresias was wise and inspired, positively omniscient, did *he* not answer the Sphinx?[6] Why, after the death of Laius and arrival of Oedipus, did he say nothing about the connection?[7] Creon's answer to this last is sage and temperate (569):[87]

> I do not know. And where I have no idea I prefer
> to keep quiet.

But it does not take us far. Is it not, rather, that Oedipus is the man who must find, and condemn, and punish himself? As for the question, why did Tiresias not answer the Sphinx? Grant that it was awkward of Sophocles to raise this, or the other question, when he would not, or could not, answer. In this second case, the Sphinx is one of those barbarous primeval figures who haunt the edges of tragedy. An amorous[8] she-fiend who asks childish riddles and destroys those who cannot answer serves with effect as a vaguely indicated background

---

[4] Line 743.

[5] For instance, why had Oedipus never gone even superficially into the question of the murder? Some awkwardness is felt and shown in lines 105–31. Or again, how could Jocasta know *nothing* (lines 774–75, often and justly admired) about the stranger she married?

[6] Lines 390–400.

[7] Lines 558–68.

[8] On sphinxes and sirens, both subsumed as types of *kēr*, see Harrison, *Prolegomena*, pp. 197–212; on the amorous sphinx, see J. Ilberg, in Roscher's *Lexikon*, IV, s.v. "Sphinx," esp. cols. 1381–85; in general, see Robert, *Oidipus*, pp. 48–50.

bogey, or as a blazon on a shield by Aeschylus,[9] but scrutinized close-up she must turn ludicrous; so, in the tetralogy of Aeschylus, she draws the satyr-play.[10] But if the question *were* answered: again, it was not for Tiresias to solve this. As Perdita is lost, so she can be found; so the Sphinx is there for Oedipus to answer. To say he was "fated" to is to overstate it with prejudice toward the grand designs of heaven; but it is a part of his pattern or story-*tychē,* which in Greek does not mean "fate," "chance," or "fortune" so strictly as it means "contact,"[11] or, say, "coincidence," the way things are put together.

The pieces fit. The missing one who has been hunted is found. This is the special sense sometimes implicated in the cry *iou iou,* the cry which Oedipus and Jocasta, and Heracles in *The Women of Trachis,* give when the truth[88] is out,[12] the hunter's cry of Socrates in the *Republic* when the quarry for which he and his friends have beaten far bushes is seen to be grovelling right at their feet.[13]

But after discovery, Oedipus does one more thing to complete the pattern. He blinds himself, as reported in the one true messenger-scene of the drama, from the anonymous Messenger who gives us, not the fact of the ruin of Oedipus, for we knew that already, but only the cruel ceremonies through which that ruin is displayed (1251–79):

> And how she perished after that I do not know,
> for Oedipus burst in, shouting aloud, and made
> it impossible to watch the rest of her agony
> because our eyes were on him as he stalked the court
> and ranged among us, crying to be given a sword,
> crying to find that wife who was no wife, that field
> that bore a double crop, himself and his children.
> As the man raved, it was some spirit showed him.
> It was not any man of us who stood close by.
> With a fierce cry, as if something were guiding him,
> he drove against the double doors, and from their bases
> buckled the panels inward and burst into the room.
> There we looked in, and saw the woman hanging, caught
> in a noose of rope. But he
> when he looked at her, moaning horribly, he loosed
> the knot from her throat. Then, when the poor woman was laid
> upon the ground, the rest was terrible to see.
> Tearing the golden pins by which her dress was clasped
> out of the robes she wore
> he raised them, stabbed them into the balls of both his eyes,

9 *The Seven* 539–43.

10 Argument to Aeschylus *The Seven.*

11 So at least I should judge, with perhaps insufficient authority, by simply combining the senses of *tunchano*-"hit" with *teucho*-"make."

12 Jocasta, line 1071; Oedipus, line 1182; Heracles, in *The Women of Trachis* 1143.

13 Plato's *Republic* iv.432D.

crying that they should never more look on himself,
nor on the evils done to him, or what he had done,
but that their sight of those they should not look upon[89]
must darken, lest they recognize whom they should not.
To such an incantation, many times, not once,
he dashed the pins into his eyes, and from the eyeballs
the blood ran down his chin, nor was the storm an ooze
and drip, but there came both
a dark clear rain and clotted hail, and all was blood.[14]

What was the sword for? The question is left flying in the air as
Oedipus sees Jocasta, already dead. But why does Oedipus blind himself? Students of motivation will find their answer. So that the eyes
should no longer look upon the people, the things, that they should
not. Sophocles says so. He repeats it: how could Oedipus share sensi-
bilities with his fellow citizens, with whom he can now share nothing?
If he could have shut off the sources of hearing, he would have:[15] thus
making himself, we might add, the outcast who was to be banned from
the community,[16] because the murderer was to be that outcast, and
Oedipus is the murderer. We add this; but Sophocles adds that it would
be sweet for Oedipus to cut himself loose from all evils, from all his life
he knows now as evil; and then seems to contradict himself when
Oedipus cries for his daughters and calls them into his arms.[17] But by
then, the mood of frenzy has ebbed along with the strength of fury, and
Oedipus is himself again, reasoning, and justifying.

Then, for the wildness of Oedipus when he stabbed his eyes, could
we say that reasoning of any kind is too reasonable? At least we can say
that Oedipus' self-blinding can be seen from various angles. It seems to
be a punishment of what is evil (kakon), for Oedipus does not deign to
call[90] himself kakodaimōn, unlucky, ill-starred, but just evil (or vile),
kakos.[18] The evil Jocasta has escaped; the fury turns on himself with, as
we have seen, the formal mode of transfixing those socketed balls of
his eyes.

But blinding still serves one more purpose. The riddle of the
Sphinx spoke of man feeble as a baby, man strong as grown man (walking on two feet), man feeble in old age. And we have had Oedipus as
baby, and Oedipus as grown man, a strong traveler walking on his two
feet.[19] We need Oedipus old and enfeebled, and he is still a man in his
prime, and appallingly strong. Only such a catastrophic self-punish-

---

[14] The text is uncertain here, and I do not try to give more than the general
sense, which seems to combine blood (dark but clear) and fragments of matter (not
clear, also bloody), the rain and hail respectively.

[15] Lines 1384-90.

[16] Lines 233-51.

[17] Lines 1480-81.

[18] The word kakos is used many times in this play, but the most interesting ap-
plications of it may be found at lines 76, 822, 1063, 1397, 1421.

[19] Line 798.

ment can break him so that, within moments, he has turned into an old man, who (1292)

> needs strength now, and needs someone to lead him.

So he has lived the three stages. The riddle of the Sphinx was the mystery of man. But it was the specially private mystery of Oedipus. This—the Sphinx might have meant to him—is the mystery of you. Solve it. *Gnōthi sauton.*

In this sense, but I think in this sense only, Oedipus is Everyman. Stories such as these have shapes of their own which force action rather than shapes which are forced by reason or character; and hence, romantic comedy tends to refine plot at the expense of personality, with stock or pattern situations generating stock characters.[20] But this does not have to happen. Eteocles in *The Seven* is also bent by the shape of the story but generates a momentum which makes his necessary act his own. So is Oedipus. He is the tragedy tyrant driven by his plot, but he is more, a unique individual and, somehow, a great man, who drives himself.

Oedipus Tyrannus is a tragical tragedy despite its frame[91] of romantic comedy, and we should be slow to type Oedipus himself. He is an intellectual man, but not *the* intellectual of the time (Pericles or another). He prides himself on his insight and wit,[21] but for a man of great intelligence he makes disastrous mistakes. Partly, it is a combination of hasty temper and a passionate reliance on quick judgments, which makes him rush to Delphi, then rush away from Delphi indignant with Apollo for not answering his question,[22] or jump to the conclusion that Jocasta's distress is caused by snobbery and anguish for having married a man who was not, after all, a king's son.[23] When he leaves Delphi, he is so sure of his assumptions that he does the two things he should never do: he kills a man who could well be his father, and marries a woman old enough to be his mother. Partly, he makes mistakes through the obsessions of a tyrant—that others are jealous and work through bribery and treachery to unseat him. This makes him assume, wrongly, that the outside brigands who killed Laius must have been suborned from inside Thebes,[24] and suspect that Polybus died through conspiracy.[25] It makes him break into the whole action against Creon and Tiresias. So far, he is the tragedy tyrant, like Creon in *Antigone* or Theseus in *Hippolytus*. But no farther. Oedipus condemns Creon without trial, but lets him off at the pleading of the Chorus,

---

20 On these matters in general, see Kitto, *Greek Tragedy*, pp. 270–71.
21 *Gnōmē*. See lines 393–98.
22 Lines 785–97.
23 Lines 1062–85.
24 Line 124.
25 Line 960.

though he is sure they are wrong. And Oedipus can answer to the
vague threats of Tiresias against him (443):

> I do not care [what happens to me] if I save this city.

No tragedy tyrant could say that; and such a man is rewarded by the
love and respect of his people (the Chorus)[92] such as no tragedy tyrant
ever earns or gets.[26] Oedipus is a tyrant, not *the* tyrant, and unique as
he is, he is unique again because he adds one more aspect: the lost
child, the strange, hunted creature who came from the mountain and
will go back to the mountain.

All combine in the most puzzling stasimon in *Oedipus*—the second
—after all has been called into question: the honesty of Creon, the good
sense of Oedipus, the official report of the murder of Laius, the identity
of the murderer, the truth of oracles, the value of religion (863–910):

> May it be always given me to know
> guarded purity in all speech,
> in all action. For this, ordinances stand high
> in the bright mountain
> air where they were born. Olympus
> is their sole father. It was no
> mortal growth of men brought
> them forth: nor shall indifference
> store them away in sleep.
> Here the god stands great, ageless forever.
>
> Lust breeds the tyrant man. Lust,
> when fed and puffed with vanity
> on what disaccords with the time's advantage,
> clambering the sheer height
> goes over the drop, where nothing breaks his fall,
> where no firm foothold serves
> longer. But I pray god
> not to break that hand hold which serves
> well the community.
> I shall not loose my hold upon the god, my guide.
>
> But if one, gazing too high
> for thought and action, advances[93]
> without fear of justice, without
> caution, where spirits live,
> may a bad fate seize him,
> his wages for ill starred lusting,
> if he gains unfairly his advantage,
> nor refrains from the forbidden,
> if he lays lewd hands on secret things.

---

26 The outbursts at lines 660–64 and 689–96, spoken in the midst of disagree-
ment and disapproval, are among the most moving, certainly the most moved and
selfless, utterances of a Sophoclean Chorus I can find.

What man shall hold off the bolts of god
from his life, in such action,
or if such works go unpunished, why
should I go through the ceremonies of worship?

No longer shall I go to the earth's
secret centerstone, religiously,
nor to the temple which is at Abae,
nor yet to Olympia,
no, unless this code is put together
to be manifest before mortals.
Then, oh Power, if Power is what you should be called,
Zeus, lord of all, oh give heed,
let your domain, ever immortal, not ignore.
For the old oracles for Laius are dying
out; men throw them aside
now, and nowhere is Apollo regarded.
God's worship is going.

To begin with the last: we are almost irresistibly forced to think that this belongs to the time, about 426,[27] after the death of Pericles and after the plague came out of nowhere to waste Athens. Apollo had promised the Peloponnesians he would help them against Athens; the city was full of oracles; the enlightened, one supposes, ignored them. Apollo must show them. He showed them. He struck, absurdly, unpredictably. The plague came. The failure of[94] the intellectual, as of the tyrant, is to insist on his *own gnōmē*. Pericles was both intellectual and essentially tyrannical. But I go no further, for Oedipus was not Pericles. But his tragedy is the intellectual's tragedy: his tragic flaw, if you must, that his wit can not cover, foresee, account for all, and nonsensical forces can make nonsense of it; or, as Aeschylus put it, "Science is weaker than Nature is."[28]

Now to go back. The intellectual's tragedy is the tyrant's tragedy. "Lust breeds the tyrant man." Or is it "lust"? The word is *hybris*. Should we say "violence"? We have just emerged from the scene where Oedipus is most tyrannical. In the famous debate on forms of government in the third book of Herodotus, *hybris*, "lawless violence," marks the tyrant,[29] both the insane, bloody acts of Cambyses and the unscrupulous intrigues of Magian nobodies. *Hybris* combines with "jealousy" (*phthonos*) to make the tyrant suspicious of good men, vindictive, one who kills without due process of law, as Oedipus has just been saved from killing Creon.[30] Oedipus is too great to refuse his Chorus, but this

27 The play is usually dated shortly after 430; see Whitman, *Sophocles*, pp. 49–50; 429 is often preferred, but it seems a little too close to the plague, and 426 is slightly supported by Aristophanes *Acharnians* 27.

28 *Prometheus Bound* 530.

29 Herodotus iii.80–82.

30 Herodotus iii.80.5-*Oedipus* 623.

is a personal favor; the almost crazy, uneasy suspicion remains.[31] But *hybris* not only characterizes the tyrant in action, it produces him; for escaping the violent tyrant, we may fall into the hands of the violent rabble or the violent nobles who by their violent disorder set up the situation for a redeemer and liberator—the tyrant again. Violence breeds the tyrant.

In a general sense. But we can get a still stricter meaning on another interpretation: the reference is to Jocasta and (it is only fair to add) Laius. The tragedy of incontinence: lust breeds (plants, begets) the tyrant. Against this, it can[95] be argued that the citizens (the Chorus) do not know that the child of Jocasta and Laius, who lusted and must breed, is now their tyrannical tyrant; they do not even think he is alive; and they and Jocasta have been working together in complete sympathy so that it would be strange for them to turn suddenly on her.

Yet I think it does apply to Jocasta,[32] since Sophocles fits the words to her, and the audience can pick up and follow. Like Oedipus again and again through the ironies of the play, the Chorus say more than they know. All meanings are combined: the civic violence which breeds the tyrant, the tyrant's violence which makes him tyrannical in action, with the violence of lust breeding the tyrant, the child who should never have been born[33] and who, born in defiance, lays hands on secret places and defiles his mother,[34] the wife who is no wife.[35]

Along with this, we have the persistent imagery of the climber on the mountain, in high places where spirits live and the overdrop is sheer, danger natural and supernatural, where the climber must use not only feet but hands, and[96] needs a guide—ideally a divine guide.[36]

---

31 Lines 658–59, 669–70.

32 At line 719, Jocasta says that Laius cast out the infant "by the hands of others"; at lines 1171–74, the Theban Shepherd says that Jocasta gave him the infant. Lapse by Sophocles (conceivable) or intention?

33 On the birth of Pisistratus, tyrant of Athens, see Herodotus i.59.1–3. In regard to a portent, Chilon the Spartan, a wise man in general and in particular an anti-tyrant, warned Hippocrates against rearing a son, but Hippocrates would not obey him. See also Herodotus v.92β–δ for the story of the birth of the predestined tyrant-child Cypselus, the emissaries sent to kill him, and the concealment of the child by his mother. In the lost *Oedipus* of Carcinus (Nauck, p. 798) Jocasta put off the man who was trying to find her son. This may mean that Carcinus followed a version which combined the foundling-theme with the outline of a dynastic drama, for which indeed the Oedipus legend contained the materials; see Robert, *Oidipus*, pp. 305–11.

34 Hippias the tyrant, son of Pisistratus, dreamed that he lay with his mother, Herodotus vi.107.1. See Sophocles *Oedipus* 980–82. My translation of line 891 is influenced by Sophocles' *The Women of Trachis* 565.

35 Line 1256.

36 While I cannot exclude the idea of a mountain climber from my mind, I am far from claiming that this is the sole and all-sufficient clue to the passage. All the key terms have multiple meanings.

No recorded Greek ever climbed a mountain for the sport of mountain-climbing, and the notion of finding the hardest way up a peak is peculiarly gothic or baroque for an Athenian, or, as Spengler would say, Faustian; but there were occasions, religious and military occasions at least, when mountains had to be climbed. The mountain-climb figured early, from Hesiod on, as a symbol of the slippery, punishing, dangerous quest for achievement or excellence (aretē) which stood at the top;[37] just as, in this stasimon, the laws of righteousness stand in the thin, pure Olympian air.

The Greek wilderness is the mountains. All cultures have their wildernesses. The northern foundling might be a child of the great forest, but Greece is not a land of flat forests; its wilderness, whether of woods or scrubby barrens or cliff and boulder, is of the big mountains which are scarcely ever out of sight anywhere in mainland Greece.[38] These were the domain of emptiness, spirits, wild beasts, and tough shepherds; the Athenian city man knew little of them, not that he did not lead a hardy life of military service that would seem impossibly strenuous today, but the citizen-spearman was a fighter of the plains and more at home on a warship than on a mountain top.[39] [97]

The mountains were the wilderness. To Athenians thinking of Thebes, *the* mountain was Cithaeron, visible from Athens; invisible in fact from Thebes, but seen from the near hills as a bold black trapezoid dominating the Asopus Valley. Parnassus is higher, steeper, and snowier, but a sacred mountain with civilized Delphi perched in its under-slopes. Cithaeron is all wild.

On such mountain sides the Chorus imagine the outcast murderer (463–82):

> Who is he, whom the magic-singing
> Delphian rock proclaimed
> the bloody-handed murderer
> whose crimes were too deep to tell?
> Run, he must run now
> harder than stormy horses,
> feet flying in flight,
> for the armed god is after him, leaping
> with fire and flash, Apollo, Zeus' own,
> and the forbidding Death-
> Spirits horribly haunt him.

[37] Hesiod's *Works and Days* 287–92, the original steep and thorny way opposed to the primrose path; Simonides, frg. 37 (Diehl); Pindar *Ol.* 9.107–108, with scholia. For Prodicus' fable of Heracles at the crossroads see Xenophon *Memorabilia* ii.20–34, where the Hesiodic passage is also quoted, but the image of the difficult way is not concretely developed.

[38] See Carpenter, *Folk Tale, Fiction, and Saga in the Homeric Epics*, pp. 18–20.

[39] For the discomfiture of Lacedaemonian hoplites in rough, precipitous country, see Thucydides iv.29–38; of Athenian hoplites caught in a mountain defile, Thucydides iii.95–98.

The message shone, it showed
even now from the snows
of Parnassus. Manhunt the hidden
man. After him all.
He lurks, a wild bull
in the wild wood, in the holes
of the rock side
lonely-footed, forlorn wandering,
dodging aside from the mid-centered
prophecies, which, things alive,
hover to haunt him.[98]

In the first long angry response of Tiresias, where the chief image is of a ship come home to harbor (obvious enough), the mountain, and the stalker on the mountain, project, even obtrude (412-23):

I tell you, since you have baited me with my blindness:
you have your eyes, and do not see where you are standing
in evil, nor where you are living, nor whom you are living with.
Do you know whose son you are? Unconscious enemy
of your own people, here on earth, and under the ground,
the double-goading curse, father's and mother's in one,
shall stalk you on its feet of horror from this land,
you who see straight now, but shall then see only dark.
What harbor shall not be full of your cries,
what Mount Cithaeron shall not echo to them soon
when you learn what that marriage is, that awful haven
where, after your fair voyage, you brought in your ship?

The foundling, in Greece, was the child of the mountain side. The foundling was often protected by divine wild spirits of the place, or he might have been a spirit himself, or even a great god, Dionysus, Hermes, even Zeus.[40] The Chorus fancy Oedipus, the mountain-child, fosterling of Cithaeron, as by-blow of some mountain-walking god, Pan, Apollo, Hermes, or Dionysus, by one of the nymphs of the mountains.[41] Oedipus, in answer to the doubts, as he thinks, of Jocasta, identifies himself with nature (1076-85):

Let her break forth her tempers as she will, but I
will still find out what seed made me, although it be
humble. She being proud, perhaps, as women are,
thinks the obscurity of my birth is some disgrace.
I count myself the child of Fortune. While her gifts
are good, I shall not call myself degraded. I
am born of her. She is my mother. And the months
my brothers marked me small, and they have marked me great.
So born, I would not ever wish I had been born
anything else, to keep me from learning who I am.[99]

40 See Harrison, *Themis*, pp. 1-49.
41 Lines 1098-1109.

Tychē, Fortune or Coincidence, is here the way in which things come out or work, that is, another Greek way of saying Nature. The natural son is the child of Nature. After the catastrophe, it is to nature and the pathos of places that Oedipus chiefly appeals (1391–1403):

> Cithaeron oh Cithaeron, why did you take me? Why
> did you not kill me when you took me? Thus had I
> never made clear to men the place where I was born.
> O Polybus and Corinth and my father's house
> of old, as men then called it, what a festering sore
> you fed beneath my outward splendor, I who now
> have been found evil in myself, and evil born.
> O three roads, hidden valley,
> oak wood and narrow meeting at the threeway cross,
> who drank the blood of my own father which was spilled
> by my own hands, do you remember still
> what things I did to you, and then, when I came here,
> what things I did again?

It is as if Oedipus had been set free from ordinary city life when he was put away into the hands of the mountain Shepherd. It is natural that the child of the wilderness who lived in the city should go home to his wilderness to die—to ask to go, even though the story has not told that he did so; and thus we have come back to our beginning (1449–54):

> But let it never be thought right that I should stay
> in the city of my father, and be part of it,
> but let me go to the mountains and live there, where stands
> Cithaeron, called *my* mountain, which, when they still lived
> my mother and my father gave me, for my final tomb.
> So let them kill me at last, for they destroyed my life.

We have completed the circle but we have not resolved all the play. Never think that. We can read *Oedipus* as many[100] times as we like, and every time find new truths and throw away old falsehoods that once seemed to be true. There is always a dimension that escapes.

While it is true that *Oedipus* is a particularly compact combination of themes, where themes of foundling, mountain-spirit, murder, manhunt, tyrant cohere because we are constantly led from one into the other, yet in this play one can, perhaps more clearly than elsewhere in Sophocles, separate the poetic from the dramatic. Or at least we can separate the "daemonic" or "barbaric," because it is not absolutely needed. There are splendid characterizing lines and rhetorical effects, without this kind of poetic material. And the daemonic is not "so." The finished play is not about any nature-child or mountain-spirit. He exists only in the imagination of the players. The Oedipus of the action is a perfectly plausible, too human man, and the closest he has ever come to being a child of Fortune or Nature, or Year Spirit with the months for brothers, is to be handed from one kindhearted Shepherd to another, in a summer of babyhood on the high pastures. The play King, with his greatnesses and his faults, does not need to be a splendid barbarian at heart, like Ajax. He is a homicide: but on the level of discourse we may see him as thinking himself so set upon, so right in his defense, that the deadly brawl at the crossroads has scarcely troubled his conscience since. He never was a hunted monster, something like a great, wild beast, fierce but scary, driven among the high rocks. That is all the imagination of old men. We can so play trenchant characters that all seems motivated, and we can forget that what first drove the action was the shape of a universal pattern story from the childhood of men.

Oedipus is acted today, often professionally, and more frequently, I believe, than any other Greek play. It is commonly given in what almost passes as an authorized version[101]—that of Yeats—which has cut down or cut out those daemonic passages we have been considering.[42] It is good theatre, and it is truly dramatic, but it is no longer haunted.

In a stasimon of *Antigone*,[43] also, among the moralities we see an image of the high snows of Olympus where Zeus is forever, deathless and sleepless, with his laws; and by contrast, an image of the pit below, this time the darkness of the sea stirred to waves that batter the promontories. The gods of Sophocles are there, but remote, unattainable as the snows of Olympus; we can only see the effects, and are closer to the dark underpit. The tragedies of Sophocles concern resolute, intelligent, civilized people, determined to understand everything; they never do, because there is a dark nonsensical element in things, which eludes their comprehension and, often, destroys them; but which has its own wild beauty.[102]

42 See above, note 3.
43 Lines 582–625.

James Schroeter

From "The Four Fathers: Symbolism in
Oedipus Rex." In *Criticism*, Vol. III, No. 3
(Summer 1961). Reprinted by permission of
the publisher.

Ernest Jones, in his book *Hamlet and Oedipus,* points out that
"myth," dream, and imaginative literature share a "mechanism" known
as "decomposition," the opposite of another one known as "condensation," which together have been responsible for bringing about "a
great part of Greek mythology." "Condensation" involves the fusing of
attributes of several people to form one composite figure. In "decomposition" attributes of one individual are disunited and several other individuals are invented, each endowed with one group of the original
attributes. "In this way," says Jones, "one person of complex character
is dissolved and replaced by several, each of whom possesses a different
aspect of the character which in a simpler form of the myth was combined in one being; usually the different individuals closely resemble
one another in other respects, for instance in age."[1]
     Unfortunately, Jones does not apply his generalization to Soph-
ocles' *Oedipus,* even though the title of his book suggests that he might.
Concerned with speculating about Hamlet's unconscious processes as
either historical realities or the counterpart of Shakespeare's, he never
engages in a detailed investigation of Sophocles' play, apparently assuming that the insights of his mentor, Sigmund Freud, were wholly
adequate and that no more need be said. Had he turned his attention
to such an examination, however, his theory of "decomposition" might
have provided him with a clue to some of the finest and most unsuspected subtleties of a play which has often been regarded as the "greatest" in all dramatic literature.
     It will be recalled that *Oedipus* has five choral passages or "odes"

1 Ernest Jones, *Hamlet and Oedipus* (New York, 1955), pp. 149–50.

which divide the action into six parts. The first part or "prologue" sets forth the general situation from which the action develops: Thebes is polluted by the presence of an unknown murderer, the responsibility for whose detection and punishment is placed by the[186] people in the hands of their leader, Oedipus. The last part or "exodus" presents the dénouement, the expiation of the murder. The four central parts or "agons" present the crucial action, the swift, intensely dramatic uncovering by Oedipus of the true murderer and of his own identity. Each of these four agons consist of a conflict between Oedipus and another character: the first between Oedipus and Teiresias, the second between Oedipus and Creon, the third between Oedipus and the Messenger, and the fourth between Oedipus and the Herdsman. All four adversaries—Teiresias, Creon, the Messenger, and the Herdsman—bear signs of being "decomposed" versions of a complex archetype. They are, in Jones' language, "disguises" of a single character.

The first clue to their fundamental identity is their age. Two of them, the Messenger and the Herdsman, figure as adults in actions taking place at about the time that Oedipus was born, and are therefore a generation older than he. Three—Teiresias, the Messenger, and the Herdsman—are repeatedly addressed or referred to as "old" or "old man." Creon's age is nowhere mentioned, but that he represents the older generation, the father's rather than the son's, seems clear in that he is Oedipus' uncle.[2] Thus, all four of the adversaries must be old men and, since Oedipus is in middle life, about the age that Oedipus' father would have been had he been alive.

Critics, scholars and producers of the play, all of whom have apparently overlooked this fact, should not be unduly censured, since the age of the adversaries is not altogether apparent from an examination of the literary document.[3] On the other hand, neither can Sophocles be accused of having failed to make his intentions clear, nor need one necessarily assume that a definite idea as to the age of the adversaries formed no part of his intention. We must suppose that, like any playwright ancient or modern, he relied upon the skill of actors and director to create the visual appearance or "spectacle" upon which his meaning depended, and that, whenever his language failed to keep the contrast between the age of his adversary and protagonist to the fore, the production of the play itself might vividly, and more appropriately than the speeches, supply the lack. It is likely that, just as old men were symbolized by white and young men by purple costumes in traditional Roman drama, the ancient Greek drama used some similar con-

---

[2] It should be noted perhaps that the avuncular is a substitute for the paternal role in many examples of imaginative literature.

[3] One critic, Gilbert Murray, pointed out that *Oedipus* has "a large share" of old men in it, but apparently attached little importance to the fact.

vention to clarify the contrasts of generations.[4] Indeed, unless such a contrast be made (and there can be no reason to suppose the ancient acting version did not make it), an important aspect of Sophocles' meaning, which depends on sensing some analogy between the adversaries, is lost, as I believe it has been in modern productions.

The second clue to the fundamental identity of the four adversaries lies in their relationship to Oedipus. Besides being old, they function in some conserving or protecting capacity towards him that can be referred to, at least metaphorically, as "life-giving."[5] Oedipus' fate is or has been in their hands; he has depended on their good offices somewhat as a child depends on its father's. Teiresias has a knowledge of Oedipus' true identity possessed by no one else. Had he at any time chosen to divulge this knowledge, Oedipus' happiness would inevitably have been utterly destroyed. Creon's conserving role is more direct. A politician, he has acted practically and in accordance with both family and national loyalties for Oedipus' political good, journeying to the oracles, summoning Teiresias, advising and generally sharing the political authority and rule. Without Creon's support the young and inexperienced Oedipus could not have gained the throne or, having gained it, could not have held it long. The Messenger's conserving role is still more direct. When Oedipus was a small baby, the Messenger carried him out of Thebes into Corinth, where he placed him in the hands of the king and queen, who nurtured and educated the infant and brought him safely to manhood. Had the Messenger not done so, Oedipus would have existed, at best, animal-like, as a shepherd or slave on the slopes of Cithaeron. The Herdsman's role is most direct of all.[6] When Oedipus was three days old the queen gave the Herdsman the baby with his ankles bound and ordered him exposed on the hill to die. The Herdsman, however, taking pity on the baby, unbound him and gave him to the Messenger to take out of the country. Had he not done so, Oedipus must surely have perished. Thus, each of the four is a surrogate father, performing some[188] part of the complex paternal function: Teiresias fostering Oedipus' psychic good (his happiness), Creon his political good (his rule), the Messenger his social good (his nurture), and the Herdsman his biological good (his physical existence). Together they share in the perfecting of the mature and kingly Oedipus we see at the beginning of the play.

So thoroughly disguised that few if any commentators have noted analogies between them, the adversaries are thus "decomposed" versions of a complex archetype and may be regarded as symbolic fathers.

---

[4] See Allardyce Nicoll, *The Development of the Theatre* (New York, 1957), p. 57.

[5] See Richmond Lattimore, *The Poetry of Greek Tragedy* (Baltimore, 1958), pp. 85–86. Including five characters—Teiresias, Creon, the Messenger, the Herdsman and Jocasta—rather than four, Lattimore speaks of them all as "helpers" or "rescuers."

[6] Lattimore, *loc. cit.*, calls him the "true" or "original" helper.

The hypothesis that the adversaries are fathers gives unexpected support to the most divergent views and interpretations of the play— views I will call the "psychoanalytic," the "anthropological," and the "poetic"—and reciprocally receives support in return. The psycho- analytic interpretation, initiated by Freud and subsequently pursued by a number of his followers, including Jones, investigated *Oedipus* and other ancient plays and myths as expressions of hidden psychic processes. Writing in *The Interpretation of Dreams*, Freud claims that *Oedipus* "is what is known as a tragedy of destiny," the chief effect of which is "said to lie in the contrast between the supreme will of the gods and the vain attempts of mankind to escape the evil that threatens them." However, his point is that this "contrast," despite the general opinion to the contrary, is not really the tragic stuff of the play. *Oedi- pus* moves a modern audience only because of "the particular nature of the material on which that contrast is exemplified," that is, the "curse" laid upon Oedipus at birth that he will "slay his father and marry his mother." Theorizing that all men are so "cursed," since we are all fated to wish for the murder of our father and union with our mother, Freud explains that the power of Sophocles' "material" is due to its revelation of a universal psychic predisposition, in which the two acts, Oedipus' murder of his father and marriage with his mother (the "Oedipus com- plex"), fulfill the "primeval wishes of our childhood."[7]

These two actions, both of which occur prior to the opening of Sophocles' play, have occupied the attention of the psychoanalysts to the exclusion of those actions Sophocles actually represents—in his pro- logue, exodus, and agons. However, if one grants that the adversaries are fathers, the entire play rather than merely its antecedent[189] action is brought crucially into the arena that the psychoanalysts have been interested in exploring. Rejecting Teiresias' dark prophecies, Oedipus attacks the old seer in the first agon. Accusing Creon of treachery, he attempts to destroy the old politician in the second. Concerned over his own clouding private fate, Oedipus unconsciously upsets the Messen- ger's entire purpose in making his journey in the third. Frightened and at the limits of his patience, he tortures the old Herdsman in the fourth. Thus, Oedipus commits some violent or destructive act against each of his fathers, exhibiting a pattern similar to that in the ante- cedent action at the crossroads, when he had unwittingly murdered his real father, Laius. Ignorant or unconscious of his "debt" to each father, partly because of the danger they pose (just as, for the same reason, he had been ignorant of his "debt" to Laius), Oedipus in his actions re- peatedly reveals that same paradoxical "contrast" which Freud prefers to translate from cosmic or religious into biological or psychological terms. Thus translated, each agon becomes a disguised murder of the

[7] Sigmund Freud, *The Interpretation of Dreams* (New York, 1955), p. 262.

father by the son in which both the nature of the father and of the murder are transformed or "repressed."

Freud thought that Shakespeare's *Hamlet*, which he claims "has its roots in the same soil as *Oedipus*," demonstrates a "changed treatment of the same material" as that in *Oedipus*, and thereby reveals "the whole difference in the mental life of those two widely separated epochs of civilization," the Greek and the Elizabethan: that is, "the secular advance of repression in the emotional life of mankind." In short, he believed that whereas the "child's wishful fantasy" of Oedipus is "brought into the open and realized," Hamlet's "remains repressed" and is only symbolically rather than literally represented.[8] Although an interpretation of the adversaries as symbolic fathers takes away the primal simplicity with which Freud wanted to endow *Oedipus*, and makes it seem closer to *Hamlet*, more "civilized" and "repressed," than he had suspected, it also, in addition to corroborating the psychoanalytic theory of "decomposition," provides a striking confirmation of Freud's theory as to the actual nature of the material with which Sophocles was dealing and the reason for its universality of appeal. Reciprocally the Freudian theory gives weight to the theory that the adversaries are fathers and helps supply a level of meaning to the play that, without the theory, might be largely unsuspected.[190]

The anthropological school, including Gilbert Murray and those following James Frazer's lead, have interested themselves in *Oedipus* and other ancient plays as myths, as outgrowths of primitive religious rituals. Whereas the psychoanalytic critics have investigated these documents as clues to hidden psychic processes, the anthropological critics have sought to find hidden rites and ceremonials in them—the "aition" (explanation of a rite) or the "sparagamos" (ritual dismemberment) of tragedy, or the "gamos" (sexual union) of comedy, elements of which they have uncovered in a number of plays and myths. One of the most crucial of such rites, according to the anthropological school, was a prehistoric ceremony involving a struggle or "agon" between two characters, one of them young and the other old, in which the young character or "protagonist" represented the son or king-to-be and the old character or "antagonist" represented the father or "pharmakos" (old king). The ceremony was concluded by a representation of the slaying of the old by the new king, thereby symbolizing the cycles of social and political change, of the generations (old age giving way to youth), of the seasons (winter giving way to spring), and, more generally, of the eternal mystery of life renewed. As the anthropological commentators have demonstrated, this ceremonial, with all of its profound religious and civic significance, has persisted vestigially in a great many ancient Greek plays, but most notably in those dealing with the stories of Orestes and Oedipus.

8 Freud, *op. cit.*, p. 263.

Although the only part of Sophocles' play which the anthropological critics have suspected to bear a relationship to the prehistoric rite is that antecedent action which also intrigued Freud and Jones, Oedipus' killing of Laius at the crossroads, each agon will be seen to bear a relationship once the symbolic nature of the four adversaries is recognized. Each involves a struggle between two characters, an old antagonist and a young protagonist; each concludes with a "destruction" of the old antagonist at the hands of the young.

Obviously there are great differences between Sophocles' agons and the primitive ceremonials described by the anthropologists, and these differences should not be minimized. Clearly the agons represented by Sophocles are immensely more refined than the struggles represented in the primitive rites. Perhaps the difference is not essentially greater, however, than that between the raising of Lazarus as described in the Gospels and, say, Dostoevsky's symbolic representation of it in *Crime and Punishment,* in which the hero, Raskolnikov, is morally regenerated under circumstances that Dostoevsky wants his reader[191] to associate with the sacred ones described in the Gospels. In the Gospels, the regeneration is physical, in Dostoevsky moral; in the Gospels it is effected directly by Christ, in Dostoevsky through the intermediation of Sonia, a prostitute; in the Gospels the account is given simply in a few paragraphs, in Dostoevsky at the length of several hundred pages involving countless subtleties and ramifications. Despite the enormous transformation, no one contests that the parallel exists and is of great importance in understanding *Crime and Punishment.* There should be little difficulty, then, in assuming that Sophocles may have drawn upon rituals, perhaps no less sacred to his culture than those of Dostoevsky were to his, however more difficult for a modern audience to recognize, and of equal importance in understanding the meaning of *Oedipus.*

A symbolic interpretation of the adversaries thus helps confirm the anthropological conviction that the primitive rituals were a pervasive influence on Greek drama by supplying previously unsuspected examples of them, while, reciprocally, the anthropological researches give added support to the theory that the adversaries are symbolic, and help provide a deeper level of meaning to the play.

The poetic critics, including such relatively recent scholars as H. D. F. Kitto and others, either ignoring or reacting against the excessive tendencies of the earlier genetic schools, have interested themselves in *Oedipus* and other Greek plays as conscious, artistic constructs rather than as expressions of hidden psychic impulses or collections of vestigial rituals.[9] Assuming that the plays are best viewed as more or less carefully thought-out poetic structures, they have attempted, using a method not unlike that of Aristotle in the *Poetics,* to account for the

[9] H. D. F. Kitto, *Greek Tragedy* (New York, 1954), p. v.

parts—the actions, characters, and speeches—by showing how they contribute to the unity of the whole rather than by showing where they come from, whether that origin is viewed as a "mechanism" of the imagination or as a certain religious or dramatic tradition. Translated into Aristotelian terms, *Oedipus* can be described as a "complex" tragedy in which each episode contributes in either a "likely" or "necessary" way to the "recognition" which occurs at the end of the last episode. Providing one or more clues to Oedipus' identity, each episode is "likely" in the sense that it follows plausibly from what came before, and also is "necessary" in that it prepares for what is to come afterwards by making inevitable the recognition scene on which the tragic catharsis mainly depends.[192]

Oedipus' "hamartia," when that term is used in the etymological sense of a "mistake" or "missing of the mark" rather than in the customary nineteenth-century understanding of it as a "flaw in character," seems most obviously and clearly applied to those two acts which occur outside the play, Oedipus' murder of his father and marriage to his mother. Like Clytemnestra's murder of her husband in *Agamemnon,* Orestes' murder of his mother in *The Libation Bearers,* or those various killings Aristotle discusses in his chapter on the "hamartia" in the *Poetics,* these acts constitute Oedipus' violation of the "laws that live on high," and, besides being the cause of the chain of events presented in the play, are the subject of his discovery. Consequently, their importance from a dramatic point of view is difficult to overestimate. Despite this importance, Sophocles had to make the "hamartia" external to the drama in order to avoid serious artistic weaknesses. Had he included the incest and parricide, first he would have been involved in what Aristotle calls an "epic" synthesis, with the problem of representing not only a long span of time (many years) and geographically separate places (Phocis and Thebes), but a double rather than a single action. Second, in representing events so sensational and shocking, he would have produced what Aristotle calls the "monstrous" rather than the "humane" or "tragic," one consequence of which would be that the dignity and nobility of Oedipus' character would suffer or be greatly weakened. Third, as Aristotle specifically points out, he would have emphasized rather than minimized the single implausibility in the play, the fact that Oedipus, after the passage of many years, is so uninformed about Laius' death that it comes as a dreadful surprise to him when Jocasta tells him the time, place and manner of it.[10] Thus, in externalizing the "hamartia" Sophocles also externalizes the horrible and the implausible on the one hand, and clears the way, on the other, for a highly unified concentration on the single action that interests him, Oedipus' recognition.

The dramatic problem is that, having taken out the "hamartia,"

---

[10] *Poetics,* Chap. 24, 1460a, 30.

Sophocles must then put it back again. One way he does this is through Oedipus' narration of the murder. But, if his play is to be unified rather than episodic, the "hamartia" must be something "organic," internal to the very nature of the hero and his action rather than merely an isolated accident lying outside the plot. Introducing the adversaries as fathers, Sophocles solves the problem by symbolizing the "hamartia." He makes it integral to the action by repeating it, in a modified form,[193] in each agon, reconstructing the original set of factors both in terms of Oedipus' character and the circumstances under which it acts. Thus the four fathers, although certainly "accountable" from the psychoanalytic and anthropological views, can also be *poetically* explained as a necessary means by which Sophocles achieves artistic unity.

One possible objection to the theory that Teiresias, Creon, the Messenger, and the Herdsman are fathers is that it is incomplete, ignoring as it does the bulk of the poetic detail with which Sophocles has portrayed the four. Although the theory satisfactorily accounts for the two similarities between them, their age and "life-giving" functions, it does nothing to explain their many differences. Yet these differences far outweigh the similarities, so much so that the similarities have scarcely been noticed, perhaps "disguised" by the more strongly-drawn and obvious differences. Indeed, the more closely one examines the play the more pervasive, striking, and important these differences appear, whether one compares the adversaries from the social, the moral, or the intellectual points of view.

Socially, Teiresias and Creon represent the upper order, the Messenger and the Herdsman the lower. Teiresias, as an embodiment of divine and supernatural power, is highest in order of importance as well as first in order of appearance. He is regarded by the city, as expressed in the choral passages, with great reverence and awe. Although of royal blood, Creon stands at a lower level. As a representative of the ruling family he is respected and loved but neither feared nor venerated. The Messenger is of distinctly lower status than Creon but of higher status than the Herdsman. Unfortunately, one can only guess at how he was to be costumed or the accents with which he was to speak, but his appearance must be such as to explain Oedipus' astonishment when he learns that the man was once employed at so lowly an occupation as sheep-herding.[11] His city has entrusted him with an important mission, and his assured manner indicates a man who, if of lowly origin, has come up an important step in the social hierarchy. The Herdsman, by contrast, a slave and a shepherd, stands on the very lowest rung of the social ladder.

Morally the contrasts are equally pronounced. Teiresias, who is

11 *Oedipus*, 1. 1029.

both fearless and proud (in the sense of knowing his proper worth),[194] represents justice or "dike," justice in that humanistic and self-assertive sense characteristic of Greek morality rather than the forgiving and self-effacing sense characteristic of Christian morality. When attacked by the king, he does not hesitate to return, retributively, Oedipus' scorn and insult with greater scorn and insult of his own. Creon displays moderation and prudence, lower virtues than those of Teiresias but higher than those of the Messenger. Whereas Teiresias counterattacks, Creon when attacked merely defends himself. His morality is dictated by considerations of honor rather than of justice. The Messenger's morality is dictated by expediency. We can safely assume that his reasons for bringing Oedipus out of Thebes many years before were self-interested; he knew his king and queen were childless, and he has evidently benefited from supplying their lack. Clearly hoping, in the third agon, to gain some benefit to himself for his "good news," he is alternately sycophantic and impudent depending on the direction in which he sees his own advantage. The Herdsman stands at the opposite extreme from Teiresias. Fearful rather than fearless, abject rather than proud, and uncomplicated by considerations of justice, honor, or expediency, he shows the proper "virtues" of a slave rather than a freeman.

Sophocles, as is appropriate in a play of "recognition" turning on the opposition between ignorance and knowledge, makes his most important contrasts depend on the intellectual differences between the fathers. Teiresias is divinely inspired. He has a profound insight into the past, present, and future, into "things teachable and things which cannot be spoken," into matters earthly and matters heavenly. He speaks in an apocalyptic poetry—lofty, enigmatic, powerful. Creon is wise but speaks from facts which can be immediately perceived. He has a knowledge of things of the earth but not of things of heaven. His reason takes the form of demonstration rather than intuition, and his language the form of logic rather than truth, of rhetoric rather than poetry. The Messenger's intellect is calculative rather than demonstrative or intuitive. He represents human cunning as opposed to Creon's political or Teiresias' divine wisdom. The Herdsman, who accidentally lets slip the information he is trying to conceal, shows least intellectual ability of all. Dull and simple, he is ungraced with sufficient cunning to protect himself.

Writing in the *Politics*, Aristotle says that the man "who is unable to live in society or who has no need because he is sufficient for himself[195] must be either a beast or a god."[12] These two poles, Beast and God, may be said to define the extremes between which mankind ranges. Many cultures, both simple and highly civilized, have tended to view man in such a framework—as mediant between God and Beast,

---

[12] *Politics*, Bk. I, Chap. 2, 1253a, 28.

Angel and Animal—but the scheme is strikingly reflected in Greek art and thought of the fourth and fifth centuries and provides a clue to the contrasts Sophocles has drawn between his fathers. Two of them live within ordinary society; the other two live outside of it. Creon and the Messenger, the intermediates appearing in the second and third agons, live within it but function there on two sharply divergent levels, the upper and lower, as ruler and ruled, showing the social virtues appropriate to their stations. Teiresias and the Herdsman, the two extremes figuring in the first and last agons, live outside of human society and must be summoned from their respective isolations before they appear. Although equally isolated, they live apart from the rest of mankind for opposite reasons. Teiresias is *above* human society, a man who inspires fear and whose associations are with the gods rather than his fellow men. The Herdsman is *below* human society. Living outside the "polis" tending sheep, he has retreated from human society because of fear, and his associations are with animals rather than gods or men.

The contrasts that Sophocles develops, rather than being random "disguises," give every appearance of having been carefully thought out and systematically differentiated socially, morally, and intellectually. Graduated from high to low, God to Beast, they reflect a total, cosmic view of man's condition. In addition to symbolizing fathers, the adversaries, therefore, may be said to represent the four stages of man. A background against which Oedipus' actions can be projected, they provide these actions with the widest possible significance.

Like the chief figures of other national literatures, myths, and religions (e.g., King Arthur, Moses, Mohammed, Christ), Oedipus is brought up by foster parents. Although the son of a king, Arthur is raised by humble parents. Moses, a Hebrew, is raised by Egyptians; son of a subject people, he is brought up by royal parents. A posthumous child, Mohammed is raised first by a wealthy grandfather and then by a poor uncle, while Christ, the Son of God, is raised as the son of a humble carpenter. Each becomes a political or religious leader—Arthur of the Britons, Moses of the Jews, Mohammed of the Moslems, Christ of the Christians—and each, by having a double set[196] of origins, assumes a special, universal significance. As an "ordinary" man (the "child" of a lowly knight, subject people, poor uncle or humble carpenter), he shares the common folk origin of the people he will lead. As the son of a divinity or king, he enjoys an origin superior to that people. Partly mortal and partly divine, partly commoner and partly king, he both shares and transcends the ordinary lot. Similarly Oedipus has two sets of parents, which, like those of Moses, represent two nationalities. Like the others his background ties him intimately both to royalty on the one hand, and to the "common folk" on the other. But Sophocles introduces an additional refinement into the picture by making the "fathers" symbolic of all stages of mankind. Rather than having been formed by any one or two of these "stages," Oedipus is a product of them all and is of far wider significance than any one of them. Embracing paradoxically the divine and the animal, his status is first that of a king and then that of a slave; his actions are god-like in his pursuit of truth and justice, and bestial in that he kills his father and cohabits with his mother; his knowledge is both prophetic and divine when he solves the riddle of the Sphinx and less than human in that, animal-like, he is ignorant of his own parentage and identity. Thus Oedipus singly exhibits the same wide human spectrum as do his fathers jointly, and his tragedy is "universal"—for and of all men, of whatever condition or degree.

In a penetrating observation on *Oedipus,* Freud said that the action can be likened to the "work of a psychoanalysis" in that it "consists in nothing other than the process of revealing, with cunning delays and ever-mounting excitement," that Oedipus is "himself the murderer of Laius."[13] Had Freud continued, he might have pointed out that the play presents Oedipus' mental voyage back to his buried, traumatic past—ultimately back to the point at which the three-day-old infant was "cast out" by his parents, so that the "process" he refers to represents the recovery of increasingly earlier and therefore more deeply buried memories, exactly as in a psychoanalysis. Rather than being dredged from Oedipus, as in a psychoanalysis, the memories are supplied by the adversaries. Therefore, if one is to fully accept Freud's analogy, he must regard the fathers as projections of Oedipus' own mental levels, ranging from the "conscious" on the one hand, to the "unconscious" on the other.

Oedipus' "psychoanalytic" journey has a clear "anthropological" analogue. Whereas in psychoanalytic terms the play represents[197] Oedipus' descent into his dim mental past, in anthropological terms it represents his journey downwards towards the dark beginnings of the race. Thus the fathers can be viewed as "levels" ranging between the two anthropological poles, "civilized" and "primitive," as well as levels between the psychoanalytic poles, "conscious" and "unconscious."

Although equally plausible and suggestive, both interpretations represent a peculiarly modern "twist" in, or reduction of, Sophocles' scheme. Oedipus' "descent" is most properly defined by the religious "God-Beast" rather than the psychological "conscious-unconscious" or cultural "civilized-primitive" polarity. It will be recalled that in the first agon Oedipus chooses to battle with Teiresias on the grounds of wisdom rather than political power. The issue at stake is "truth," and Oedipus, twice reminding the blind prophet of his own super-human wisdom in answering the Sphinx, makes of the battle a struggle between two prophets rather than prophet and king. Accusing Creon of treachery and political chicanery, Oedipus makes the struggle between them turn on the question of who has the greater honor in the eyes of

13 Freud, *op. cit.,* pp. 261–262.

the people. Rather than involving two prophets, the battle between them involves two rival politicians. Sophocles portrays a private "drama of cross purposes" in his third agon. Neither Oedipus nor the Messenger, each strong in his own hopes and fears, is able to see fully the motives of the other, with the result that each unconsciously defeats the other. The Messenger is concerned with his self-advantage in the form of a reward for his good news and favor in his king's eyes, and to that extent acts in a private rather than a public capacity; but Oedipus, no longer acting as prophet or politician, is also concerned with his "private" fate rather than that of his "polis." Cringing and afraid, the Herdsman in the fourth agon is concerned mainly with his physical safety, but it is his physical person that Oedipus attacks. Trying to get the old man to speak because of the urgency of his own fears, Oedipus descends (for the first time) to physical coercion, while at the same time he is himself close to the immediate prospect of physical harm. Paradoxically diminished by each "victory," Oedipus descends in each agon to the successively lower stages symbolized by the fathers.

The poetic significance of this descent cannot be understood fully without comparing it with an opposite movement in the last episode or "exodus," in which the blinded, suffering king says farewell to his children and banishes himself from the city over which he had[198] ruled. Commentators point out that Sophocles, by displaying his hero at the extreme limits of suffering and pain, here completes the "reversal" (from happiness to misery), but they seldom point out that he also completes the "catharsis" of his play (purging of pity and fear) by "raising" as well as "lowering" his hero. It is true that Sophocles does not dramatize in this play that part of Oedipus' life following his exile in which he becomes a divinely inspired prophet living apart from the rest of mankind and possessed of oracular wisdom; he deals with that part of the legend in *Oedipus at Colonus*. But Sophocles presents a sufficiently complete set of clues before the conclusion of *Oedipus Rex* to indicate clearly a parallel between Teiresias, symbol of the highest "stage of humanity," and the "resurrected" Oedipus. First and most obviously, Oedipus, like Teiresias, is blind (an infirmity conventionally associated with seers and prophets), having put out his own eyes in a deeply symbolic gesture. Second, like Teiresias, Oedipus is to live outside of the "polis" (living apart from normal society is also conventionally associated with prophets), having exiled himself according to his own edict in a second profoundly symbolic gesture.[14] Third and most

---

[14] Oedipus' self-inflicted punishment (exile and blinding) is double, as was his *hamartia* (parricide and incest). The first punishment, exile, is a fulfillment of a public pact Oedipus made with his subjects, in accordance with his own edict, while the more terrible blinding is a private act akin almost to madness, perhaps fulfilling some unwritten prescript of the gods. Whereas the first punishment can be considered a voluntary deprivation of the highest good—citizenship—conferred by the political community which a man has the power to take from himself, the

important, like Teiresias he possesses the oracular knowledge of a prophet, having painfully gained it through his own unremitting search into matters which another kind of man would perhaps have preferred to leave unexplored. Thus he has arrived at a higher stage of humanity through a series of apparent descents into more degraded stages of humanity. The catharsis or emotional reflexivity of the play depends on the fact that Oedipus has come full circle. Just as Teiresias is not to be feared for or pitied, even though blind and solitary, because he is in a sense above pity and fear, so Oedipus, morally sublime in his self-caused blindness and self-willed exile, is too great a figure for pity or fear—a man magnificently equal to his fate, however terrible and unforeseen that fate may be.[199] The point is that the stages of Oedipus' "resurrection" as well as of his descent are clarified and defined by analogy with the fathers, taking on color and meaning from it. Hence, the entire tragedy depends on the conception of man's potentialities that is implied by the fathers' four "human stages."

The adversaries, therefore, in addition to serving as unwilling vehicles of the knowledge, both creating and destroying, which provide Oedipus with the basis for his ultimate regeneration, act as seldom-suspected but important symbols. On the one hand they stand for the father Oedipus has killed and whom he symbolically kills again. On the other hand they jointly symbolize the four stages of humankind (ranging comprehensively between the two poles, God and Beast), thereby defining both the "universality" of Oedipus as a man and the full meaning of his descent and resurrection.[200]

---

second can be considered a deprivation of the highest good conferred by the gods which a man has the power to take from himself. The first seems a fitting expiation for the parricide, while the second seems to fit the more private and yet more hideous crime of incest.

John Crossett

The world has long agreed to call the *Oedipus Rex* one of its very greatest plays. So much has been said about the play, and so well has much of this been said, that my work here is reduced. I need not demonstrate that Sophocles is a great playwright. What I propose now is to confirm this judgment by placing the *Oedipus Rex* where it belongs in the development of Sophoclean art and thought, for the very things that make it great make the other plays great too. . . .

If the *Women of Trachis* showed one extreme of the relationship between character and situation, an extreme indicated by the very title, the *Oedipus Rex* shows the other extreme. Here we have a perfect congruence of character and situation; here the myth is perfect for Sophocles' purposes; here the character who gives his name to the situation is the hero and victim of the situation, doer and sufferer, agent and principal. All difficulties that arose in the previous plays from the choice of myth disappear now; the defects of the so-called *diptych* construction cannot be charged against Sophocles. Instead of main characters who never meet, but who are connected by framework and *exempla*, or by contrasting parallels, or by messengers and verbal clusters, we have one character who has never met himself, but who experiences that meeting in the play—in this sense the *Oedipus Rex* is a *diptych* play—who is his own *exemplum*, his own contrasting parallel. Messengers and verbal clusters and oracles form a part of the play, but are not made the subject of virtuoso exercises. Every element that we have praised, and censured, in earlier plays is present here in its most perfect form. The material outside the drama is used with consummate skill. No wonder critics and readers have so admired the play.

A diagram of the play would be a straight line; or, since there is a contrasting parallel here, two lines moving in opposite directions but superimposed on each other, for they are one line, as they are one life. The play exemplifies perfectly a motto from Aristotle:

To de telos tés praxeos kata ton kairon estin.

The end of an action is implicit at the critical moment.[1]

. . . The play deals with only one day of Oedipus' life *after* he has fulfilled his terrible *moira* [destiny]. The action (*praxis*) which Sophocles imitates is an action of knowledge;[2] Oedipus finds out that he has done what he has done. It is absolutely essential to remember that Sophocles is not dramatizing the whole of Oedipus' life; with all that life to choose from, he chooses to start, and finish, on this one day, which occurs after those events to which most readers and critics devote their attention. The beautiful tact of Sophocles' art is conspicuous here, if tact can be called conspicuous: by starting at this point, he relieves himself of responsibility for showing how Oedipus could naturally commit the mistakes he does, those mistakes that even freshmen see, at least in part, as implausible. For Sophocles, these are *données,* the situation. It does no good to accuse Sophocles of failing to persuade us that Oedipus could have done what he did, for the myth, not Sophocles, is responsible. All that Sophocles is responsible for is to show us that Oedipus could plausibly and naturally act as he does *in the play.* The *telos* [end] he is concerned with is the *telos* of this *praxis.* As we shall see, Oedipus, by his decision at the opening of the play, makes this *telos* implicit. That decision, however, is the natural consequence of a whole series of decisions made at critical moments (*kairoi*) throughout his life, and even before that, for there is an action outside the life as well as outside the drama.

We may now begin to define this series of *kairoi,* starting with the one at the beginning of the play. Here Oedipus decides to help his people. Does he have a choice (*proairesis*)? I do not think that the most fatalistic of critics can argue that the gods make Oedipus decide to help his people, or to help them in the way he does.[3] Those are consequences of his character. Of course, *qua* king he has no choice. It is his job, a job that he took on voluntarily, as a just reward for his courageous intelligence—and, ironically, as an unjust reward for his action in killing the former king, his father; for the throne is rightfully his by virtue (vice?) of that act. At the beginning of the play he comes into his own in two senses. As he had saved Thebes once, so he must

---

[1] *Nicomachean Ethics,* III,1,6: Aristotle is discussing free will and choice. It is difficult to distinguish here whether Aristotle is referring only to the temporal relationship of action and end or, perhaps also, to the moral relationship.

[2] The pseudo-Platonic *Definitiones* defines *hamartia* as a *praxis* contradictory to right reason: 416a.

[3] The gods do, of course, force him to act when they send the plague, but they do not force which action he is to take. Though it is hard to see, and harder to accept, I shall argue that in sending the plague they are helping both Oedipus and the cosmos.

save it again, and by the same virtues—or vices—courage and intelligence.

This is the first *kairos* in the play. There follow and precede it, however, a whole series of *kairoi*, which, like points, make up the line that is Oedipus' life. The irony and tragedy of his life are that every point, every critical moment, is the same. He has innumerable chances to avoid his destiny, and in every case he makes the "wrong" decision. Each decision is made for good and natural reasons, and yet each decision confirms the *telos*, the end, that is implicit in the moment of decision. I have said that Oedipus' life may be diagrammed as a straight line; it may also be envisioned—for we could not draw it so—as a multitude of superimposed points.

The *kairos* before the opening of the play with which we must first be concerned is the solving of the Sphinx' riddle. At this moment Oedipus saved Thebes—only to destroy himself—got a throne, and obtained a wife by one and the same act. His decision to tackle the Sphinx is characteristic of the man, for it shows a kind heart, a bold nature, and extreme intelligence. We may add, if we like, a suicidal despair: perhaps he did not care what happened to his life, which seemed meaningless because it was so meaningful. Critics have said that he is not especially reflective, or he would have seen the truth earlier. Such a view seems to me a complete misreading of the evidence: anyone who has watched Oedipus ask one of his series of pointed and bulldog questions knows that he is shrewd and tenacious. He never wastes a question. His intelligence is not reflective, but that is not the only kind of intelligence. In every decision he makes his intelligence is manifest; he does not see the truth in each case because of the pressure of circumstances, a pressure critics tend to forget about as they look back from the vantage point of complete knowledge. What defeats their criticism is the ironic fact that by making the "wrong" decision, Oedipus ends, in every instance, in the right place. What difference would it have made to Oedipus' life had he spotted the truth earlier in the play? The horrible deeds are done. That he does not discover them earlier seems to me perfectly natural, although unbearably horrible, in view of his character and the situation. In point of fact, Oedipus' salvation lies in not discovering the truth earlier. Otherwise he would have killed Jocasta and would not have blinded himself, and would thus have failed to fulfill Teiresias' oracle. And for any Apollonian oracle to fail of fulfillment means, as the chorus will say, the end of moral order, of any order, in the cosmos. Would this course of action have been better, either as drama or philosophy? Would it be more lifelike than what does happen?

But to return to Oedipus outside of Thebes. It is difficult to see how he could have solved the riddle and avoided the throne and wife. He is not a modern picaresque hero, who can never stay in one town he has saved, and who must always be drifting on to see what lies on the other side of the hill. Oedipus is looking for a safe place to live, and yet one worthy of his talents and birth: he is the son of a king, and has been trained for the throne, even if he does not know which king and which throne. Thebes offers him that safety and that position, and he has earned the right to claim and to accept them. The logical implication of his solution to the Sphinx' riddle does away with the criticism made against the play, that surely Jocasta would have discussed the former king's death. In the crisis the Sphinx caused, all thought of Laius was forgotten, for Creon tells us (126–127, 567) that an investigation was vain. The excitement is enough to make even Oedipus overlook the matter, just as in the play itself, Oedipus becomes so excited over the mystery of his birth that he forgets to question the shepherd about the death of Laius, although it was for this purpose that he called him. In addition, we should remember that Sophocles portrays Jocasta as a person who does not care to dwell on unpleasant subjects: it is best to live at random, she says, as one can (979). In the rejoicing over the city's deliverance and in the festivity of the wedding, such a topic of discussion, even if remembered, would have been most indecorous. Oedipus, as we see, is not a man to ask idle questions or pursue irrelevant subjects, and he is not likely to have brought up the matter. What would he say to Jocasta by way of introducing the question—"A funny thing happened to me on my way to the kingdom"? Or how would Jocasta have brought the matter up, how and why? Once the marriage was consummated, the oracle was fulfilled. It would not matter when Oedipus asked questions. That he does not ask them for many years is part of his tragedy, and part of Sophocles' tragic views of time. Of course he should have asked, even though it was perfectly natural for him not to. He does not ask, and the failure is an ironic comment on the limitations of his great intelligence.

The *kairos* before the Sphinx is the slaying of Laius. Once again a virtue of Oedipus' is his downfall; where he had displayed intelligence in answering the Sphinx, he displays courage in confronting Laius. Falstaffian discretion would have kept Oedipus from meeting either crisis; but then he would not have been Oedipus. In the play itself the two virtues coalesce, and the downfall is greater. Singly they lead to triumphs; together they lead to doom. To symbolize the small part that intelligence played in the murder of Laius, Sophocles has the quarrel take place near a crossroads, that traditional symbol of uncertainty and possibility (801). What caused the two to arrive there at the same time? What would have happened had they met at the crossroads itself? Which way would he have turned who arrived first? Did they meet on Laius' side of the crossroads, towards Thebes, or on that of Oedipus, towards Delphi? Oedipus was fleeing from Delphi; Laius was going there, for he was on a pilgrimage to Delphi, as Creon tells us (114–115). Oedipus was fleeing not to some place, but away from Corinth; he had no destination, though he had a destiny. He was, he tells us (795), measuring his path by the stars—perhaps a hint of astrological influence is intended here. If he and Laius met on the Theban side of the crossroads, then Oedipus had already crossed and was on his way to Thebes. There are, we remember, three roads at this crossing: three, that number Sophocles was so fond of.[4] If they met on the other side, then Oedipus had not yet had a chance to decide which way to turn. What caused the meeting—chance, fate? Sophocles does not say, and the ambiguity is, I think, intentional. The meeting does not cause the murder; it merely provides the *kairos*. If Oedipus and Laius never meet, the story has no meaning; but the fact that they do meet does not cause Oedipus to slay his father. It is fatefulness of character that causes the quarrel and the murder. In defending his right of way, Oedipus acts like the prince he is. He does not strike first, but he does strike back. The act is natural, even if not wise: for no man attacks five men and expects to escape a fight. We may perhaps sense here another suicidal impulse in Oedipus, the despairing act of a man who no longer cares to live because his life is ruined—the same impulse that led him to take on the challenge of the Sphinx. That Oedipus slays four of the five men is a tribute to his courage and strength, good qualities in a king. That he lets one escape was apparently not his intention; he thinks he slew them all (813). His failure to do a complete job is his downfall. Yet the man who escaped deserved to escape; for it was he who had saved Oedipus' life as a baby. His escape, however, will doom the man he has saved.

The *kairos* before this one occurs at Delphi. Here Oedipus came to ask who his real parents were.[5] The god does not reply, and instead tells him that he is to murder his father and marry his mother. Oedipus runs away in fear. The act is again natural; he is probably quite young, perhaps not yet twenty, and the shock must have been overwhelming. Speaking with the knowledge of his whole life that we have, we can blame him for lack of intelligence. He should have followed up the drunken slander that he was illegitimate. Later in the play he will follow up the slander; but to wait as many years as he does is dangerous, for the relevant witnesses may die. As a matter of fact, he himself nearly kills the key witness. Yet the circumstances at Delphi do not

[4] See H. St. John Thackeray, "Sophocles and the Perfect Number," in *Proceedings of the British Academy* (London, 1930), XVI, 15–44.

[5] The *kairos* at Delphi is the least plausible of the *kairoi* that come before the opening of the play; Oedipus does not seem to have a reason for not continuing his original investigation. To explain his failure we must be a little sophistical, and argue that it is more than possible for him to take the oracle's failure to answer his question as confirmation that Polybus and Merope are his real parents; or else have recourse to psychology and explain his action by remembering his youth and the uncertainties and fear natural to that age. Still, one sees in his failure to follow up his original quest a foreshadowing of his failure to do so in the play.

compel investigation; those at Thebes do. The very ambiguity of the Delphic response can be construed as confirmation that Polybus and Merope are his real parents. Once again we see that Oedipus' decision at a *kairos* is natural even if wrong. Polybus and Merope have denied the slander. As in Thebes, excitement caused by a crisis makes men forgetful of the most rational courses of action. We who do not experience that excitement must allow for it in our judgments.

The gods could not be fairer than they are: they warned Laius and Jocasta, and Oedipus, of what is to come. All the interested parties have all the essential information, or the means to get that information. In the *Ajax* and the *Women of Trachis* the oracles had not been made explicitly conscious and clear to all the persons concerned, but that charge cannot be made here. Not knowing is painful, Deianeira had said, but what can be painful in knowing? Among other things, the *Oedipus Rex* deals with exactly that question. Sophocles' art has improved in the *Oedipus Rex:* in the *Women of Trachis* the problem had been only verbally dramatic; in the *Oedipus Rex* it is made implicit in the situation. Hence there is no need to vocalize the question.

. . . By being given, the oracle produces the end it warns against. Once that end is produced, the moral necessity for exposure is incumbent on heaven, which does not fail to live up to its responsibility. The characters involved—and they number more than Oedipus—must know what they have done and what has happened, even if that knowledge involves them in tragic suffering. As we shall see, especially in the *Oedipus at Colonus*, the tragic suffering which knowledge brings also brings tragic illumination, and that illumination, terrible as it is, most men would judge to be better than ignorant sinful bliss. The ultimate irony of the *Oedipus Rex* itself is that both knowing and not knowing are terrible. Not knowing does no good, if by "good" we mean being able to avoid the predicted evil. Knowing, although it is somehow better than not knowing, also fails to avoid the horrible reality of the sin. Yet between the two terrible states, knowing and not knowing, one would always choose knowing—at least a Greek would. And Oedipus, in his passionate desire to know the truth, is pure Greek. By knowing, man becomes like the gods; the gods know *moira,* even though they may regret it. Zeus, we remember, weeps tears of blood over the *moira* of his son Sarpedon, which he can but must not change. Man, knowing his fate, has every power that the gods have except the power to change his fate.[6] And although the gods have that power, they do not use it. As Hera warns Zeus in the *Iliad,* if he violates destiny by saving Sarpedon, the other gods will do the same; and so Zeus, to pre-

---

[6] In point of fact, by telling man the future the gods give him a godlike power of changing that future. The difference between man and the gods may lie just here: that the gods willingly refrain from altering the future, at least in any serious way, while man, by willingly trying to alter it, brings it about.

serve the cosmos, the system of *moirai*, upholds an order that is personally painful to him. In some ways men are better off than gods. Priam, when he looks down from the towers of Troy and weeps for the imminent death of his son Hector, weeps only human tears, for he has no power to save him. Zeus weeps tears of blood, and his pain is the greater because of his power to save. . . .

The *kairos* before Delphi is that produced by the drunken slander in Corinth. Here Oedipus confronts his supposed parents with the slander, and is reassured by them that it is false. He still doubts, and goes to Delphi. Is he wrong to do so? Do the gods force him? Or is this not the earliest sign we have of that passion for truth which is his greatest virtue and his greatest vice—a passion that leads him to his doom, and whose abandonment, in the shock of the knowledge brought by Delphi's oracle, also leads him to his doom?

The *kairoi* before this are not Oedipus'; they belong to the shepherd and to Laius and Jocasta. The shepherd should have obeyed orders, but did not. He showed humanity, but to what an inhumane end! Yet would we be satisfied to have the baby Oedipus die? Would the defeat of the oracle by this means satisfy us? The horror of his life is excruciating; but his death as a baby would be unbearable. Laius and Jocasta should never have had children, but they did. Once born, the child should have died—it is interesting that they never had another child; continence seems to have been possible for them psychologically as well as physiologically. It is a life like that of Oedipus that makes the dictum of Theognis, echoed by Sophocles, so valid: The best thing is never to be born, the next best, once born, to die as quickly as possible. . . .

Would we really prefer that Oedipus never had any *kairoi*, that the drunk never spoke up, that Polybus and Merope told the truth, that Delphi answered his original question, that he never met Laius . . . ?

Although all of these *kairoi* are outside the drama, and although most of them refer to a time before the double sin is committed, they are the same kind of *kairoi* that occur within the drama. Oedipus makes the same mistakes here that he made before he came to Thebes, and because of the same virtues. He has not changed over the years; his character, like his *moira*, remains constant, and so continues to produce the situation that is his doom. As Tom S. Driver points out, Greek literature is not concerned with the development of character in the way that modern literature is—Dostoyevsky, for example.[7] As we shall see, even in the *Oedipus at Colonus* the character of Oedipus does not

[7] *The Sense of History in Greek and Shakespearean Drama* (Columbia University Press, 1960), pp. 133–135, 157–158 and *passim*. The point must be pushed too far: clearly the Achilles we see at the end of the *Iliad* is a different man from the one we saw at the beginning. Oedipus, however, remains consistent in both plays.

change; there is no transformation which, growing out of the suffering, illuminates and redeems the human life. Such a notion is Christian.

The terrible difference between the *kairoi* inside the drama and those outside is that the inner decisions are all practically vain and meaningless: the doom predicted by the oracles has been fulfilled. The two most important *kairoi* of Oedipus' life have passed: the slaying at the crossroads and the marriage with Jocasta. Nothing that happens in the play can alter or undo these. By starting his play after these events Sophocles is doing something entirely new. In the earlier plays he has been interested in dramatizing efforts to escape oracles and in showing how vain such attempts are. Dramatic situations of this kind lead to pointed and intricate construction. In the *Oedipus Rex,* however, Sophocles takes up the life of his hero after the oracles have been fulfilled, and the vanity he is dramatizing becomes at once more severely simple and more agonizingly terrible. It would have been possible to write a play that dealt with the murder of Laius, the solving of the Sphinx' riddle, and the marriage with Jocasta: can one think of a more grisly and horrible irony than such a play, which would end with the marriage feast and crowning of the new king and husband and son? For Sophocles, in his third period, such a treatment would hold no interest. His Oedipus has no chance to escape, at least not in our sentimental sense of the word "escape"; the play is not like the *Ajax* or the *Antigone* or the *Women of Trachis,* which all hinge on the efforts men make, just too late. Sophocles has passed beyond this simple and Hardy-like kind of irony to a new "ethical" irony: this play is almost the supreme example of the third style, "ethical" and "best." I say "almost" only because it is, in a way, unfinished; it has not the satisfying finality of the *Electra* or the *Philoctetes* or the *Oedipus at Colonus.* We should perhaps note that the plays of the second period all end in moods of frustration or despair; any satisfying compensations that may exist come outside the drama, like the apotheosis of Heracles. The plays of the third period, after the *Oedipus Rex,* all end in happiness and reconciliation, and the satisfying compensations take place within the play. The *Oedipus Rex* lies on the borderline: it seems to end in despair, yet the very vanity of the despair, as we shall see, holds a promise of something more. . . .

The *kairoi* of the *Oedipus Rex,* then, do not lead to Oedipus' doom—for that has already come—but to his tragic recognition of that doom. We may, when we first hear or read the story, think that recognition the worst part of the doom; but a little thought will show us that only by recognizing what he has done can Oedipus ever "escape" that doom. The downfall is the salvation. It is for these reasons that the play does not end in death or crumbling futility, like the ends of Ajax or Creon or, apparently, Heracles. The end of *Oedipus* is inconclusive, at once the most terrible and the most optimistic of Sophocles' plays. I do not know that anyone could have predicted the *Oedipus at*

Colonus, but I think it would not have been difficult to see that Sophocles had to return to the theme. Both he and the reader face the problem of the play's ambiguous conclusion: what happens to Oedipus, and what can happen that will make sense of his life? It is no wonder that the *Oedipus Rex* did not win first prize; its imperfection, perfectly as it has been composed, teases the mind out of existence. One can see in it the defects and the virtues of the single play as opposed to the trilogy.

The action, which the play imitates is, then, only a part of the hero's life: a period of one day.[8] Yet that one day embraces the whole of the hero's life up to that point. Never before has Sophocles had a theme which so perfectly allowed him to play with the contrast between long stretches of human life and the short span of one day. As we shall see, his treatment of Oedipus consists of dramatizing two days out of the life, each coming at the end of a long period of time. The first period is largely empty of incident but happy; the second, coming between exile from Thebes and salvation at Colonus, is largely empty of incident and unhappy.[9] Each of the days dramatized gathers up the whole of the period or periods before it and fills them with meaning—or at least comments on their pointless emptiness. By the time we are through with all the Oedipus plays, we will have seen the story not only of Oedipus, but also of the house of Labdacus, treated with both dramatic and philosophic completeness; at the end of the *Oedipus Rex* we have only dramatic completeness.

As a play the *Oedipus Rex* is perfect in every way, except that it does not satisfy; the mind and the heart cry out for an explanation, for the explanation which the play offers does not satisfy even Oedipus. He may accept his fate at the end, but we do not. His fate is not death —and no one I know thinks that Oedipus ought to die at the end of the play, that such an end would be morally and philosophically and psychologically appropriate. We are not, however, satisfied with the reasons Oedipus gives the chorus for not committing suicide. They may have been his immediate reasons for not killing himself, but they scarcely explain why he must go on living. As long as he lives, both he and the audience must ask Why? Although the *telos* implicit in the *kairos* at the beginning of the play has been reached, the *telos* of his life has not been reached, not in any sense of the word *telos.* More *kairoi* must come before that. What those *kairoi* are we shall see when we come to the *Oedipus at Colonus.* Whatever the nature of that *telos* is, it seems in some way to be supernatural, as the oracles themselves

8 See Driver, pp. 155–156, 208.

9 Although many *kairoi* occur in Oedipus' life before the opening of the play, they are all crowded into a short space of time; for most of those years Oedipus' life is tranquil and happy. Similarly there is considerable episode within the two years or so after the *Oedipus Rex,* yet most of those intervening years are characterized by monotonous suffering.

suggest. No *deus ex machina* is needed here, however; no explanation given in human terms, even if given by a god, would be enough. What Athena tells us in the *Ajax,* and what Heracles tells us in the *Philoctetes,* satisfies us because the problem created by the interplay between character and situation remains human. The problem created by the suffering of Oedipus, however, transcends the human; and so we need an answer in terms beyond the human. That answer the *Oedipus at Colonus* gives—or says is given.

We may now return to the *kairos* at the beginning of the *Oedipus Rex,* in order to trace the *kairoi* that occur in the play. Each one confirms the decision made at the beginning, and each is in natural conformity with the character of the hero. And yet the natural turns out unnaturally. In the opening scene Oedipus reveals himself as a merciful, concerned, kingly, intelligent, and brave man.[10] Before the first scene is over, he will have shown what qualities co-exist with these: a love of truth, revealed in his inexorable ability to ask the most relevant questions in brutally logical sequence; a capacity for indignant anger, shown in the terrible curse he pronounces on the head of the murderer; and a suspicious nature, attendant on his position as king and engendered by the apparently tyrannical source of his authority; for he is not the rightful king—or so he thinks. His anger, if in some ways unreasonable, is not unreasoning. He never does things without a plausible motive, even if it is not the correct one. We can see the correct act, but we are not in his situation, nor have we his character. We must always remember, too, that what we would call the correct decision would lead to a frustration of Apollo's oracle and hence to a destruction of the divine order of the cosmos.

The condition laid down by the oracle which Creon brings from Delphi is the source of Oedipus' next *kairos:* the murderer of Laius must be found and cast out of the country before the sterilizing plague can be cured. Oedipus is polluted by his acts, and religious law required that the punishment for such pollution be exile. His first decision, then, is whether or not to increase the punishment as a means of encouraging citizens to bring in evidence. He decides for the increase, and pronounces his terrible curse. The suffering that he undergoes at the end of the play is thus in large part his own doing. He could have been content with exile.

The question Oedipus next sets out to answer is, Who murdered Laius? By the center of the play his relentless questioning has started

---

10 Of course he is also passionate and impulsive; he allows Creon to relate the Delphic oracles in public, even after the diplomatic Creon suggests that privacy would be better; the decision, generous, frank, noble, yet leads to the increased ferocity of the curse.

certain actions which will lead him to know the murderer's identity—
and his own, though this last is not part of his original intent. The
attendant who escaped from the slaughter at the crossroads has been
tracked down, despite opposition from Teiresias and Jocasta, though
none from Creon. It is to Oedipus' credit, both as man and as king, that
he does not listen to their persuasions to stop or divert the investigation. His suspicion of a conspiracy between Teiresias and Creon is also
a cause of delay in the investigation. He is angry at them for two reasons: first, because, if true, it is a complication of the immediate crisis;
and second, because the threat may be real. Too many critics have accused Oedipus of excessive anger here. I would argue that his anger is
excessive only because we know Creon and Teiresias are innocent.
Oedipus did not know. His position as king is self-achieved, and is thus
subject, as tyrannies always are, to overthrow. What better time for a
revolution than when a crisis puts the government under strain and
allows the malcontents both an occasion and a reason for conspiracy?[11]
. . . Teiresias knows the truth and has every reason to be calm.
Oedipus does not know, and his anger is understandable. Teiresias'
language to Oedipus is no less scornful and savage than that of Oedipus
to Teiresias. Creon, of course, is a logical suspect. Oedipus' anger does
cloud his reason, but the anger is not irrational. There lies the
irony. . . .

The quarrel between Teiresias and Oedipus breeds the quarrel between Creon and Oedipus; the two quarrels lead to the intervention of
Jocasta, whose efforts at reconciliation produce the next *kairos*. Her
attempts to prove that oracles are foolish include the story of the oracle
given to Laius; but instead of allaying Oedipus' suspicions of Teiresias,
it merely shifts them. I say "merely." The shift, however, is of central
importance, for it puts Oedipus' attention on the shepherd who saved
him as a baby and who was the key witness of the murder at the crossroads. He seizes at once on the central point of the story: the question
of whether there was one or more murderers. Jocasta, who does not
know that the shepherd made the murderers plural because he recognized Oedipus in Thebes, is confident that he will disprove Oedipus'
suspicions. It is a nice irony to think that the shepherd recognizes
Oedipus as the murderer, but not as the baby he saved. Had he known
this fact would he have kept silent? Oedipus is partly swayed by
Jocasta's confidence, but insists that the shepherd be sent for. With
that the center of the play is reached, where we find, as we have come
to expect, a great central ode which will illuminate the meaning of the
play. The ode will deal with faith in oracles: it is ironic to think that
Oedipus, who starts with absolute faith in oracles, comes, in the center

---

[11] The same theme turns up in the *Antigone,* where Creon voices the same
suspicious fears. The condition was endemic in Greek political life.

of the play, to lose faith just as they are about to be completely and terribly justified.

The chorus begins with a prayer that destiny (*moira*) will find them pure in all words and deeds. This conventional association of "word" and "deed" (*logos* and *ergon*) is not merely conventional here; Oedipus and Jocasta, by their contempt for oracles, have just been irreverent and impure in word, and yet if the oracle is true, Oedipus will be impure in deed. His verbal doubt of the oracles is itself an impure deed. It is in this dilemma that the chorus is caught. Hence their use of both words, together with "all." They do not, however, merely make a vague wish for absolute purity. Instead they specify the kind of words and deeds they have in mind: those which "lofty-footed laws sanction." The word "lofty-footed" is one of the many words in the ode referring to feet, and we cannot fail to see that they glance at Oedipus, he of the swollen feet. As we shall see, Sophocles plays with both roots in the name Oedipus. The laws the chorus intends are those unwritten and divine laws which Antigone praises, which exist outside of time: "a great god is in them, and he does not grow old" (870–871). These laws are the children of god, not of man, and are not subject, like man, to vicissitude. Oedipus calls himself the child of chance (*tyche*), the essence of random vicissitude; but were he so, the eternal laws could not exist. Before his life is over, or at the moment of its close, we and he learn that he is as much the child of the great god as the lofty-footed laws of which he is a distorted symbol.

The first antistrophe switches subjects abruptly. Now the chorus voices the familiar Greek idea of surfeit-insolence-retribution (*koros, hybris, ate*). Their statement of the idea, which is tailored and condensed to fit the situation, makes sense only when we remember the large idea. Insolence breeds tyranny, they begin. We at once think of the *tyrannus* who is the hero of the play, and who gained his tyranny by an act of insolence (*hybris*): the slaying of Laius and the others at the crossroads. Insolence, surfeited on "many things" (Jebb translates "wealth") that are neither meet nor good, leaps from its height into an abyss of doom, "where it cannot use its useful feet" (875–880). Once again there is a grim play on the name Oedipus. Opposed to the wanton individuality of the tyrant is the rivalry or prudential craft (*palaisma*) which brings good to the city (879–881). The words suggest several things: first, the sterile and dangerous rivalry of Oedipus with Creon and Teiresias; second, the prudent craft, the foresighted counsel, by which a man supplants his adversary. In this second sense there is an ironic glance at both Oedipus and Laius: Laius did try to supplant his rival by a *palaisma;* but Oedipus' supplanting of Laius can scarcely be called either prudent or foresighted. The chorus then opposes to the insolent tyrant their faith in a *prostates:* the word they use is a political term, just as "tyrant" is a political term, though they have more than political meanings in mind. Pericles was a *prostates,* that is, a leader who, by his influence and intelligence, persuaded the city to action. Presumably the chorus means Apollo, who was called *Prostates* in the *Women of Trachis* (209). In calling Oedipus a tyrant, the chorus sees him as something different from the good king who has ruled Thebes for many years. . . .

The second strophe continues the foot image, and blends it with references to hands. "If any man walks haughtily in words or deeds," they begin. The first strophe had opened with the same collocation of words and deeds, but there the word for "deeds" had been *erga;* here it is *chersin,* "hands." The word "hands" here equals "deeds," but is something more than equal as well, for it is one of the key words of the play. The second strophe continues to echo the first as it mentions "reverence" (*sebon*) and "destiny" (*moira*). May an evil destiny seize such a man, the chorus prays. The prayer is ironic, for Oedipus' evil destiny has already come on him. . . . The chorus concludes by asking, In such a world, why should we dance (895–896)? The form of the question is artistically daring, for in the word "dance" (*choreuein,* to be a chorus) Sophocles reminds the audience that what it is experiencing is only art. Yet the image is not a sterile trick, like the comparison of the moon to a sigma: as Knox, following Jebb, brilliantly points out (p. 47), "If the oracle and the truth do not coincide the very performance of the tragedy has no meaning, for tragedy is itself a form of worship of the gods." The chorus represents tragedy, art, order, comprehension, religion; as an *orchestra* it is a symbol for perfect form.

Given their dilemma, the chorus makes the terrible but necessary choice: they ask that the oracles, no matter how horrible, be true, for they prefer a universe of fearful symmetry to one of fearful chaos. The wish is pure Greek. . . .

At this point Jocasta re-enters. This little scene of thirteen lines exemplifies Sophoclean originality at its dramatic and ethical best. The myth requires no such scene, and were it not here, who would have conceived of it? Although the great central ode points primarily at Oedipus, it includes Jocasta too. She herself has displayed signs of tyranny and insolence, not only in speaking publicly, but also in attempting to dominate her husband, the ruler of the state. Her words are blasphemous. In the closing lines of the ode the chorus pledges never again to visit the temple of the gods, for their worship is fading, oracles decline. Our expectation and our attention are on Oedipus; when Jocasta enters, we experience both dramatic disappointment and surprise. Yet she is a worthy surrogate for Oedipus. She who had left blasphemously and scornfully returns apprehensively and religiously. She had left doubting Apollo; she returns praying to him. Her change of attitude is complex, for she has not abandoned her old theory of living at random: she begins "The thought has come to me to visit the temples of the gods" (912). The word is the same word the chorus had used. They who were faithful pledge not to pray; she who doubts begins to pray. Jocasta's offhand mode of address scarcely shows true reverence. Yet she is concerned; Oedipus is so distraught that, as she had shaken his faith, so he has shaken hers. She prays to Apollo, who happens to be the nearest god at hand—an ironic example and rebuke of her theory that life should be lived at random. What she prays for is a solution to their problems; she does not see that she herself will bring that solution into being—indeed, she has already started it working. . . .

In the midst of Jocasta's prayer, as if in answer to it, the messenger from Corinth enters. He is the bearer of joyous tidings that turn out to be dark and grim. We may contrast the simple economy with which Sophocles uses the device of the messenger here and its complicated use in the *Women of Trachis*. The upshot of the messenger's news is to create a new *kairos* for Oedipus. Now he must find out the truth about his birth. The irony of the shift in aim is dramatized by the coming of the attendant who escaped the slaughter at the crossroads, now a shepherd in the outskirts of the country. Oedipus had sent for him in order to ask questions about the death of Laius; because of the peripety caused by the messenger from Corinth, Oedipus never once asks him about the killing of Laius. We should note that the messenger and the shepherd are tied together again, as the Corinthian returns the baby, now a man, that the other had given him years ago. Oedipus forgets his original aim. The irony of the forgetfulness lies in the fact that Oedipus could have answered the first question without answering the second. Had he done so, as he originally set out to do, he could have successfully carried out his curse on himself and been exiled—but he would not have known that he had fulfilled the oracle, murdering his father and marrying his mother. Once again the pressure of the moment drives him to take a course different from the one he planned, as it did at Delphi when he first consulted the oracle. Then the excitement and fear had impelled him to seek the truth further; here again they impel him. . . .

In point of fact, he cannot discover the story of his birth without finding out the murderer. Though his original aim is forgotten, it is not left undone. A true king to the last, he does save his country, most truly his country when he is no longer king. Once again we see that the end of an action is implicit in the critical moment, the *kairos*. The decision he makes in that moment is purely in character. The man who challenged the Sphinx would not quail at the mystery of his birth. . . .

The news brought by the messenger from Corinth leads Oedipus to a new *kairos:* when he finally learns the terrible truth of his past— not, however, of his present or future—he rushes into the house to kill what is already a corpse. The decision to kill Jocasta is for Oedipus his utmost moment of madness and blindness. Only when he sees her dead body, the *telos* of her "action," does he come to his senses. At that moment he confronts the last great *kairos* of his life as king: what to do in the light of his blinding knowledge? Even had Oedipus found Jocasta alive and slain her, he would still have this *kairos;* her suicide spares him the unforgivable sin of slaying his mother, for I do not think the Greeks or we would judge that murder as sympathetically as we judge the slaying of his father Laius.[12]

The agony of this last great *kairos* is unique and incomprehensible to all men but Oedipus. What should a man in his position do, standing there over the corpse of his dead mother-wife and knowing that he has killed his father? What action would be appropriate? Tears? Cries? Madness (if that be an action)? Suicide? None of these seems right. Oedipus makes his last and his best decision. He blinds himself. He does not voice the typical cry of the Sophoclean hero caught in a dilemma: What shall I do? What answer could anyone give, even if anyone were present? Later the chorus will wish that Oedipus had never found out his fate—apparently it regards the "evil destiny" that has befallen their tyrant as too great, despite its wish in the great central ode. . . . The act of blinding himself is the most perfect act, the most perfect decision, the most perfect answer Oedipus could make. His last free act turns out to be the fulfillment of Teiresias' prophecy. The verbal links of light and dark, of seeing and not seeing, of blindness and vision, that make up the key cluster of the play are here caught up and unified in one act. Yet the appropriateness of the act is not only dramatic and symbolic, but also philosophic, psychological, moral, and legal. Oedipus has been hurt by an outside force, and he is entitled to strike back. The law of action and reaction, of *tisis* (retribution) and *adikia* (injustice), as pronounced by Anaximander entitles him to; and that law is standard Greek morality and standard Greek religion. . . .

With irony that is not merely irony, Oedipus puts out his eyes. The rest of the play deals with the reasons and the consequences of that act. The writer of the ancient *hypothesis* saw the triple centrality of the act when he wrote:

> The heart (head) of the drama is the knowledge Oedipus gains of his private ills (evils, pains), the gouging out of his eyes, and the death of Jocasta by a noose.

It is knowledge, *gnosis,* that is the heart of the play. Oedipus acquires that knowledge in a blinding flash of action when he gouges out his eyes with the brooch from Jocasta's dress; the choice of weapon probably left his dead mother-wife naked before eyes that had looked too long on that they should not see. But a knowledge that is only dramatic would not be Greek; there must be a word, a *logos,* for this deed; and in the scenes that follow we shall see how much of what Oedipus knows dramatically he knows intellectually. We shall not, of

---

[12] Nor so sympathetically as we judge Orestes' slaying of Clytemnestra. After all, Jocasta is not only mother but wife.

course, find any such explicit philosophical position as I have been advancing in these pages; Oedipus understands more by his dramatic act than he does by verbal discussion of the motives and significance of the act. As Wittgenstein remarks, "What *can* be shown *cannot* be said."[13]

The messenger now describes the blind Oedipus as helpless, without strength. He has lost not only his sight, but also that courageous strength that enabled him to fulfill his doom by slaying Laius, breaking down Jocasta's door, and gouging out his eyes. The chorus says, ironically, that it cannot bear to look at him, and yet there is much that it would ask and learn and see. At this point there begins that accumulated use of the word *daimon* that Mr. Bowra has analyzed.[14] The use is ambiguous; the word comes in naturally and conventionally enough, intending to explain what has happened; it does not explain really, but it is better than no word at all. The ending of the *Women of Trachis* will not work here, nor will that of any other play. There is no surviving counter-hero, like Odysseus, to point up the exemplary hero's error, for Creon cannot fill that role. There is no painfully unrelieved and bleakly aging life that drags itself out towards a weary and useless wisdom; Oedipus' life is too intense and consuming and overwhelming to go out with a whimper. Nor is the mythic sanctification of Oedipus of the same divine and grand order as that of Heracles; Sophocles cannot let it operate as comically ironic compensation. Instead, the *Oedipus Rex* gathers up strands and elements from all the previous plays. Ajax had said that he must either live well or die well, and had killed himself because he thought that he could not live well. Oedipus does not kill himself, and, though apparently in the greatest disgrace and shame and pollution, becomes noble. Sophocles changes his solution to the problem from suicide to suffering. Jocasta, like Deianeira, commits suicide on her bridal bed—but Oedipus, unlike Heracles, is profoundly affected. His life, like that of Creon, will continue for a long time, but will end not in mere and useless wisdom but in some kind of sanctification—another resemblance to the *Women of Trachis*. Heracles, however, was the son of Zeus, and his doom, his full doom, brings him to heaven; Oedipus is mortal, and his doom is not apotheosis. Hence *Oedipus Rex* ends with every character's having a reason for blasphemy; yet no character does blaspheme. The play ends on a calm and classic note, and is both perfect and unfinished. When the chorus asks Oedipus why he gouged out his eyes, he does not use the word *daimon;* instead he says (1329–1333):

These things are from Apollo, my friends, from Apollo, who is the accomplisher of all my evil, evil woes; yet no other struck them with his own hand, but only my wretched self.

13 *Tractatus Logico-Philosophicus*, 4.1212.
14 C. M. Bowra, *Sophoclean Tragedy* (Oxford, 1947), pp. 179 ff.

No translation can do justice to the artful ambiguity of syntax here. The word *autocheir* is a kind of hyperbaton, dramatically accounted for perhaps by Oedipus' distraught condition. It means "by one's own hand," but has as subordinate meaning "one who kills himself" and "relative." The little word *nin* means "he, she, it" or "them"; presumably here it refers to "eyes." Although Oedipus has turned his own hand on himself, he is not a suicide; although two relatives have struck blows at him, literal or figurative, it is not they but he himself who has put out his eyes; although it is his hand that struck the blinding blow, the situation derives from Apollo and the gods. To this paradoxical profundity, the heart of the play's explanation, Sophocles has been driven; the *logos* that will make explicit the dramatic act of blinding can be no more logical than this. If the sentence makes sense, then the play is a philosophic as well as a dramatic success; if it does not, then the play is a philosophic failure, or at least is philosophically incomplete, though it does not therefore become a dramatic failure. If it both makes sense and does not, then the play is what it is: the greatest dramatic statement ever made of the *aporia* which Sophocles sees as ingrained in the human situation: not how can man know his destiny, for oracles can tell him that; not how can he escape his destiny, for he cannot; but what use is the knowledge either before or after that destiny has been fulfilled? Closely related is the question, What connection is there between the usefulness of the knowledge and the waste of suffering life? If the end, the *telos*, of an action is implicit at the critical moment, then the interval between the *kairos* and the *telos* serves no function. The whole of Oedipus' life, except for two days, is wasted irrelevance. The process of the action must take place in time, because that is the dimension in which man lives; but the passage of time is irrelevant to the inevitability of the end once the *kairos* has been reached. It is the sense of this waste that constitutes the essence of Sophoclean tragedy.

The *Oedipus Rex* ends, like a great Platonic dialogue, in an illumination that comes from perceiving the difficulty of the problem. Oedipus was in an *aporia,* a place with "no exit"; he created an exit by his act of self-blinding, which is simultaneously word and deed, purifying word and deed, that is, a deed whose rationale is implicit, a conception become act at the moment of conception. It is the power the gods have. The difference is that the gods create by their divine conceptions; for a man to achieve such a divine conception can only be destructive. Yet when Oedipus blinds himself, his act is not a sign of frustrated rage, but of logical perfection and fulfillment of both character and destiny.

A discussion of the motives for the act takes up the next part of the play; it cannot really explain the act—that explains itself—for it is an attempt to explain the whole of this blended word and deed, this act and conception, in terms of a part of the whole, in terms of the *logos* alone. But for Sophocles, unlike Plato, any ultimate explanation must be dramatic—that is, both word and deed. To my mind, Oedipus' blinding of himself is, next to Samson's "suicide," the greatest single theatrical and poetic act in literature; in it idea, agent, and objective correlative coincide.

Oedipus' explanation of his act is, then, unsatisfactory: "I could never have looked on my parents." Do we really believe that Oedipus deliberated and then acted on these grounds in that death-filled bedroom? Or were not the two simultaneous? He reveals the mystic joint responsibility of god and man in his cry about Apollo and his own hand; it is something that neither he nor the chorus fully understands. Nothing further is said about that cry; nothing more could be said here and now. Either the statement is the profoundest truth ever expressed or it is only an ingenious paradox; but Sophocles will say no more here. For him to have done so might have made the play philosophically explicable—though I doubt it—but it would then have ceased to be tragedy. Almost two hundred lines remain of the play, a huge proportion when we think of the shortness of Greek plays. Of the *Oedipus Rex* it is nearly one seventh. Why, if the blinding and the cry are the climax, does the play go on? Is Sophocles "bungling" again, as some think he did in the *Ajax,* the *Antigone,* and the *Women of Trachis,* failing to see what was good drama and good theater? To begin with, I think that no one could tolerate ending on so shrill and anguished an edge, for Oedipus has not yet fallen from his tyrannical height into the abyss of doom which the chorus prayed for. Unless we start with a definition of art which makes its end sensation, we must agree that an audience is better off leaving a theater calm than distraught, and that Aristotle was right when he said that the purpose of tragedy was to purge men of pity and fear. Classic art always ends on a quiet note; and it is in the *Oedipus Rex* that Sophocles begins to be truly and perfectly a tragic artist. . . . Oedipus and the chorus must both grow calm, even if all passion is not spent. To achieve this end a variety of incident is needed, all of it domestic and in a minor key. Sophocles provides that variety, all of it natural and consequential to the main action: we have, after the lyric interchange of Oedipus and the chorus, the interview with Creon, the farewell to his daughters, and finally his departure from the stage, to go for the third time into the house. The incidents follow a line of decreasing tension, as Oedipus declines from his superhuman agony and descends into a world that is "normal," that is, in which he must live.

First, Oedipus asks to be cast out of the land, in accordance with the oracle and his curse; he describes himself as the most hateful to the gods of all mortals. Yet he will not be cast out, in violation of the oracle and his own curse; and there is no evidence that he is hated by the gods. He has done horrible things, but against his will: it was his fate, his *moira,* and *moira* transcends morality. The gods do not blame

Oedipus for his deeds; they only said he would perform them. The chorus, less humane than the gods, then wishes it had never known him, never known the twofold savior of their city and themselves. Oedipus has solved both problems: the Sphinx and the plague. After the first they praised him; after the second, they blame.

He then curses the herdsman who saved his life; both he and the chorus overlook the virtues of what they condemn. The herdsman, innocent, fearful, pitiful, could twice have prevented Oedipus' fate, once all of it and once half. He saved the baby, and then, years later, refused to identify him as Laius' murderer at the coronation and wedding. Oedipus then wishes that he had died, and the chorus agrees. . . .

Oedipus next talks to his children, and voices a sentiment that recalls our earliest extant play by Sophocles, when Ajax makes his suicidal farewell to his son. There (553) Ajax said that the sweetest life consisted in not thinking.

The sentiment is violently unGreek, a denial of the beauty and efficacy of the *logos*. Here, in a similar suicidal mood, and about to say farewell to his children, Oedipus repeats the idea (1390); it is the nadir of his depression just as his "decision" to kill Jocasta had been the nadir of his madness and mental blindness.

It is sweet for our thoughts to dwell outside the world of suffering.

He is, of course, referring to his now eyeless mind, no longer struck by the sight of horrible reality; but in a larger sense such voluntary isolation in the cave of self is a denial of the *logos;* we may think of Plato's myth of the cave, and the pleasant ignorance of those within, pleasant but deadly. It does not matter that Oedipus thinks such an existence sweet, for it is impossible for man to live so. In suffering is wisdom, Aeschylus had taught Sophocles and Athens; ignorance may bring sweetness but never wisdom. The wish for things to be otherwise resembles the frequent choral laments of Greek tragedy, in which the singers wish to be birds, and to fly away from the horrors of existence. But such a wish is sentimentalism; and Oedipus, like Sophocles, is ultimately no sentimentalist, no matter how tempting that weak desire is. He comes back to his senses when he recognizes his predicament and asks again to be cast out of the city. Cast me out or kill me, he begs; the alternatives are confused, as he has not yet fully recovered his mental powers; he seems to regard both alternatives as means of escape. He will not kill himself—we can know that now as he must know it. That moment passed over Jocasta's corpse. The closing part of the play, in addition to allowing for the quiet end which is the essence of classic art, also allows Oedipus to recognize that violent death is not for him, that his life, like the piece of classic art it is, requires a calm close. He has not yet recognized this truth, but it will become clearer to him during the next two scenes, with Creon and his children.

Creon now enters, and Oedipus repeats his request for exile. That he does not ask to be slain is a small sign of his growing recovery. Creon refuses his request. He, who has every reason to obey the gods' behests, now argues that since the gods' behests have led them to this predicament, it will be best to learn anew what course they ought to follow. Though they now know the whole truth, they do not know enough, for they know only the whole truth of the past, not of the future. Oedipus then requests proper burial for Jocasta; his concern contrasts with Heracles' callous oblivion of Deianeira. He repeats his desire for exile, to Cithaeron, as a fitting place for his expiatory age. There is something he begins to know—note how he grows in wisdom and calm together—that neither disease nor anything else can destroy him (1455–1456). The use of "disease" (*noson*) may again remind us of Heracles in the *Women of Trachis*. The words are prophetic of his fate, and of the *Oedipus at Colonus*. Yet Oedipus does not express hope, for he says that he had been saved from death for some terrible evil (*deino kako*). The language is ambiguous: the word for "evil" is pessimistic; yet the word for "terrible" means both "strange" and "terrible," and suggests that what happens to him will be appropriate for his strange and terrible life. That the world should be a congruent propriety would, for a Greek, be a good thing. Heracles' life, we remember, had been congruent to his character. Despite the many technical differences between the two plays, we can clearly see a thematic development. Oedipus ends this cryptic vision by saying "let my fate (*moira*) go where it will." His thoughts have turned from Jocasta, the dead, to himself, the living dead (*thneskon esothen*, 1457); and will end with the living, his "children." Even here we see the progress towards calmness and recovered sanity. The three centers of attention correspond to the three closing scenes. He continues, despite his new knowledge, to think of them as his children, and to call them such. I do not think that anyone will blame his assertion of the relationship: it is, for all its monstrosity, the only way we can conceive of them, and he remains in our eyes primarily their father. In the scene that follows he shows both his tenderness and his realism; he predicts their future life for them, a life of agony and solitude. Like Teiresias, the blind Oedipus sees clearly now, for such is what their life turns out to be.

Creon, who had started by ordering him out of the sun, because of his pollution, now more tenderly urges him into the house. The sun is sacred to Apollo, and Oedipus can, for all his pollution, never escape that eye of God. He obeys Creon, and in that act of obedience shows his new mood of acceptance. The act of blinding himself had been an instantaneous and impulsive deliberation; the act of yielding to Creon is a resigned and reluctant deliberation. Yet, as we shall see, resignation and acceptance are not the solution to his problem; they will only serve to pass that waste stretch of time between the two ends of his life, the *tele* that are dramatized on this day and on his last day. Oedipus says that his obedience is not pleasant. The loss of his kingdom and his kingship, though not of his kingliness, which would be so great in the eyes of most men, is compressed into this one bald line. To it Creon replies in a sentence that contains one of Sophocles' favorite ironic words (1516):

> All things are beautiful in their season.

The word is *kairos*, critical moment or season; it picks up Oedipus' advice to his daughters (1513), in which he bade them live as *kairos* allowed. Given the doctrine of *kairos* and *telos* as advanced in these pages, which I have drawn from Aristotle's remark in Book III of the *Nicomachean Ethics,* we can appreciate the magnificent irony of Creon's words. Oedipus' life has been a series of *kairoi;* would Creon call them "beautiful"? Would anyone call them so? Yet before Sophocles is through with his own life, he will have answered that Creon's statement is true. Oedipus' life has a kind of beauty and rightness just because his character and his destiny are perfectly congruent. Although his destiny, up till now, has been monstrous, it is not yet over; and only the *telos* will enable us to judge whether it was happy or not.

Oedipus has, however, violated the *moirai* of others besides himself, those of his children. For these violations he must pay, and will, and his children will be the agents of that exaction, as we shall see in the *Oedipus at Colonus*. Their mere existence is a part of his payment, and in the closing scenes of the *Oedipus Rex,* their tender and harrowing separation is the beginning of that payment. "Do not take them from me," he pleads to Creon. And Creon replies, "You must not expect to be master; the mastery that was yours has not followed you through your life." Except for the choral close, these are the last words spoken in the play. They remind us of Oedipus' fall from glory and power. The reminder is ironic, however, for had he ever had mastery, this child of chance, this creation of destiny, this self-made man whose self was doom?

The choral ending has disturbed many critics, who find it flat and unworthy of so great a play. The chorus concludes (1528–1530):

> Let no one call any mortal happy while he is fixing his eyes on the last day which one sees, until he has crossed the boundary of life experiencing no pain.

This is the last time that Sophocles will use the sentiment either to close or open an extant play. It is all he can say here; his dramatic thought, and his life, have gone no farther, and must wait for time to bring his *telos,* the *Oedipus at Colonus*. But that *telos* was implicit in the decision to write the *Oedipus Rex*. Oedipus has not consciously denied the principle of vicissitude laid down by Athena in the first of our extant plays, the *Ajax;* but his life has been both an attempt to escape the truth of that law, and a pursuit of its fulfillment. One day has produced reversal for him, and a more terrible vicissitude never occurred in one day. Yet the germ of hope is present, for Oedipus does not die, like Ajax or Heracles, but will live for some kind of sanctification. We can see in his life the promise of those later comedies which we are about to examine, the *Electra* and the *Philoctetes*. Yet on this one day nothing has happened, no action has occurred to bring about the vicissitude. All that brought it about is knowledge, a knowledge that Oedipus had all along, both before and after the reality. The reality itself had happened long ago, on a day—whichever day it is that one decides was the ultimate and initial *kairos*. There remains ahead of Oedipus that waste expanse of suffering which comes between this day and his last. In the *Antigone* Sophocles regards that waste time as the most terrible and tragic of man's sufferings; he will change that view by the end of his own life, in a play which is to him what the *Tempest* was to Shakespeare—though I should say that the appropriateness of the *Oedipus at Colonus* is more perfect than that of the *Tempest*, for it comes as the last play of a long life.

William Arrowsmith

From "The Criticism of Greek Tragedy." In *Tulane Drama Review*, Vol. III, No. 3 (March 1959). Reprinted by permission of the publisher.

My purpose here is to do a little superstitious rapping in the hope of persuading into existence something a little different in the kind of criticism we normally bring to bear upon Greek tragedy. If this seems pretentious, blame the subject in part: Greek tragedy requires, I think, a formidable apparition by way of an adequate criticism and certainly a larger one than I can summon up, though also a larger one than presently attends the scene. What I want to do is to outline the nature of the job to be done, as I see it, and to discuss what seems to me inadequate in both the traditional and contemporary ways of writing about Greek tragedy. I think I see—though vaguely—the kind of criticism to which Greek tragedy points, though I recognize that this may turn out to be merely a mirage made up to answer imaginary needs, or an old familiar ghost in a new murk, or even something that concerns no one but students of Greek tragedy. Whatever the results, I am convinced that the need is real; that we have reached some kind of impasse in the study of Greek tragedy in which neither the older nor the newer criticism, nor any compromise between them, is really adequate; and further, that the need is general. . . .[31]

. . . In the last years it is abundantly clear that criticism has returned to classical scholarship; if the New Criticism as such is not yet, in classics, the heavy industry it has become in English studies, its pressure is clearly visible and especially among the younger generation. The direct influence of the critics themselves upon classical studies has mostly been oblique, and, more often than not, unfortunate: Francis Fergusson's able but unconvincing piece on the *Oedipus Rex* is some kind of exception, extraordinary in its perceptivity, but crippled in its too great reliance upon theories of the ritual origins of tragedy. And neither Kenneth Burke's strange essay on the *Oresteia* nor Edmund Wilson's perversion of the *Antigone* provides reliable models. But the New Criticism is writ large in Goheen's study of the imagery of the *Antigone,* diffused throughout Kitto's *Greek Tragedy* and Lattimore's superb introduction to his translation of the *Oresteia,* or Owen's fine commentary on the *Iliad,* and everywhere visible in the spate of dissertations which study single plays or single metaphors or the master-tropes of tragedy, and in the insistent emphasis upon the key terms of the New Critics: irony, ambiguity, symbol, tone, image, texture, formal structure and myth. . . .[33]

Up to now the most conspicuous failure of both the traditional and the new critics in respect to Greek tragedy has been the failure to realize turbulence: turbulence of experience, turbulence of morality in the process of getting made, and the turbulence of ideas under dramatic test. If any one charge can be brought against the older criticism, it would be, I think, that it has seemed to ask too little of Greek tragedy, and asking so little, has rarely discovered much. Its crucial failure has come at the point where all criticism is finally tested: the ability to transfer complex experience from one period or language to another, and to get the substance of that experience—its turbulence as well as its final order—into language. This is, of course, in the end, impossible, but it is the ideal by which we measure the adequacy of any interpretative criticism. Where the older criticism failed was in the deeper skills of the very humanity it professed, the point where passion is used to make the experience from which any great image of humanity, like the Greek one, is made. Intensely obsessed with history and[34] politics, the traditional criticism failed to show how history and politics got into tragedy and what they did there in relation to the humanity of the heroes; concerned with man and his destiny, it could never quite conjure up the complex reality of experience and suffering that in the Greek plays gives human passion its meaning; committed to the task of clarity, it failed on the whole to remove that dense patina of stiffness and strangeness and austerity that makes Greek tragedy so formidable to our first impressions, or translated it into sentimental commonplaces and limp passions.

Who, after all, is really stirred by the standard interpretations of the *Antigone*—that tidy passion of a perfect heroine caught up on the gods' errand and hindered by a brutal Creon, a conforming Ismene, and a dunderheaded chorus with an inexplicable gift of tongues? And who believes the fashionable reverse, with its stubborn and presumptuous Antigone, its tragic Creon and its misunderstood Ismene? These interpretations are, to my mind, not credible because they so clearly violate the emotional experience of the play or reduce its difficulties to the vanishing-point. What has not gotten into them is the play's real turbulence and complexity and what they express is rather the superficial order the play throws up as its terms or its field, not its subject or solution. What is missing is what, to my mind, the play insists upon in both action and character: the way in which Antigone, trying to uphold a principle beyond her own, or human, power to uphold, gradually empties that principle in action, and then, cut off from her humanity by her dreadful heroism, rediscovers herself and love in the loneliness of her death; not the opposition between Antigone and Creon, but the family resemblance which joins them in a common doom; not great heroism justified by great principles, but conduct in the fateful grip of principles, making out of courage and love a deeper principle altogether. And if you look to the *Oedipus Rex* or the *Agamemnon* or the *Bacchae,* it seems to me you find the same impoverishment: what is real or turbulent in the life of those plays is for the most part expelled, either because the critic has let his own principles of order usurp the play, or because his own experience is unequal to it, or because he refuses the act of criticism once it gets near the difficult edge of experience. How many interpretations of the *Oedipus Rex,* for instance, have come to grief on the fruitless quest for a tragic flaw that will justify the hero's suffering simply in order that Aristotle be justified. How commonly the cry of botching is raised against Euripides because his plays refuse to conform to the critic's expectations of proper organic structure. And how little of the full turbulence of the *Orestes* or *Bacchae*—those great pitiless mirrors of the terrible political and social desperation of late fifth-century Hellas—does our criticism[35] get, largely because we ask so much less of tragedy than it requires.

Thanks to the New Criticism, we can hope to see the turbulence of language and rhetoric restored to tragedy, for the New Critics are nothing if not keen-nosed where verbal subtlety and density are concerned. And we have, I think, everything to hope for from the thorough examination of the rhetorical habits of Greek tragedy. But I sometimes wonder whether a keen nose for metaphor, irony or ambiguity is much to the point when the spoor is as old and crossed as that of Greek tragedy. It is, for instance, extremely difficult in fifth-century literature to distinguish between metaphor that is genuinely fresh and metaphor that has hardened into idiom or *cliché;* we simply do not possess the linguistic evidence that might allow us to tell them apart. How fresh, for instance, are those yoke and ship images which run like master-tropes through all three tragedians? Or are these simply the metaphorical idiom of an agricultural and seafaring people? The answer, of course, lies in a desperately difficult tact, but that tact comes far harder in Greek and Latin than it does in a living literature like English where we understand stress and tone as we never can in Greek. And the chances are high, of course, that tact will disappear before the critic's drive for conceptual consistency: I know of at least one treatment of the symbolism of the *Oresteia* where the interpretation derived more from the itch for conceptual rigor in the imagery than from the emotional experience of the play. And this risk seems to me particularly high for the New Criticism in its academic setting, where the old insistence upon methodology and the student's necessary economies with complexity combine to harden method into mere formula.

I would not, of course, like the consciousness of risk to damage the enterprise: we badly need in Greek tragedy just that refinement of rhetoric which has been the success of the New Criticism. We need to know, for instance, just how those *sententiae* with which Greek tragedy is so lavish and which so embarrass modern producers of Greek plays, arise from the action; the structure of *stichomythia,* that brisk staccato exchange of single lines for up to a hundred lines at a time, is badly in need of work; I suspect that the relation between metaphor and dance-figures is crucially important; we know very little about irony in tragedy, so little that the tone of whole scenes and even whole plays is in question; the language itself, with its curious alternation between stiff archaism and colloquial speech, its habits of rhetorical movement, from the big jaw-breaking, piled-up compounds of Aeschylus to the deceptive simpleness of Euripides, is still *terra incognitia;* and I suspect that we have barely started to do the work required by the choral lyrics. Beyond these jobs, it is my personal conviction that the[36] study of tragedy would enormously benefit from a shift in perspective; we need to question, that is, our tacit assumption that Greek tragedy is staged in a religious context or represents a kind of collective worship, for the assumption vitally affects interpretation. And it seems to me that nothing but chaos can come from the fashionable notion that because Greek tragedy begins in ritual, its structure is therefore ritual dramatized, its hero a ritual scapegoat, and its action a shadow play of the death of the *Eniautos-daimon* or god of the year. The more I read of Greek tragedy, that is, the more I am impressed with its very distance from its ritual origins and its stubborn refusal to behave as honest ritual should. And there is something violently improbable about an image of the Greek theatre which does the kind of damage done by Gilbert Murray's recanted theory of its ritual elements and more recently by Francis Fergusson in his study of the *Oedipus.*

If we require an idea of the Greek tragic theatre at all, it seems to me that the clue might best be taken from the very charge of rhetoric so persistently brought against tragedy, and against Euripides in particular ever since the time of Schlegel. Over and over again, that is, the late fifth-century tragedy seems to suggest as its informing image a theatre shaped more by the law-court than by the altar. In this theatre, the *agon* is viewed essentially as a trial, and the characters, with all the tricks of sophistic rhetoric, put their cases in opposed speeches—often of identical length, as though timed by the waterclock of the Athenian dikastery. The audience in this theatre sits as jurors, not merely a panel of five hundred jurors, but the full *Heliaea,* the sovereign judicial assembly (*ekklesia*). No appeal, no matter how emotional, is debarred, and each character in his plea speaks with the formal passion of a man whose life and fortunes hang upon his words. But it is a formal and rhetorical passion, below which we can glimpse, as the jury must, the personal passion and the real motives glozed by the rhetoric and often exposed in action. Such a theatre, of course, is most appropriate to Euripides, but in some degree, I think, to Sophocles also, especially in the later plays. I find tentative confirmation of this not merely in the number of Greek tragedies which openly stage formal trial scenes, but in the very structure of Euripidean drama: its persistent avoidance of the single hero in favor of the *agon* of two chief characters—Pentheus vs. Dionysus, Phaedra vs. Hippolytus, Orestes vs. Menelaus, Ion vs. Creusa—and the corresponding division of so many plays into two almost disparate actions; the flat assertion of the intention to make a formal plea; and, most important, the constant impression of the plays as problem plays in which the judgment is never asserted, but left, as it were, to the audience of jurors. If they understand the play, they make the right decision, or better, understand that no moral[37] decision is relevant because the problems are beyond the reach of moral judgment, i.e. are both tragic and true. If this is correct, it is understandable why the constant imposition upon Euripides of Aristotelian structure and the notion of a religious theatre so regularly distort him. I throw this suggestion out, not as a developed thesis, but merely as a hint. For it seems to me that in the study of tragedy, as in almost any other human study, the discoveries come in that slight shift of perspective which we get when we examine those prejudices and assumptions which are so close to habit that we are almost unaware of them. And both our almost unconscious Aristotelianism and our deep assumption that Greek tragedy is finally religious tragedy are habits which I think need severe scrutiny by any serious critic of Greek drama.

The last charge which I should like to bring against the New Criticism is related to just this refusal to examine one's oldest habits. It is finally full interpretation of the plays and the tragedians that we want, and I find it puzzling that the newer criticism of Greek tragedy so seldom undertakes the full job. This may be modesty, but I suspect it is the old illusion of objectivity in fancy dress; and between *Quellenforschungen* and metaphor-snooping, both uprooted from the values they are intended to discover or reinforce, I can see very little difference. It is not merely that the New Critics have failed to take up the job of full interpretation, however, that I find distressing, but the fact that their analyses proceed more from the habit of old interpretation than the fresh act. I am not by this proposing that the New Critics should make their fortunes by systematically inverting all traditional criticism, but that analysis, wherever possible, should free itself from the immense authority of the standard interpretations. A book I admire, Goheen's analysis of the imagery of the *Antigone,* originally written as a dissertation and suffering the handicaps of that impossible genre, ably illustrates just how much the New Critics have to offer in enriching our criticism of tragedy. But unless I am mistaken, Goheen's close analysis is subtly hindered by the authority of the nineteenth-century *Antigone,* whose shape guides the analysis where it needs to go, but not where it might have gone were its destination a little less certain. This is not slyness, of course, but the necessarily blinkered gaze of good conviction: you look where you are going, not askance. But the one metaphor Mr. Goheen overlooks—the metaphor of alienation, Antigone as *metic* or peregrine—a casual sport so far as his theory is concerned, seems to me the one metaphor that most illuminates the key word of the play—*philia* or love. Habit is hard to shed, of course, but in the case of Greek tragedy where critical habit has hardened into cultural habit, I think it is crucial to any hope of a fresh and exacting criticism.[38]

In this connection one point deserves mention. Greek tragedy is, *par excellence,* a sacred cow, even more sacred, I suspect, than Shakespeare, since it is seldom produced or else produced via the atrocious medium of Mr. Robinson Jeffers and Broadway; and most students get introduced to it in the killing atmosphere of reverential hush that attends the reading of any classic in our general humanities courses. Worse, fewer and fewer literary men read Greek nowadays or read it with sufficient security to challenge the scholars on their own ground, as Goethe challenged Schlegel and Matthew Arnold challenged Newman with enormously fruitful results. And in scholarship, as I suggested earlier, unconscious timidity in the face of the accumulated judgments of dead scholars is a deep critical habit. In evidence of this attitude of blind deference to Greek tragedy, let me cite the production not so long ago on Broadway of two Greek plays by a modern Greek repertory troupe: night after night, audiences and dramatic critics, unable to understand a word of the productions, but deeply impressed with the performance of their cultural duties, willfully applauded on the curious assumption that Greek tragedy is mostly gesture anyway, and that a modern Greek company, by virtue of being Greek, somehow must possess the secrets of ancient Greek tragedy. Against adulation like this, it may be beyond the power of criticism to help, and the critic himself may be insensibly drawn into the work of justification rather than criticism. But it needs to be pointed out that we are in real danger of taking over almost intact the canon of Greek tragedy which the nineteenth century established. Who, after all, except classical scholars, now reads any Aeschylus except the *Oresteia* and *Prometheus*, any Sophocles except the Theban plays, and what Euripides besides the *Alcestis, Medea, Hippolytus* and *Bacchae?* I am not, of course, suggesting that these are not great plays, but that the canonizing of them into a cultural monument damages the chosen eleven as much as the excluded tragedies.

Worse, the difficulty is not merely that we have adopted an old taste, but the habits that accompany that taste as well, and especially the nineteenth-century habit of making Sophocles the norm, if not the ideal, of tragedy—a habit which has done great damage to Aeschylus and almost irreparable damage to Euripides. It is no accident, for instance, that the favored plays of Euripides are precisely those which appear to meet the standards of so-called Aristotelian structure, that is, the "organic structure" which critics think they find in Sophocles. Against this tendency, I can only argue that it botches Sophocles as badly as Euripides, and that it cuts off our access to a power in Euripides that meant very little to the nineteenth century but everything to the twentieth—I mean that part of Euripides that is concerned with political desperation, the corruption of power, and the corrosion of the civilized virtues[39] into a set of specious slogans for demagogic consumption. We need not only the *Bacchae,* but the *Hecuba,* the *Heracles,* the *Orestes, Electra, Supplices* and *Trojan Women*—all plays in which we should sense the full turbulence of one of the very greatest of dramatists in a context that very easily becomes our own. But this means production as well as criticism, since nothing hinders the critic's right perception of a play more than the perpetual unavailability of his material in living form. At the moment, I can think of no greater service to Greek tragedy than the regular production of those plays that lie outside the canon and are so commonly regarded as undramatic, and particularly the plays of Euripides, whose structure is censured by critics who have never seen them performed. But such a service needs to be regular, a continuous repertory production, and not merely those sporadic productions which derive from a duty to the classics; but it is a service I hope some lively academic theatre may be encouraged to perform, since Broadway offers even less to Greek tragedy than it does to the modern playwright.

What, in the meantime, should criticism do? I spoke earlier of the turbulence traditional criticism missed, and, at its most general, the charge I have preferred against the criticism of tragedy is its incompleteness. What was incomplete in the older criticism was that it over-generalized experience and missed whatever was complex and particular in human passion; it took the particular turbulence for granted, that is, and thereby leached its own generalizations of what should have given them life. What the newer criticism missed was meant to be implied by what it got—turbulence of language; but the implications, trapped by the New Criticism's notorious penchant for the autonomy of the work and its deep embarrassment in the face of value, only rarely succeeded; experience got swamped in the generalizing drive of the symbolism or the technique of the dramatist's work. What I want to restore to the criticism of tragedy is a sense, a feel, a look of significantly lived experience, particular before being general, the turbulence of the actual disorder of experience as it moves on to make the dramatist's order. To restore depth and passion to the terms of experience—the notion of a personal fate, responsibility, purpose, the emotions before and after their moralizing, illusion, necessity and reality; to show how values burgeon out of structure and plot; to know again why the plot is the "soul of the play", not its skeleton; to see that any character in a play who lives and uses his passion is prior to anything he may stand for; to refresh the simplicity of reason through the complexity of passion, not the other way around: this is a part of what I mean by turbulence, the turbulence to which both the critic and the producer are responsible. Unless the criticism of tragedy can make itself big enough to talk about[40] experience at the level it proposes, it is doomed to even greater inadequacy than even criticism must normally expect. To talk about literature at the level of experience implies a criticism large enough to contain what is chaotic in experience as well as what is orderly. And it is my conviction that criticism of Greek tragedy, too heavily committed to the criteria of orderly reason and the rhetoric of intelligence, has dehumanized its heroes by cutting them off from the condition in relation to which they win their meaning. The hero, cut off by an inadequate criticism from the actual power and anguish of the condition he can never quite escape without destroying himself, loses the terrible tension and redeeming dignity of his equivocal status. . . .

II

I suggested earlier that one refreshment of perspective might be found in a shift in our traditional idea of the Greek theatre, at least as that idea affects Euripides. And I should like to suggest further that we need much more precision in dealing with the hero and a different purchase on that central and elusive concept. What is most urgently needed is some sense of flexibility and variety in the ways heroism is manifested, and more attention to the *dramatic* use of the hero. The difficulty is not merely that we fail to distinguish between generic kinds of heroism or between the heroism of one dramatist and another, but that discussion begs almost all of the questions that affect the *dramatic* status of the hero in relation to his own humanity and also skirts whatever experience is relevant to the earning of heroism. Attempts to meet this problem with a unitary concept, as in Whitman's recent book on Sophocles, have been Procrustean in result: it is, of course, a pleasure to be rid of the view that Sophocles was an enlightened bishop and his heroes Anglicans in trouble, but a Nietzschean Sophocles with a Zarathustrian Antigone hardly helps us much. But most commonly heroism is treated in drastically abrogated moral terms, or made to satisfy the Aristotelian theory of the hero's tragic flaw, or reduced to the protagonist, or hypostatized and used as a critical *deus ex machina*. The crucial questions relevant to[41] heroism, however, seem to me to be the following. First, how is heroism asserted in tragedy and how is it sustained, both morally and dramatically? What skills of experience or reality distinguish the hero from the other characters and from his former self? What is the relation between the achieved dramatic reality of the hero and his symbolic dignity? What is the cost of heroism to the hero in contrast to the values of what his heroism asserts? How does the hero's mortality affect his morality? What are the *legitimate* limits of the hero's responsibility for his nature or his acts? What is the relation between necessity and illusion in the hero's ability to rise to, and even surpass, the meaning of his own experience? . . .[42]

My point, then, is the simple one that heroism is too complex a term to be handled loosely, and that, if mishandled, it generates trouble in other directions. We need a tact with our terms which can distinguish when a particular concept is demanded and when it is superfluous; so far as heroism is concerned, we particularly need precision when we attempt to relate it to *dramatic* movement, plot, genre, and a particular dramatist. Where our definitions tend to be static rather than dynamic, or uprooted from a single type, or abstracted from one dramatist and imposed upon others, we impoverish tragedy in the critical act. . . .[45]

III

Unless I am mistaken, tragedy is also in deep need of some new perspectives in the matter of its operative moral terms as well as in structure and plot. And particularly, I think, we need to question again the relevance of Aristotle on at least two points—the so-called tragic flaw and the putative Aristotelian theory of tragic structure, the structure that draws its sanction from the *Oedipus Rex* and is reinforced by our modern preference for the organic. Aristotle is, I know, a rough customer: he has of necessity immense authority, and one is never quite sure whether one is talking about Aristotle or about something that has borrowed the authority of his name. But I have never been able to satisfy myself that the *Poetics* is the purely inductive treatise that scholars claim it is: again and again, that is, what is inductive in the *Poetics* seems to me to be directed by what is not, the pervasive notion of a purposive and rational universe and all that such a notion implies for tragedy and for the structure of tragedy. Thus for Aristotle a tragic fall is grounded in a consistent and harmonious sense of a man's responsibility for his nature and his actions: when the hero falls, he falls for his own failure, and behind the rightness of his fall, working both pity and terror by the precise and relentless nature of its operations, stands the order which society and a god-informed world impose upon the individual. What the law requires, the world requires too, and so the Aristotelian play portrays, like an image of human life, the individual torn and suffering between his nature and an objective world-order.

The tragic fall is, of course, in the common reading of Aristotle, based upon the hero's possession of a tragic flaw; and whether as doctrine or habit, the attempt to find a tragic flaw in Greek plays seems to me a persistent stumbling-block. If you really look at the *Oedipus,* for instance, it is immediately clear that Oedipus' tragic flaw is hard to discover: one wants to know—if you begin with the Aristotelian habit—just what in the hero's nature or his acts makes him suffer as hideously as he does, and the obvious answers—his anger, his treatment of Creon and Teiresias, his attempt to avoid his fate—are all unsatisfactory, or if satisfactory, indict the gods that could afflict a man so grievously for such offense. One recent critic of the play, an Aristotelian by conviction as well as habit, recognized his dilemma immediately and proceeded to solve it by the suggestion that Sophocles in this play has generalized *hamartia* into something like original sin: Oedipus has no particular flaws but suffers in the very flaw of his humanity. I suspect that very few classicists, whatever their religious color, will be happy with this[50] theory, and I hope that even Aristotelians might object. But I use it to illustrate the kind of trouble that the expectation of a tragic flaw can create even in the treatment of a play which Aristotle regarded as the paradigm of his theories.

I cannot myself pretend to understand that mysterious play, but I wonder if we are perhaps not the better off for proceeding from the play rather than from Aristotle. Freed from our own *a prioris,* the experience of the play may at least propose itself in different terms. Thus it has always seemed to me that the single most pertinent fact of the *Oedipus* was not the hero's flaw, but his refusal to accept a ready-made fate: he wants his own fate, not the gods', and though his personal fate may be cut short by his doom, Oedipus at the close of the play insists upon distinguishing his own responsibility by blinding himself. It is the magnificence of his own declaration of responsibility that makes him so heroic: his fate is *his* and no one else's. His anger is anger, neither more nor less; it is not the source of his doom, but the irritant that he exhibits on the road to doom; and if he has a *hamartia*, it is not sin or flaw but the ungovernable tragic ignorance of all men: we do not know who we are nor who fathered us but go, blinded by life and hope, toward a wisdom bitter as the gates of hell. The cost of action is suffering, and heroism is the anguished acceptance of our own identities and natures, forged in action and pain in a world we never made. Whatever the final merits of this suggestion, it at least, I think, preserves the dignity of human passion in the play without violating in the name of a crude automatic justice the mysterious destiny that rules the play.

But crude or vulgar Aristotelianism[1] has hurt all three dramatists, and Euripides in particular, and one of the most urgent tasks for the criticism of tragedy is the thorough re-examination of Euripidean structure; once we get Euripides straight, we may be in a position to see just where we have subtly distorted Aeschylus and Sophocles in the name of a misunderstood Aristotle. But here again, I think, criticism might best begin from the obvious—the long insistence of critics that Euripidean plays lack unity, fall into disparate actions or are merely episodes strung together. We start, that is, from the fact of dislocation and attempt to see whether dislocation might not be deliberate method

[1] Much of contemporary dogmatizing about what Aristotle did or did not mean seems to me to rest squarely upon uninformed or unimaginative interpretation of what Aristotle actually said. I am encouraged in this opinion by Professor Gerald F. Else's magisterial *Aristotle's Poetics: The Argument* (Harvard University Press, 1957), surely the most important book on Aristotelian criticism in the twentieth century and one which will inevitably shape and alter the whole tenor of modern explication of Aristotle.

At my request, Professor Else has provided me with a brief statement of his views of what Aristotle actually said, and I quote him verbatim in the conviction of complete agreement. He writes: "There is no doubt that the root and center of Aristotle's theory of tragedy, indeed of all poetry, is the idea of an action (N.B. *"an* action," not simply "action"). It should be easy to say what he means by an action, since he talks about it so much; but there are obscurities and ambiguities. Perhaps the key is that an action is a *trans*action, the living out of a decisive turn of events by a significant human being. Aristotle seems to say that neither *people* nor *situations*—suffering, hopelessness, demoniacal possession, or whatever—are tragic in themselves. Involvement in action is the sign-manual of our human condition and our passport to happiness; it is also the warrant of our possible ruin. Without action a man can be, but he can neither win nor lose; and the winning or losing (not having-lost or being-about-to-lose, or even being-such-as-to-lose) is the tragedy. What is tragic is neither the potentiality nor the actuality of suffering, but its actualization. Tragedy cannot be *displayed*, but only *enacted*. It would seem to follow that the tragic action, though involved with universals—character (type), characteristic acts, pattern of events—is irreducibly a particular. Whether or not Oedipus is a type, the hell into which he enters is his individually, for *only he has entered it through this action*. But it is not clear whether Aristotle is aware of this further corollary. What he does do, beyond any ambiguity, is to insist on the primacy of the action."

rather than the hit-or-miss *ad hoc* work of a genius who consistently botched. What is immediately apparent if we start from this point is the real coherence of the plays so far as structure is concerned; what is most obvious in the *Heracles* or *Hecuba* is true also of the *Bacchae*, *Hippolytus* and *Medea*: all lack the kind of unity which the organic theory requires, all exhibit dislocation. If we ask why this is so, I think we find it mirrored by a curious doubleness in the action or in the given and created realities of the plays. Thus the *Heracles*[51] shows two successive plateaus, the first a reality appropriate to legend and old convention, i.e. a world of mythical illusion, the second the full created tragic reality out of which heroism is born. If we look, say, at the *Orestes,* we discover a play which freely invents its own reality and then confronts the action so created with an epiphany of Apollo in which the whole motion of the play up to that point is flatly contradicted. We get a head-on collision, that is, between the action of the play and the traditionalizing impossible *deus ex machina,* and no attempt is made to modulate or explain these incompatible sequences. The same is true of the *Iphigeneia at Aulis,* and also, I think, of the *Medea* and *Electra:* their conclusions are simply at variance, as real events, from the whole tenor of the action. In the *Hippolytus* and *Bacchae* this doubleness is used in a different and less violent way: both plays dramatize the full incredibility of a traditional account of Olympian anthropomorphism—it is incredible that gods, real gods, should act as Dionysus and Aphrodite do. But once the familiar reality has been exposed and displaced, both plays proceed, in a symbolic manner, to hint at a deeper meaning and a different reality for these displaced gods. What I am trying to suggest is that again and again in Euripides, what makes the plays dislocated in structure is a deliberate juxtaposition of antithetical realities—the reality of the material which the play takes from legend and myth, and the new reality which the dramatist forces, as action, from his old material. We get the same kind of jar, that is, that our lives receive when they proceed upon inadequate conviction and are suddenly confronted with difficulty too great for the old conviction. But to my mind our understanding of Euripidean structure rests firmly upon our ability to understand the dramatic experience that bridges the two or even three plateaus of reality that most Euripidean plays exhibit. In the *Heracles,* for instance, we get between the two actions no *propter hoc* connection of the kind Aristotelians insist upon, and yet the connection seems to me, if not quite necessitous, at least valid with whatever validity the conversion of human experience possesses.

If heroism happens to arise from a fortuitous and accidental eruption of the irrational in the nature of things—as in the *Heracles* or the *Hippolytus*—the very fact that it *is* in the nature of things makes the eruption necessary or probable: we tend to disbar it only because our Aristotelian habits predispose us to a dramatic world like that of

Sophocles, where the apparent irrationalities of experience are explained by a divine order we cannot comprehend. But as applied to Euripides, these habits and their corollary in a crude notion of the tragic flaw can only complicate chaos further. We need rather a theory of Euripidean structure which starts from[52] dislocation and attempts to show the relation of this form to a world of moral disorder. Unless I am mistaken, such examination must also show the irrelevance of *propter hoc* structure to Euripides, whose sense of necessity in drama derives more from the motion of the human mind under stress and the patterns which men's convictions make when confronted by adventitious realities. A man's character may be his destiny, but for Euripides destiny is often dependent upon and defined by circumstances the hero never made, nor the gods either. Unless we can restore an understanding of the importance of the dramatist's assumed world for his form, Euripides must stand perpetually condemned or be explained with all the willful improbability of Verrall. At least the latest book on Euripidean structure—Gilbert Norwood's *Essays on Euripidean Drama*—makes the implicit claim that these dislocations of plot and internal inconsistencies in the plays are best explained as the work of fourth century redactors. This seems both unfortunate and unnecessary.

One final point. Nothing, I think, more effectively hinders our understanding of the experience of Greek tragedy than the inadequacy and crudity of meaning which critics and translators assign to the operative moral terms of Greek tragedy—*sophia, hybris, anankē, sōphrosunē, aristeia, timē, authadia* and the like. For in much criticism of tragedy these terms are used as though they possessed simple English equivalents, without, I think, adequate reference to the experience with which they were meant to cope. Alternatively, they are exposed to static definition without regard to the transformations which tragedy may force upon them as the hero moves from a situation of conventional morality and reality to an ordeal for which the traditional wisdom of the Chorus may be utterly inadequate. In such situations it is my conviction that the old moral terms are employed with a meaning so turbulent with fresh or restored experience that they are no longer the same terms, nor the hero to whom they apply the same man. *Timē*, for instance, is normally translated as *honor*, but its root meaning is price, or valuation, and in most tragedies where the concept is important—the *Antigone*, for instance—the word operates very much like the deep sense of our word "respect." Thus when Ismene claims that Antigone has not shown *timē* to her, and that Creon has not shown *timē* to Haemon, she means, not that she and Haemon have been dishonored, or insulted, but that they have not been respected: they have been disallowed the dignity of a fate and their dignity as individuals. They have, as it were, been priced all wrong, and this charge is, of course, central to the play, since Antigone claims to act for *philia* because she wishes to give *timē* to Polyneices. What, the play seems to suggest, is the assertion[53] of *philia* worth without *timē* too? And what is a *philia* which, in order to respect one person, shows disrespect to another, both equally claiming the rights of *philia*?

Or consider the word *sophia,* which we badly translate as "wisdom," as it gets into the *Bacchae.* Among other things, *sophia* means a knowledge and acceptance of one's nature and therefore of one's place in the scheme of things. It presupposes, that is, self-knowledge, an acceptance of those necessities that compose the limits of human fate. It also means the consequent refinement of feelings by which a man recognizes and respects the sufferings of others before necessity: it issues in compassion.[2] *Sophia* is further contrasted with its opposite, *amathia,* a deep, brutal, unteachable, ungovernable self-ignorance which breaks out in violence and cruelty. If the *sophos* is by definition susceptible to the feelings of civilized humanity, a compassion learned in fellow-suffering, the *amathēs* is callous and merciless, a barbarian by nature. But it is these meanings which crowd into the *Bacchae* and everywhere provide, through dramatic action and testing, the play's missing principle of order. For in the course of the action, through the very brutality which they use to support their claims to *sophia,* both Pentheus and Dionysus utterly expose their own *amathia.* . . .[54]

. . . In my opinion the same widening and deepening of the operative moral terms of Greek culture is to be found everywhere in tragedy—*philia* in *Antigone, sōphrosunē* in *Hippolytus, eugeneia* in *Heracles, aristeia* in *Orestes,* etc.—and it would be surprising if it were not so. But upon our sense of the play off the traditional or lazy meanings of these words and the definitions which the tragic action makes lies, I think, much of the turbulence now missing from the criticism of tragedy.

Let me close with a brief note on necessity, for necessity seems to me the crucial center of Greek tragedy, just as Greek tragedy seems to me unique in the firmness and sharpness with which it follows necessity into human action. In its basic aspect, necessity (*anankē*) is that set of unalterable, irreducible, unmanageable facts which we call the human condition. Call it destiny, call it fate, call it the gods, it hardly matters. Necessity is, first of all, death; but it is also old age, sleep, the reversal of fortune and the dance of life; it is thereby the fact of suffering as well as pleasure, for if we must dance and sleep, we also suffer, age and die. It is also sex, the great figure of amoral Aphrodite who moves in the sea, land and air and as an undeniable power in the bodies of men, compelling and destroying those who, like Hippolytus, refuse to accept her. Or it is Dionysus, the terrible ambiguous force of

---

[2] Cf. *Electra,* ll. 294–5, where Orestes states that pity (*to oiktos*) is never to be found among the *amatheis* but only among the *sophoi,* i.e. compassion is a true component of "wisdom."[57]

the *Bacchae*, "the force that through the green fuse drives the flower," and who[55] destroys Pentheus who lacks the *sophia* that accepts him. It is the great god-sprung trap of the *Oedipus* and also the nature of Oedipus himself, that stubborn human courage of pride that drives him relentlessly into the trap. It is the necessity of political power which, in corruption, destroys Hecuba and Iphigeneia and Cassandra and Polyxena. It is the inherent hostility of blind chance, the incalculable daemonic malice which in the Euripidean *Heracles* calls out to the hero to die and tells him that there is no hope and no moral order in the world at all. Suspend necessity in the form of the play, and you get such charming, romantic plays as *Iphigeneia at Tauris* and the *Helen*. Romantic, that is, because not tragic; and not tragic because necessity, the mainspring of tragedy, has been, for fun, for entertainment and experiment, removed. Where men are freed from the yoke of necessity, their lives cease to be tragic, and with the loss of suffering comes also the loss of dignity and *sophia*.

For it is in the *struggle* with necessity that heroism is born, and even the hero, if he is to retain his humanity, must accept necessity. Ripeness is all. And so we see Orestes discover purity and compassion in the face of a necessity that threatens to deform him as it has already deformed his father and mother and as it inevitably deforms the weak, the flawed, the average human nature. So too Antigone accepts her necessity, the consequence of her own act, humanity pushed to the extreme, and thereby comes again upon her humanity in the very act of acceptance and recognition of loss. So Oedipus by asserting his total utter responsibility for his own fate, wins the victory over a necessity that would have destroyed a lesser man. And so Heracles claims a moral dignity forever out of reach of the amoral powers that persecute him. There is a magnificence here in the power to rise, in the anguished acceptance that must always, in Greek tragedy, precede the winning of dignity. For it is here before necessity that old morality is unmade and then remade into a new thing. Thus Orestes, having discovered at least that compassion that made him hesitate, enables justice to be born. And so too at the close of the *Hippolytus* and *Bacchae* we see the suffering human survivors of the play discover, under the awful yoke of an intolerable necessity, the love and *compassion*, the shared suffering that makes men endure with love in a world which shrieks at them to die. Learn wisdom through suffering, says Aeschylus, and if we are loyal to the turbulence of Greek tragedy, we can see what he means. For, stripped to the bone, the essential *action* of the greatest of the Greek tragedies is an enactment of lives lived out under the double yoke of man's own nature and a world he did not make; the weaker fail or are deformed; the strong survive, and by surviving and enduring, liberate the[56] dignity of significant suffering which gives man the crucial victory over his own fate.

Glossary of Greek Terms

adikia: injustice.
agon: an action involving conflict.
amathia: ignorance.
anangke: necessity.
anomalia: irregularity, deviation from rule.
antistrophe: "counterturn" in a choral dance; second section of a choral
    poem. (See *strophe*.)
archon: city official who supervised the Greek play.
arete: excellence, virtue.
aristeia: prowess.
ate: madness, infatuation.
authadia: wilfulness.
choregus: financier who met choral expenses for a play.
choreuein: dance as a chorus.
comae: villages.
commos: wild lament (in a play, of actors and chorus).
coryphaeus: dance leader of a chorus.
daimon: divine spirit.
deinos: terrible.
demoi: city divisions of Athens.
desis: complication of a dramatic plot.
drama: a doing, from *dran,* to do or act.
eisodos: stage entrance to a theater.
ekklesia: Athenian assembly.
ekkuklema: wheeling stage machine.
Eniautos-daimon: "spirit of the year," fertility god honored annually.
epeisodia: recitative dialogues of actors.
erga: deeds.
exodus: exit song of chorus.
gnome: perception, wit.
gnosis: knowledge.

gnothi seauton: "know thyself" (Socratic and oracular maxim).

hybris: violence, pride, overreaching.

hypothesis: plot summary.

kairos: proper time, decisive moment, high point of a sequence.

kakos: evil.

koros: surfeit, excess.

logos: word, story.

lusis: loosing of a dramatic plot, dénouement.

mechane: stage machine.

moira: allotted portion, fate.

nomos: established law.

noson: sickness.

oidipous: swell-foot.

orchestra: dancing place.

paraskenion: wing-platform.

parodos: side entrance to stage; entrance song of the chorus.

pathos: suffering; the process of undergoing suffering as one acted upon (rather than as an agent).

peripeteia: reversal of action in a play.

philia: friendship, love.

philos: friend, dear person.

phthonos: envy.

praxis: action.

proaeresis: predilection, choice.

proagon: fore-action, preview of a play.

prologos: opening of a play up to the first chorus.

proskenion: stage platform.

prostates: representative.

sebon: that which is reverent.

skene: stage building.

sophia: wisdom.

sophrosune: prudence.

soter: savior, rescuer.

stasima: choral songs recited by the chorus at intervals.

stichomathy: line by-line repartee.

strophe: "turn" of the chorus in a dance; opening section of a choral ode.

symbola: signs, clues.

telos: end, goal.

timē: honor.

tisis: retribution.

tyche: chance, fortune, coincidence.

tyrannos: autocratic ruler.

xenos: foreigner, outlander.

Questions for Study

THE GREEK THEATRE

1. What effects might the physical structure of the Greek theatre have had on its audience? The presence of the chorus? The relative bareness of the stage? The masks worn by the actors? The restriction of speaking actors on stage to three at a given time?

2. Even though we do not have the music of the Greek plays, what do you think the presence of music would contribute to a dramatic performance?

3. The commentaries of the choruses interrupt the speeches of the individual characters in a Greek play. The choruses do not affect the action directly. What effect do they have on the dramatic progress of the action? On our interpretation of the action?

OEDIPUS—THE MYTH AND THE PLAY

1. What parts of the Oedipus myth did Sophocles select?

2. What parts did he leave out?

3. What reasons might be given for his beginning *Oedipus Rex* at the particular point of the myth he chose?

4. How would you compare his treatment with Homer's summary?

5. Robert Graves' interests resemble those of an anthropologist. What might Sophocles' reaction be imagined to be in the face of an anthropological interpretation of a myth?

6. In what ways does the myth—a traditional story with primitive roots—add to the play what an ordinary story would not?

7. What is the effect of opening the play with a crowd scene? At the precise moment that Thebes is expiring from the plague?

8. Can any dramatic irony be found between Oedipus' apparent situation and his actual one in his first speech? In the priest's speech?

In Oedipus' second speech? In line 58, when he calls them again, as in the first word of the play, "children"?

9. What does the tone of Creon's speech do to the mood established between Oedipus and the priests?

10. In the opening chorus (*parodos*, 151–215) how is Creon's mood echoed and transmuted? What is the attitude of the chorus to events thus far?

11. What difference can Oedipus' proclamation (216–270) make to Thebes? To himself?

12. In the dialogue with Tiresias (300–416), what faults does Oedipus first reveal? How does the quarrel between them start? What information is the audience now given for the first time?

13. The chorus (463–512) states its disbelief of Tiresias' charge, but only at the end of its speech. Why? How has their mood now changed?

14. How does Creon bear himself toward Oedipus (513–679)? What does his bearing reveal of his values?

15. Is Jocasta's initial anger (634 ff) justified? What seems to have motivated it? Does her tone change after Creon's departure?

16. What leads Oedipus to tell his story to Jocasta (771–833)? What may be concluded from his failure to do so all through their marriage?

17. Why does the chorus (863–910) speak in such generalities? How does the thought "Pride breeds the tyrant" happen to appear at this precise moment in the play? Has its attitude toward fate and the gods undergone any transformation?

18. Jocasta (911–922) is at the same position now, a suppliant looking toward Oedipus, that the priests were at the outset of the play. What is the dramatic effect of this? What relation does her speech have to the succeeding announcement of Polybus' death? Why does Sophocles have this news transmitted first to her?

19. Why does Sophocles keep this messenger on stage? What values does the messenger already reveal?

20. At what point does Jocasta seem to realize the whole truth about the past? What steps does she take to conceal it? Why does Oedipus not wish to do this too?

21. Why does the chorus (1086–1109) speak so briefly? Why so optimistically in the face of what has happened?

22. In the dialogue between the Theban herdsman and the Corinthian messenger (1110–1185), how is the conflict between the values and awareness of the two made to carry dramatic weight? Why is the final revelation given in the play to such relatively minor characters? Why does Oedipus force the servant?

23. What effect does the abrupt reversal of events have on the tone of the chorus? Has their attitude toward fate and the gods

undergone any further alteration? Do they associate themselves with Oedipus as a fellow human being, or do they shrink from him?

24. How does the second messenger (1237–1285) editorialize his account of Jocasta's suicide and Oedipus' self-blinding?

25. Why do the verse rhythms of dialogue and of chorus, hitherto kept fairly separate, now merge and interfuse? Why does the chorus switch to "blank verse" (lines 1312 ff) when Oedipus speaks in choral odes? Why does Oedipus himself return to blank verse in line 1365?

26. What new attitudes does Creon show? How does Oedipus react?

27. What is the dramatic point of introducing Oedipus' daughters?

28. What dramatic effect does the chorus's new tone and rhythm have in their final speech (1523–1530)?

CRITICISM

1. Take Aristotle's six elements to be found in a play, and describe how each is present in *Oedipus Rex*.

2. *Oedipus Rex* has often been called Aristotle's model for a drama. Why is this so?

3. The ancient scholiast applies the line "Pride breeds the tyrant" to Jocasta. Is he justified in doing this? Are there other interpretations possible? In view of the Greek title *Oedipous Tyrannos,* in what sense could we apply the line to Oedipus himself?

4. Can a case be made for Voltaire's view of *Oedipus Rex* as a play with "many imperfections?"

5. Is Dr. Johnson right to resolve Sophocles' idea of Destiny back to the "ancient and popular notion"?

6. How may Schiller's emphasis on the pastness of the main action in *Oedipus Rex* be taken to modify the idea of an Aristotelian flaw in the protagonist?

7. How does de Quincey's application of the riddle of the Sphinx to Oedipus himself have a bearing on the central concerns of the play?

8. How does John Moore's interpretation of *miasma* shed light on the problem that faces Oedipus and Thebes at the beginning of the play?

9. Why does J. J. Letters emphasize the improbabilities in the plot of *Oedipus Rex?*

10. Does James Schroeter's Freudian interpretation of Oedipus' "agons" with four older men illuminate the central situation in the play?

11. How, in Richmond Lattimore's view, does the poetry contribute to the drama in *Oedipus Rex*?

12. What are the main dramatic moments (*kairoi*) that John Crossett finds in the play? On what basis does he choose them? How does he relate them to the "heart" of the play?

13. William Arrowsmith feels that recent critics have not done justice to the complexity of Greek tragedy. How is the "turbulence" he discusses present in *Oedipus Rex*?

QUESTIONS AND TOPICS FOR PAPERS

1. Discuss how the *roles* of the main characters—Tiresias as priest, Creon as adviser, etc.—affect the play's action and meaning through what the characters do and say.

2. Examine the choruses in the play and show how the chorus's response to the action is not random but forms a pattern in itself.

3. It was a rule of the Athenian stage that no more than three main speaking actors appear on stage together. Take one or more of the *epeisodia* and show how this restriction works to throw a character's position into relief.

4. Oedipus' view of himself changes through the play, and his mood also changes. Describe how these two changes are related. Are they always related in the same way?

5. The chorus, as representative citizens of Thebes, stand, as elders, for the mature view of a majority. Analyze and discuss their final view. Is it reflected in the views of any of the characters?

6. At the climax of the play, slaves move to the fore and become crucial to the action. Discuss the conclusions that might be drawn from this fact.

Selective Bibliography of Additional Works in English

Bowra, C. M., *Sophoclean Tragedy*. Oxford: Clarendon Press, 1944.

Brooks, Cleanth, and Heilman, R., *Understanding Drama*. New York: Holt, Rinehart & Winston, Inc., 1948.

Carroll, J. P., "Some Remarks on the Questions in the Oedipus Tyrannus," *Classical Journal*, XXXII, No. 7 (April 1937), 406–416.

Earle, M. L., *The Oedipus Tyrannus*. New York: 1901.

Fergusson, Francis, *The Idea of a Theatre*. Princeton: Princeton University Press, 1949.

Freud, Sigmund, *The Interpretation of Dreams*. New York: Random House, Inc., 1938.

Goodman, Paul, *The Structure of Literature*. Chicago: University of Chicago Press, 1951.

Haigh, Arthur E., *The Greek Theatre,* 3rd ed. Oxford: Clarendon Press, 1907.

Kitto, H. D. F., *Greek Tragedy,* 2nd ed. London: 1950.

Knox, Bernard, *Oedipus at Thebes*. New Haven: Yale University Press, 1957.

Mullahy, Patrick, *Oedipus, Myth and Complex*. New York: Hermitage, 1948.

Nietzsche, Friedrich, *The Birth of Tragedy*. New York: Doubleday & Co., Inc., 1953.

Norwood, Gilbert, *Greek Tragedy*. London: Methuen, 1948.

Pack, R. A., "Fate, Chance, and Tragic Error," *American Journal of Philology*, LX (1939), 350–356.

Pickard-Cambridge, A. W., *Dithyramb, Tragedy and Comedy*. Oxford: Clarendon Press, 1927.

————, *The Dramatic Festivals of Athens*. Oxford: Clarendon Press, 1953.

Wheelwright, Philip, *The Burning Fountain*. Bloomington: Indiana University Press, 1954.

Whitman, Cedric H., *Sophocles*. Cambridge: Harvard University Press, 1951.

Other Translations to Consult

Fitts, Dudley, and Fitzgerald, Robert. New York: Harcourt, Brace and World, Inc., 1948.

Grene, David. Chicago: University of Chicago Press, 1942.

Jebb, Richard. Cambridge: Cambridge University Press, 1883.

Knox, Bernard. New York: Washington Square Press, 1960.

Yeats, W. B. London: Macmillan, 1928.